parklife

Also by Nick Varley

Golden Boy: A Biography of Wilf Mannion

NICK VARLEY
parklife

a search for the heart of football

MICHAEL JOSEPH
LONDON

MICHAEL JOSEPH

Published by the Penguin Group
Penguin Books Ltd, 27 Wrights Lane, London W8 5TZ, England
Penguin Putnam Inc., 375 Hudson Street, New York, New York 10014, USA
Penguin Books Australia Ltd, Ringwood, Victoria, Australia
Penguin Books Canada Ltd, 10 Alcorn Avenue, Toronto, Ontario, Canada M4V 3B2
Penguin Books (NZ) Ltd, Private Bag 102902, NSMC, Auckland, New Zealand

Penguin Books Ltd, Registered Offices: Harmondsworth, Middlesex, England

First published 1999

10 9 8 7 6 5 4 3 2 1

Copyright © Nick Varley, 1999

The moral right of the author has been asserted

Set in 10/13pt Monotype Concorde
Typeset by Rowland Phototypesetting Ltd, Bury St Edmunds, Suffolk
Printed in England by Clays Ltd, St Ives plc

A CIP catalogue record for this book is available from the British Library

ISBN 0-718-14362-0

For Marianne

In memory of Joe McCarthy and ninety-five others

contents

acknowledgements

I'd like to thank all those who agreed to be interviewed, especially Colin Auton and Niall Scott, and those whose input and help, although unquoted, were invaluable in various ways: Andy Limb, the John Pearson and Ian Baird of the Kop; Rowland White, the John Sheridan and Eddie Gray of editors; Patrick Walsh, the Vinnie Jones of agents; John Williams of Leicester University; Rob Nicholls of *Fly Me to the Moon*; Philip French of the Football Trust; Craig Brewin; Martin and Rachel in Manchester; Bill Borrows; Piara Powar and Ben Tegg at *Kick It Out*; Daniella and Graeme in Glasgow; Graham Courtney at Newcastle United; Nobuaki Tanabe and Jonathan Watts in Tokyo; Kev Miles and Alison Pilling, for France especially; likewise, Karine and Delphine Rus; Kath Viner, Paul Kelso and anyone else who helped at the *Guardian*; and, of course, Mum, Dad and Ade.

changes

What is required is the vision and imagination to achieve a new ethos for football.
Lord Justice Taylor's final report into the Hillsborough disaster, paragraph 59

It used to be easy. About noon on a Saturday I'd stuff some money in my pocket and pull on a coat as I went out the door. For a couple of years when optimism got the better of me, and before geography did so too, I had a season ticket to remember as well. But generally all I needed was cash and cover. That was it. I was off to the match.

Today I set the alarm clock for 9.30 a.m. – even though it's Sunday. When I banish the last of my sleepiness by slamming the front door as I leave, I've got my credit card in one pocket, cashpoint card and loose change in the other.

It used to be cheap too: £3 in and perhaps a tenner to cover the cost of a couple of pints, a programme and train and bus fares for a ninety-minute journey to the ground. That season ticket set me back £65, if I remember rightly, so little that if I didn't fancy watching the Plymouth game, say, or Shrewsbury, I simply stayed at home without worrying about the cost. The resulting empty space behind the goal mattered even less; there were always plenty of those.

Now I withdraw £100 from the bank to cover all eventualities – even though transport will cost me nothing as I'm walking the mile or so to the ground.

But it used to be so empty as well. Tickets didn't cost much, the side was doing OK, yet there were fewer than 15,000 in a lot of the time. Most were similar to me: young white men grouped together on the terraces. There were some older fans in the main stand, a few even accompanied by wives and families, but, to be honest, they probably would have been better off – warmer at least – huddled with us.

Four days into 1998 I stroll along with husbands and wives, mums and dads, boys and girls, all traipsing towards a sold-out 35,000-capacity ground, while millions of others tune in televisions and radios for exhaustive live coverage – despite the ungodly hour.

Back then, only a decade ago, it would have seemed like a dream: football all-conquering and hip, but also a massively profitable multi-million-pound business. By the late 1980s the game was, in the entirely accurate words of the *Sunday Times*, a 'slum sport played in slum stadiums'. Fences had gone up to contain crowds, while the crowds themselves were half the size of a generation before – a fall partly explained by facilities, which had barely improved in those years. Finally, as incompetence and inhumanity combined to produce a disaster which many had forecast but no one had forestalled, almost a hundred people died just going to a match.

Today it seems impossible that such a tragedy could happen again. It seems almost incredible that Hillsborough ever did. The crowd for what was then one of the best-attended games of the season is now exceeded every time the country's premier club opens its doors. And it's so obviously inconceivable that anyone watching New Football at Old Trafford could die there that it's barely worth saying. Fans travel from as far afield as the Far East and Scandinavia to shop before, sit during and visit the megastore or museum after the action. Ninety minutes is merely the anchor for a pleasant day out at the Manchester United experience, not the cause of a near-death one.

The surreality of the dream goes on: Chelsea, where I'm heading, managed in the 1980s by a succession of nondescript track-suits, have one of the world's greatest players as their coach and chief clothes-horse. Ruud Gullit is good-looking, coined the phrase sexy football and advocates it passionately, has his own brand of leisurewear and, not least significantly for those who remember the bad old days, is black. His players, successors to the likes of Micky Droy, have been recruited from Norway and Nigeria to Romania and Uruguay. His goal-keepers are Dutch, Norwegian and Russian.

And on: Gullit earns an estimated £1.5 million a year from a lucrative portfolio of commercial deals before his club salary is even considered. The squad, assembled at a cost of more than £20 million, has a wage bill put at £13 million. And the man O King the expenditure has seen the value of the club he bought for £1 in 1982 top £175 million and profits approach £10 million a year. Ken Bates, whose love of Chelsea is such that he was once chairman of Oldham and on the board at Wigan, is also overseeing a £200 million redevelopment at the club's Stamford Bridge home. Even their best-known supporter and the self-proclaimed Voice of All Fans, a politician taking an electorally enforced rest, who also used to support another side, is rich and adds to his pile at an estimated rate of £500,000 a year.

And on: the Bridge itself, once one of the worst grounds in the upper echelons of the league, has been rebuilt and recast as the focal point of the redevelopment which pushes football further yet into a brave new world of hotels and restaurants, penthouses and fine wines, not to mention Harley-Davidsons in club colours. Where it used to look like a down-at-heel builder's yard, the stadium is now a semi-permanent building site, incongruously renamed Chelsea Village, where glass and chrome tower over the grass of the pitch. Eventually there will be nine restaurants, including one named after the Shed, the notorious area of terracing where football's verbal, and other, bad odours once regularly rose from the crowd. Its former inhabitants will be able to reminisce about the good old days over a glass of club-labelled Pouilly Fumé or a champagne ideal to toast the launch of a new kit, to celebrate a booking-free appearance by Graeme Le Saux or to pop at David Mellor if you spot him in the posh seats.

Sadly, not all dreams come true.

On a fine early summer's day those ten years ago, the Chelsea Headhunters and their less regimented but still-hooligan disciples were ready for action. The potential victims from Middlesbrough, trapped in the away end of the Bridge, were rejoicing at their side's promotion to the First Division at the expense of the home side. A handful of the jubilant Teessiders scaled the perimeter fences, jumped on to the pitchside track, ran to the players and were dancing around as the first movements towards them began.

A few in the home end had started pushing past static colleagues and down towards the gates in the wire caging at the front before the final whistle. They gathered at the yellow-painted openings on to the pitch, ill-intent obvious by their presence. But the swell only gained real momentum and hundreds of members, getting noisier and angrier, as Boro celebrated. Those already at the gates were joined by scores and scores more. Then the gates swung open and the mob burst through, its members shoving past each other and towards the enemy, with the unmistakable guttural roar of a crowd in full battle cry.

The players sprinted for the safety of the dressing room; the stray Boro fans fled too, back into their end, which was soon being showered with whatever missiles had come to hand – bottles and stones mostly – by the mob which had run the length of the pitch. For a few terrifying seconds, as the gates which were all that separated the two sides were attacked, the spectre of an all-out, face-to-face, fist-to-fist riot loomed, until, belatedly, police moved in to force the Chelsea fans back down the pitch. For half an hour the skirmishes flared, getting slowly more distant from the Boro end, injuring one policeman badly – and then engulfing the ambulance called to take him to hospital – as well as another twenty people less seriously, and resulting in 102 arrests. Eventually the young Boro players re-emerged for a celebration which was flanked by officers warily watching the terraces, as unsure about if and where and when a new offensive might erupt as they had been caught unawares when the first exploded.

In truth the riot was an entirely predictable end to what had already been an ugly day. The away fans had been sped through the underground system to the ground on special non-stop services which couldn't be ambushed; at Fulham Broadway, the first and final stop, they emerged into the sunlight to be surrounded by police deployed to protect them from the baying, goading, threatening crowd lining the streets; and inside the Bridge the 400 Boro fans with seats in the stand were moved to the away terrace after finding themselves unsegregated, and under attack, amidst 6,000 home supporters. Among the besieged was the mayor of Middlesbrough, who eventually walked out in disgust at lack of action from police and stewards; a Teesside MP and the players' wives, who were pelted with missiles; and a primary schoolboy whose big day out almost ended with him being thrown over a balcony with a seventy-foot drop to pitch level. And the remarkable thing was that none of it seemed very remarkable.

I had heard the shapeless roar of the pitch invasion rumble through the quiet Saturday afternoon streets where I was visiting a friend and realized almost immediately its certain venue and likely cause, if not its specific ingredients. That night we drank in a pub dotted with bitter Chelsea fans drowning their sorrows and none of our group bothered to discuss the events of the afternoon despite being surrounded by some of those who had at the very least witnessed it; the riot was routine. Such end-of-season brawls were just another part of what football had become: a canvas for clusters of violent young men hell-bent on fighting to indulge themselves in an atmosphere of near anarchy. Some incidents were big enough to seep, via the news, into the fabric of national life, like the bloodstains decorating the shirts of some of the Chelsea fans; others were all-but-invisible blemishes, confined to word-of-mouth reports from those who had witnessed them. The major ones were recorded, just like championships and cup wins; the minor ones quietly ignored. Either way, the game moved on – and waited for the inevitable next.

For twenty years, since the first reports of knives and beatings, the story had been the same. New levels of outrage were reached season on season: a pitch invasion by a few dozen Leeds fans intending to attack the referee, 1971; three pitch invasions followed by a riot by Rangers fans in Barcelona during, and after, their side's victory in the European Cup-Winners' Cup, 1972; mass pitch invasions aimed at causing the abandonment of crucial games at Manchester United and Newcastle, 1974; the destruction by Spurs supporters of part of Feyenoord's ground during the UEFA Cup Final, again in 1974; Leeds, again, pillaging Paris during and after the showpiece European Cup Final, 1975; Black Saturday, 1976, when fifty-five Manchester United fans at Stoke, sixty Rangers at Ibrox and a hundred Chelsea at Luton were all arrested – the latter after a pitch invasion which concluded with one steward stabbed, another suffering a broken nose, and the home goalkeeper punched in the head; and on and on. And these were just the major incidents, not the run-of-the-mill individual assaults, terrace skirmishes or train trashings.

All were lumped together under the euphemism 'trouble', a catch-all word which included everything from a couple of punches being thrown to premeditated stabbings. At one match it might mean a bloody nose and a black eye; at another, a slashed face and a deep knife wound. It encompassed the actions of both groups who would fight anyone foolish enough to identify themselves as opposition fans and others who went out of their way to ambush or confront like-minded devotees of violence. Yet its linguistic flabbiness somehow lessened its physical consequences, soaking away some of the bloodstains, almost reducing acts of medieval-style barbarism to modern-day capers.

The perpetrators were only a minority – albeit sometimes a significant one – of any crowd, but 'trouble' affected all parts of it. Those fans who had never been, and would never be, involved in any incidents were still subjected to stern policing, which increasingly came to resemble a military operation rather than a public-order one to merely ensure safety at a sport. Those who walked or ran away from the fighting still faced the risk of being caught up in it the next time, inside or outside the ground. And those who turned up week in, week out saw their sport taken away from them – literally when games were periodically forced behind closed doors as punishment.

Then there was the impact in the game as a whole: on the players, whose efforts could be overwritten by pitch invasions and who were themselves sometimes threatened; on the managers, who were reduced to impotent despair, like Jack Charlton when he wept with helpless rage as rioting fans of his Sheffield Wednesday side ignored his pleas to stop; and the administrators, directors and FA officials, who regularly issued angry statements condemning the enemy within but proved simply incapable of confronting the problem effectively.

And there was the impact on society too: the policemen who were targeted with cloudbursts of spittle, loose change, sometimes pre-sharpened, and the occasional dart as they patrolled the perimeter of the pitch, nothing more than slowly moving targets; the town-centre shopkeepers and their customers who had to endure frequent and fearsome invasions; the train drivers who had to deliver carriages of ill-intent into stations all over the country; and everyone who involuntarily hung their head in shame when their countrymen went on the rampage abroad, again.

At home hooliganism was trouble; abroad it became our national disease and our best-known 1970s export. At home metal fences were introduced in the middle of the decade to cage fans away from the pitch and away from each other. In Europe, where fewer physical restraints, less aware policing and duty-free drink provided an incendiary cocktail, the violence flourished at the away games of the English clubs in continental competition; the authorities were soon regularly punishing those whose fans misbehaved with fines, games forced to be played at neutral or empty grounds, even bans. Then the hooligans also began to join up for England internationals and the national side, the nation, gained a reputation to rival that of any club.

In the first half of 1985, a century after its birth as a professional sport, football finally seemed to be on the point of being consumed by the disease.

First, there was a riot at the Bridge as Chelsea were beaten to a place in the League Cup Final by Sunderland. Home fans invaded the pitch during the game and tried to attack Sunderland scorer, and ex-Chelsea player, Clive Walker. Mounted police were caught in a downpour of seats, bottles and other missiles. Afterwards Bates announced the most infamous proposed solution in the history of hooliganism, one inspired by his cattle farm: electrifying the pitchside fences.

Weeks later Millwall's visit to Luton brought the scale of football's malaise into every living room in the country. Television cameras, then still a rarity at matches, were there to record who won through to the semifinal of the FA Cup, but instead captured a twenty-five-minute pitch invasion, two smaller ones during the game and then a final one, the worst, at full-time. Scores of away supporters spewed across the pitch, lobbing vivid orange plastic seats ripped from the stand at the police as they went. Officers with dogs and batons drawn counter-charged; the fans just regrouped, reclaimed spent orange ammunition and charged again, unabashed. And all back and forth across a pitch meant for football. FA chairman Bert Millichip described the night as 'probably the worst in the long catalogue that has blighted our game over the last twenty years' and conceded the inevitable immediate result: England's bid to stage the 1988 European Championships was over.

But the worst was still to come – and this time in the biggest game of the season, on live television, when the European Cup Final was turned into a real-time horror movie. The logistics were straightforward: Juventus fans ended up in a supposedly neutral zone next to Liverpool fans in the Heysel Stadium, in Brussels, thanks to ticket touts; chanting and abusive hand gestures graduated into English fans running at Italian, who fled; they ended up crammed in the corner of the decrepit terrace, desperate to reach the exits, in such numbers that a perimeter wall collapsed. When the dust kicked up on the dry summer evening finally settled, thirty-nine fans were dead, buried amid rubble and each other like victims of a bomb or an earthquake.

Everyone supposed Heysel was the conclusion of a story which had begun fifteen years earlier or more; it had to be. Football had to change. Hooliganism had to be curbed. Safety had to be improved. The judge who inquired into the disaster concluded: 'I believe that the paramount need is to protect the public by improving safety standards, and thereby restoring confidence among those who attend sporting events. This means effective steps should be taken quickly.'[1] But still the fighting continued: a brick and aerosol-spray attack on the Manchester United team in its coach at Anfield, 1986; a riot between United and West Ham fans aboard a cross-Channel ferry, later in 1986; two members of Chelsea's Headhunters jailed for ten years each, 1987; and then Chelsea–Middlesbrough, 1988.

A month later a beaming Gullit, the Dutch captain, thrust the European Championship trophy skywards. His majestic headed goal had opened the scoring in the final against the USSR, capping a tournament in which he confirmed his status as the best player in Europe, possibly the world. Alongside him, team-mates such as Frank Rijkaard and Marco Van Basten, scorer of the almost impossible volley which completed a 2–0 win, had also added to already gleaming reputations.

All three played for AC Milan, the best, and richest, club in what had been recognized for decades as the best, and richest, league in the world – the Italian one. All had collected medals there when their club won the league a few weeks before the championships in West Germany. All savoured every second of the win over the host nation in the semifinal – sweet revenge for defeat in the 1974 World Cup Final and, according to those with longer memories, the Second World War. But all treasured most winning their country's long-overdue first international trophy.

In stark contrast to the Dutch glory was the shame of one of the teams they had beaten on their way to the final: England. Bobby Robson's side lost all three games. The manager was assaulted by tabloid headlines demanding his resignation. The fans had further sullied the tournament, with more than 200 arrested following three-way clashes with the Dutch and Germans which saw the streets of Düsseldorf and Frankfurt clouded in teargas and awash with blue lights and wailing sirens. The FA shamefacedly withdrew another request, this one for the lifting of the post-Heysel ban on its clubs appearing in continental competition. An England friendly in Italy was cancelled because of security fears. Meanwhile, the government, its patience long since exhausted, seriously considered withdrawing the side from all international football, starting with the qualifying games for the World Cup in Italy.

Instead, what appeared to be a story of relentless, unstoppable descent and disgrace has enjoyed the most unlikely of happy endings. England were allowed to play on and qualified for Italy. The side which failed embarrassingly in Germany was lifted to within a couple of instants of luck of the final by the maverick skills of new addition Paul Gascoigne. His tears, his character and his life humanized the sport for new viewers; new viewers meant lucrative new television deals; and lucrative new television deals meant money for ground improvements and the purchase of well-paid, new foreign players, the very best, so that when Chelsea and Middlesbrough met once again, just seven years after the battle at the Bridge, I was sitting in a new ground in a new era, with only the game unchanged.

All around eyes blinked in disbelief, trying to take in the unfamiliar geography of the new, all-seater Riverside Stadium, and then trying to register that the familiar dreadlocked figure on the pitch really was Gullit. The ex-European and World Player of the Year performed with grace and poise in the blue of his new English club. He brought a cultured calm to the perpetual motion of the game, guiding attacks into culs-de-sac and carrying the ball from defence with the skill to deliver the required pass impeccably. But what he also brought was the confirmation of the rehabilitation, and revolution, of English football.

Another eighteen months and he brought Chelsea their first trophy in a generation too, as I completed my Chelsea–Boro trilogy at the 1997 FA Cup Final. Chelsea, featuring three Italians, a Norwegian, a Frenchman and a Romanian, beat a Boro side including two Brazilians, two Italians, a Dane and Slovakian. Back in 1988 at the Bridge, the nearest either side had got to a Serie A star was a full-back of Italian descent,

Tony Dorigo; and the closest to any sort of overseas talent was an Australian-born import, soon to become an England international, the same Tony Dorigo.

In Wembley's exclusive Olympic Gallery, where I had managed to get a seat from another innovation, the cup's sponsors, gold-medal-winning rower Steven Redgrave was an apt member of the more upmarket fans who smiled and clapped, pretty much regardless of which side they supported. Mixed together in the seats, as their predecessors had been back in 1988, there was not even a hint of trouble. Down below, the blue masses sang their traditional song, 'One Man Went to Mow' – the sort of simple ditty every club should now have so that non-English-speaking players, or fans, can quickly learn the words. Even Dennis Wise. But little else was as it used to be.

Within a mile of the Bridge, as I continued on my way to Chelsea's first match in defence of the cup, a tatty club flag had slipped down its pole in the face of the biting wind. Its position, at half-mast, was rich in symbolism of the match to come, in which Chelsea were thrashed 5–3 by Manchester United, the team of the 1990s, but not, as it would turn out, the season. As relevant to the game as a whole, though, was that the pole from which the flag fluttered was on one of the exclusive houseboats moored on the Embankment.

When football came home, it wasn't just to its traditional estates and rows of humble terraces, but also to upmarket addresses where the only previous interest had been when residents discovered that the new neighbour was a player or manager. Over the past five years fans have become older, wealthier and less likely to be unemployed.[2] At Chelsea, the trends are especially pronounced: six out of ten season-ticket holders watching the working man's game earn £20,000 a year or more and just 15 per cent of those enjoying a sport which was once characterized by its popularity among young men are aged under thirty.

Some of the newer fans were heading for the ground early: a dad with his two daughters, one in a red replica top, one in blue; mums accompanying children decked out in Chelsea strip from head to toe; and well-to-do greying men in the uniform of pressed jeans and Barbour jackets once limited to the sporting arena a little further out, at Twickenham. They all mingled between the dome of the exclusive Chelsea Harbour development and the rising pile of Chelsea Village, outside a bar called Come the Revolution. Someone should tell the owners that it's already here.

Elements of the old days lingered. Small groups of lads in what the advertisers call middle youth, but many others would call extended adolescence, waited for stragglers at either end of the cut-through to the ground. A few necked canned lager, the odd one or two even boasted a black eye or another battle scar from the night before or bygone encounters. But behind these figures from the past towered the shape of the future: the 160-room hotel and apartment complex rising in blond and red brick. It will be followed by a second hotel and a Venetian restaurant assembled in Italy and shipped to SW6. And then by the final stage, which will include a leisure centre and a sports museum, where the £1 with which Bates bought the club will presumably be framed, next to a digital scoreboard showing the club's current market capitalization, earnings-per-share yield or wine-lake valuation.

The area is to be the 'Covent Garden of west London', according to Bates. Whether this means overcrowded with spendthrift European teenagers and their multicoloured ruck-sacks, home from home to black-tied members of the élite who frequent the opera or a collection of exclusive boutiques selling overpriced designer clothes, it's impossible to say. The answer is almost certainly all three, but supposedly to fund football. 'My hobby is the pursuit of excellence,' Bates has claimed. His job, however, is clearly to make as much money as possible.

And there are so many ways of doing it. Part of the new façade at the Bridge houses one of the most obvious: the biggest club shop in the country, a £2.5 million, three-floor shrine to commercialism in chrome, glass and neon. Its stock ranges from scooters in club colours to ridiculous Ken Bates garden gnomes via a calf-bound official history priced at £595. About 3,000 other Chelsea goods, from bedspreads to mountain bikes, are distributed over more than 10,500 square feet. Ruud Jnr can wake in his Chelsea bedding, pull back his Chelsea curtains, switch on his Chelsea light to reveal his Chelsea wallpaper decorated with a Chelsea clock and a Chelsea pennant, slip on his Chelsea dressing gown and wander to his Chelsea memo-board to read: Must change name by deed poll to Gianluca.

At the store's official opening Gullit, wearing a T-shirt from his own clothing range, posed outside with members of his millionaire's club of players, holding the FA Cup while also balanced on £2,500 CFC mopeds. The stars, who had self-consciously slipped on their new-style replica shirts just before the press photo call, raised what was the most hallowed trophy in English sport – and exposed more of the new sponsors' name emblazoned on their chests. Inside, another photographer, a club man, was waiting to take a snap of fans with the cup for £19.99 a time. Kitting out a son or daughter might not be cheap – around £800 for twenty of the most likely items a child could want – but as Sports Minister and Chelsea fan Tony Banks said to me as I reported on the opening, 'What do you want – a law which stops people spending their own money?'

Sadly, that's exactly what I got when I reached it. Sunday trading laws meant it was closed. Mammon, at least for a couple of hours, remained a poor second to God, who, in turn, was clearly a poor second to football. The man behind the superstore's glass waved a dismissive finger as I tried the door in vain. Around me people hurried to their seats, but I headed back towards the aged makeshift huts which still housed the ticket office charging the highest prices in the Premiership as the hotels and restaurants went up around it.

I thought about buying a programme, but decided against it and instead went home. I didn't have a ticket, frankly never had a chance of getting one and, with even the touts invisible, had no prospect of last-minute success. My cash stayed in my pocket. All I wanted to do was watch my local team, but today that's not as easy as it sounds. Not just at Chelsea for one of the games of the season, but from Arsenal, with its five-year waiting list for season tickets, to Newcastle, with its all-season-ticket crowd, the biggest headache facing many is not the return of hooliganism, or the cost of replica kit, but just getting a ticket – and the price of it.

roots

It is small wonder that attendances at matches gradually fell off from a peak of 77 million in the season 1949/50 to about 20 million in the late 1980s.

Lord Justice Taylor's final report, paragraph 33

Who really remembers the first time? Even if you know which match it was, what can you honestly recall of it? The scorers perhaps – but most likely from the record books or a newspaper clipping lovingly kept inside the programme ever since. Some dramatic moment maybe – if there was one and if you really understood what was going on. The most likely answer, though, is not much. We were, after all, schoolboys, and primary schoolboys at that, going with our dads or uncles or neighbours. We didn't appreciate the significance of the day or the anecdotal value it would later have.

Who remembers when it started to get serious, when weekends, consciously or not, first started to be constructed around the match? When Saturday mornings began to take on a routine; when Saturday nights were made, or ruined, by what went earlier? Then when it wasn't enough to be a regular at home, but away too. Perhaps even when midweek cup ties started to mean taking a day, maybe even two, off work – just to see Oldham or Watford dump you out of the League Cup.

And, for the truly devoted, some might call them the obsessed, when holidays began to be booked around pre-season tours.

For me it came late, in my first weekend at college. A sign went up on a notice-board on the Friday night suggesting that anyone interested in going to tomorrow's game should meet in the foyer in the morning. By the early evening, when we arrived back, I knew I had a new Saturday routine.

Football was all around as I grew up, but the proper game, the professional game, was always distant.

My brother and I played with a ball in the back garden and on the grass verge opposite our house. We wore our replica strips. Mine was a gaudy number – largely red, but with yellow and green stripes running from each shoulder to the base of each leg of the shorts – which made me look like an acid casualty's flashback of a leek. One of his, a little later, was sky blue with the latest design innovation of shadow stripes. Our friends generally wore the distinctive claret and blue kit that their older brothers went to watch in its natural habitat, Villa Park.

We all spent Saturday mornings at an indoor five-a-side session taken by a coach who, we were awed to discover, had once had a trial with the Villa – an opportunity which my best friend from primary school also had when he was a teenager. He and I and our classmates played on a sloping, stony pitch at school. Dad even appeared occasionally on it when the teachers and fathers combined to put a side out – and once embarrassed us beyond speech when he dived, full-length but unathletically, to push aside a goal-bound shot. He was playing left-back.

On Saturday afternoons – at least until it became a time to be pulling on boots of one sort or another, depending on the time of year – we'd watch *Final Score* before we had our fry-up in front of *Basil Brush* or *The Generation Game*. In the evenings we'd watch the likes of Leeds and Liverpool battling it out for honours on *Match of the Day*. And on Sunday we'd watch the terminally less successful local sides on ATV's regional highlights show. But only after we'd been to church, where, a couple of years later, we'd look out for Villa's Tony Morley or Gary Shaw slipping in to Mass after it started, lurking self-consciously at the back throughout and then leaving early.

When I was older I played with new friends, kicking a succession of bald tennis balls around the tarmac parade ground at secondary school. One goal was formed by two of the buttresses of the chapel, the other by the base of steps leading up to the main school buildings. One of the sidelines was the fringe of the playing fields, but we were never allowed to take a proper ball on them as they were reserved purely for rugby and cricket. Nevertheless, we asked the games master if we could form the first ever school football team, but the answer was an unsurprising and unexplained no. So we did it, unofficially, anyway.

Dad would tell stories about his days supporting his home-town team, Blackburn Rovers, too. One of his most repeated was how he saw them robbed of the 1960 FA Cup. How he hitched to London from his National Service base in the South-West, but without tickets. How he met another fan with a spare on the morning of the match. And how their Wembley hopes were crushed just before half-time when Rovers lost one of their best players with a broken leg and – in the days before substitutes – were forced down to ten men and doomed to defeat, 3–0 in the end. One of those, of course, was a dodgy offside.

Another of his favourite tales was even more dramatic, and seemed less likely still. For years I secretly doubted that it was true – doubts which his vague telling of it did nothing to dispel. What he could remember was that he and some of his friends had travelled to Bury to see their side play away. Afterwards they had been among thousands crossing a railway bridge taking them to the trains home when its floor gave way. And one of his friends was among those hurled on to the tracks below. The rest of the group were left a few yards from the gaping hole. In Dad's version of events there were many injured, but the number and much of the other detail had long faded to leave just the outline of the story.

The blanks can be filled in from a trawl through the newspapers of 1952. The seventy-year-old wooden footbridge 'was a solid mass of good-tempered humanity', according to the *Blackburn Times*. Dad's group was delayed because the smallest of them, George Howarth, aged fourteen, had lost his ticket and had stopped to buy a replacement. He tried to make up for lost time by squeezing around and under the adults inching towards the waiting football specials, leaving his bigger friends behind to catch up. But his haste meant that he was in the section which collapsed and was one of 300 or so who tumbled, amid clouds of dust and debris, to the ground.

Somewhere nearby, among the cries of those with broken limbs and the creak of broken timber, lay retired weaver William Hargreaves, aged sixty-six, and John Fowell, aged fifty-two, a winding master at a yarn dyers. They both died. Another 175 fans were injured, including forty-five who were detained in hospital, almost thirty with broken limbs or ribs. Up above, those overlooking the gaping hole, including Dad, desperately called for those behind to stand still so that the pressure of the crowd didn't send anyone else over the edge and down towards the groans of the trapped.

If I'd ever thought about it, or ever believed it, I might have supposed, wrongly, that the disaster was part of the reason why proper football, such as Villa or the Blues of Birmingham City, was so distant; why Dad barely went to matches any more and so rarely took us. If I'd understood such things at the time, I might also have realized the main reason: that it was difficult for him to follow the Rovers from exile, with a young family, in the Midlands – and quite impossible to change teams. Occasionally he did take us to see them play – in Exeter and Plymouth, where he once used to go on the terraces with his father-in-law, my grandad, and at Derby in a cup tie once – but it was a rare treat. Of sorts. Only later did I realize that there was another factor which contributed to our absence, and one which contributed more and more: hooliganism.

The third of Dad's yarns was how the rival sets of supporters used to behave – and this one seemed the most unlikely yet, almost as outlandishly make-believe as his claims to have worn clogs to school. Fans would mingle at half-time, he said, strolling past each other in opposite directions so that each set was standing behind the goal their side was attacking in both halves. There would be no fighting, no police officers rushing in to separate the two sides and, most remarkably, no segregation to stop the mass movement.

Even to my childish ears it sounded quaintly ridiculous. I'd read the modern reality in the newspapers: cup finals marred by mass violence – regardless of the result, attacks launched from and on dedicated away ends and football specials such as he'd caught in the 1950s being destroyed by those travelling in them. Pictures in the papers and on television showed the destruction and illustrated the atmosphere at matches with shots such as the famously chilling one of a fan being led away with a dart poking from his eye. And that, for my generation, was how it had always been.

Villa Park stood as a constant reminder of the game. Throughout the first half of the 1980s I used to pass it every morning on the way to school. The commuter train I caught looped broadside to it, offering a lingering view of the stern but proud structure which dominated an area which was being largely reduced to post-industrial rubble. In the evenings, when I got the bus home, its distinctive floodlights peered above the rooftops of the rows of terraced houses running in parallel lines towards it. One summer I even had a job compiling the electoral roll in the streets around it, traipsing about in its shadows and marvelling at the size of the vast home Holte End up close, but seeing the decay not so apparent from a distance.

St Andrews was a later landmark on the train ride, perched away to the left on higher ground as the diesel engine slowed to a crawl on the approach to New Street Station. Its floodlights were as notable a feature on the skyline, to a dreamy young football fan anyway, as the Rotunda and its blinking digital clock. Yet they still came a poor second to their equivalents at Villa Park, where the bulbs were flamboyantly arranged to form a matching A and V at either end of the ground. St Andrews itself had none of the flourishes of Villa Park either, not the chic innovation of seats coloured to pick out the club initials or the grand, modern stand, all smoked glass and rippled concrete. Most of all, though, what St Andrews lacked was Villa Park's role in my life.

It was where our baby-sitter used to work. It was where Dad and my brother, Adrian, saw the League Cup Final replay between Liverpool and West Ham. Later, it was where Ade celebrated his twenty-first birthday – and so where my mum endured her only game, a dire 0–0 draw with Everton. But most importantly it was, of course, where I saw my first game, on the first day of the season in 1975, when Villa lost 2–1 to Leeds United. Peter Lorimer got both Leeds goals – or so the record books tell me.

For years I remembered the day as something that it wasn't: the game which made me swap sides. I loosely supported Villa, I reckoned, until, with the fickleness of a seven-year-old, I changed to the team which beat them. A further trick of the memory had Leeds trouncing Villa, recording a victory whose size and style, rather than just the fact of the win itself, were the inspiration for my switch. Not that it really needed justifying anyway. As I had no strong paternal or geographical ties – Birmingham might have been where I lived, but, to confuse matters further, Cardiff was, by birth at least, my home town – I wasn't betraying anyone.

The reality is less clear. I know that I was supporting Leeds before then for two reasons. The first is the numbered sock tags which the players wore when winning the FA Cup in 1972. Introduced as a marketing gimmick (along with the players' names being spelt out on their backs for the first time, but on track-suits rather than shirts), they were also an early example of football's merchandising potential – and I had to have a pair (number 4s, like Billy Bremner's). The second is because I remember the disruption caused to a family holiday in Cornwall, which coincided with the riot at the European Cup Final in May 1975, when I was banned from supporting Leeds any more.

The club's followers were already notorious. Four years earlier they had staged what was the most blatant act of hooliganism then seen when dozens of fans ran on to the pitch to confront the referee after he allowed a patently offside goal to stand. Perhaps as generally frowned upon as the thirty-odd arrests and the vehement protests by the players was the reaction of club officials. Manager Don Revie refused to condemn the fans: 'I don't blame them at all. The referee's decision was diabolical.' His chairman, a respected councillor, added, equally amorally, 'I'm not blaming the spectators. There was every justification for it.'

There were similar attempts at justification after Paris – two penalty appeals were turned down and then a Lorimer strike was disallowed for another dubious offside before Bayern Munich scored on the break and went on to win. Years later there were also rumours that the referee had been bribed. But UEFA were little impressed and banned Leeds from Europe for three years.

I had rather more luck with Dad, who relented after I threw a tantrum which was matched only seven years later when Leeds were relegated from the First Division. Then I set aside homework and sat listening to Radio Two's commentary on the vital, final game – even though it was less than ten miles away at West Bromwich Albion. At the final whistle, which confirmed the drop, I wept in angry frustration. And when the fans who were at the Hawthorns began destroying it, I wept some more. Perhaps Dad had been right all along. But, obviously, I didn't tell him that.

For years I had been calling myself a Leeds fan. In truth I was nothing of the sort. Fans could discuss the form of the side. Fans could at least recognize the players, which was impossible for those of us who just read match reports in the papers. Fans went to watch their side.

By the time I left home and moved north to go to university, I had only ever been to Leeds itself once, when Dad had some sort of sales conference in the city and extended it to a family weekend which included a father and sons trip to Elland Road. We watched one of my favourite, but until then pretty much faceless, players, Welsh international Carl Harris, score the winner in a 1–0 win over Norwich in 1981.

For the first time, though, I was also properly aware of another part of the club: the ranks of fans on the terraces. At Villa or wherever, we'd always watched from the stands, usually sitting along one of the touchlines, away from the noisy ends. At Elland Road our seats overlooked the corner flag, and just to our right were the massed faces and voices of the Kop, chanting and singing, sucking in its collective breath as Norwich went close, exhaling an exaggerated 'Oooh' when Leeds did. Animated too, with isolated eddies of movement as Leeds attacked and alive with wave after wave of motion when Harris scored. Injecting life into the afternoon, providing a soundtrack to action on the pitch.

When I first joined them, five years later, it was an unnerving, even unpleasant experience. I knew none of the rituals. I stood in the wrong place (either directly behind or, worse still, completely away from the crush barriers, which meant in each surge I was either crushed against metal or swept away down the terraces). I would open and shut my mouth in what I hoped looked like a convincing manner while desperately trying to pick up the words to the songs. I don't think I ever did pull my hands out of my pockets to clap just as everyone else stopped, but a few times it felt like I did. And all around were real fans, a few of them a daunting type I'd never come across before: burly, some of them miners or, increasingly, ex-miners, leery and beery.

But even before the end of that first game, a 3–0 win against Crystal Palace, I was starting to feel at home. I had mastered my first chants – which, given that one consisted of grunting 'Leeds' repeatedly, the other of singing 'We are Leeds' to the tune of 'Here We Go', wasn't too difficult. I recognized the players, and which of them were the favourites – generally gutsy fighters with the aggression, but little of the skill, of Bremner. I'd started to learn the routines: singing each player's name individually in the warm-up, waiting for a wave of acknowledgement and then asking for an encore via a version of 'Nice One, Cyril' personalized for each of them; a rousing chorus of the club anthem, 'Marching Altogether', before kick-off; the forearm jab into the air, accompanied by grunts of 'Leeds', every time we won a corner; and the comic impersonations of an ambulance siren's nee-nahs whenever the opposition's trainer scuttled across the pitch to tend a fallen player.

On paper, out of context, the chants lose all meaning. Some become embarrassingly juvenile, the grunts especially just plain senseless. But I mention them to illustrate the range of vocal support which was offered. There were others too, even more unreal in black and white: 'YRA', 'We're Yorkshire's Republican Army'; 'We're Leeds United. We'll Never be Defeated'; 'Que Sera Sera', reworked as a unique and violently anti-Chelsea song; and the peculiar cocktail of nihilism and obscenity which was 'Let's Go Fucking Mental' – a song, accompanied by cheery pogoing, which later became England's 'Let's All Have a Disco', but which also came to be used

as some sort of evidence against us. A match was incomplete
without most, if not all, of them.

There were the one-offs too, like when the PA played the
number-one hit of the time and thousands of voices joined in,
just like the singing of the unprompted Anfield Kop in the
1960s. Except that we were all squeaking in painfully fake
falsettos to the hummed opening of the Communards' 'Don't
Leave Me This Way'. And there were the trends as well, most
famously the inflatable craze which started with Manchester
City's bananas and got sillier from there. It never caught on at
Leeds, but the Mexican wave did, transformed into something
much more than a diversion for those in the seats when they
got bored by the game – and an irritation for anyone actually
trying to watch the game. Someone would bellow 'Sidddown'
and we'd crouch as best we could and spring up as the wave
went by, punching the air and shouting 'Leeds' again. And
this happened not just on the terraces but on buses and trains
to the game. Even in the street.

All the while there was also the constant contact with those
around, the physical support in the shifting crowd. There were
the different types of surge: the two-step tumble which was
just a readjustment to the ebb and flow of thousands of bodies;
the relocation down the terrace prompted by a near-miss on
the pitch, when all the reference points of the match – the
goal, the bloke next to you, the clock and the scoreboard –
were temporarily rearranged; and the anarchy of a goal. Only
in hindsight did any of it seem dangerous; at the time there
was nowhere safer. If you started to stumble to the floor, a
stranger would almost instantly pull you back to your feet; if
there was a crush, or the bloke beside you wasn't ideal company for the afternoon, you just manoeuvred yourself up, or
down, or to the side a bit. Only outside, at the turnstiles, did
you ever feel slightly concerned.

To appreciate the terraces fully, though, to understand their
dynamics and power, you simply had to be there. In fact, that

was the point: you had to be there. In those days it was the only statement of real support. There was no mass proxy of wearing a replica shirt in front of a giant screen in the pub (and certainly few such shirts at matches, where colours might provoke an assault from opposing fans). There was no real chance to see your side on TV, as live games were a rarity limited to just over a dozen a season. Being there meant being part of it.

And an active part of it. Every time a home player said the crowd was worth a goal start or an away one talked of the daunting atmosphere, we knew he was talking about us. The most common chant was 'We are Leeds', because we *were* Leeds. We weren't just watching. We were off-pitch players, unable to contribute on the field but doing so from the terraces. The team rarely lost at home – whole seasons would go by without a defeat at Elland Road – and we were proud of that because we knew we were playing our part, doing our job as the players did theirs. In the 1970s Leeds had been Bremner and Lorimer, in the 1980s were John Sheridan and Ian Baird, into the 1990s would be David Batty and Gary Speed, but always us.

The togetherness, the camaraderie – to use the word which always is – was unlike anything I'd ever experienced anywhere else, unlike anything I've ever experienced since. There was the grand shared history which everyone knew about, the cup and title wins, but also the less celebrated moments in the following, fallow years which bound us. Such as when full-back 'Rocket' Ronnie Robinson persisted with the offside trap at an away game in which we were already 6–2 down (in what, unsurprisingly, proved to be his last game for the club); or when Vinnie Jones scythed down a mascot with a sliding tackle in the pre-match warm-up; or laughing at West Brom's basketball player of a midfielder – little realizing we'd later pay £2.6 million for him, one Carlton Palmer.

Most memorably, perhaps, although it's a hard choice, there

was when Brighton ran out, sheepishly, at what was sometimes
called Fortress Elland Road, in a bright-pink away strip. With
the word Nobo, their sponsors, emblazoned on the front. The
only incident which matched that for mass hilarity and the
acute embarrassment of the victim was when the Tannoy
burst into life in the second half of another game to relay an
important message to someone: 'Your girlfriend's ill and so
won't be able to meet you at the station as planned.' And the
Kop, as one, gave a sympathetic, sarcastic 'Aaah.' I asked
Mum if she might leave a message at the station next time.

Looking back, I can remember many of the results, some of
the goals, but most of all instants on the terraces. When Sheridan beat England goalkeeper Peter Shilton with a twenty-five-
yard volley – which he'd teed up to himself when a free-kick
was rolled into his path – over the defensive wall and no one
moved, not Shilton, or us, as we all tried to absorb what had
happened; then the wave of human celebration which crashed
all around as he peeled away from his static team-mates in
bug-eyed celebration. Or when fans invaded the pitch at the
end of that season to chair Sheridan, again, around the ground,
acclaiming their hero for the less than regal achievement of a
3–2 win over West Brom which secured a play-off place.
Or when we equalized in the last minute of a game against
Blackburn a couple of seasons later and I found myself in the
arms of one of the burly fans I'd once found so intimidating,
jumping about and both of us lost in another of the moments
which made football what it was.

Finally, and most of all, the away game at Leicester when
we spent all of half-time engaged in a surreal massed rendition
of the whistled refrain from a De La Soul hit of the time. We
lost the match, even though we were winning at half-time,
but it was a great, great day anyway – because we made it so.
And that, as much as anything else, was what football was
about.

*

One particular game captured almost the entire experience of football in the 1980s, good and bad: the visit of QPR for a fifth-round FA Cup tie.

A dozen of us had gone to the first game, the one advertised on the notice in the foyer at college. Its author was another first-year student called Darren, who had grown up in Leeds until his family moved south. So he had the accent, the United flat cap and, most importantly, the knowledge: how best to get to Leeds, which buses to catch to the ground and where to get a drink.

We had innocently followed him into the Whip, a pub tucked off one of the main city-centre streets, which he reckoned pulled the best Tetley's in town and would be full of fans. As strangers, though, we were looked up and down on entry. As strangers without stubble as part of their haircuts, we were regarded even more suspiciously. Strangers without a York-shire accent did well to keep their voices down, I decided. Darren bought the round.

All the others from the first outing quickly dropped away, but Darren and I were back the following week and a fortnight after that and so on. We usually skipped the pub, grabbing a burger or some chips and then heading straight to the ground, but four months after our first visit, before the QPR game, we stopped for another pint – and ended up missing the biggest game of the season, the biggest home game for the ten seasons since our last run in the FA Cup. But still enjoyed one of the best afternoons of the year.

Usually we arrived at the ground at about 2.30, early enough to secure our place on the Kop – centre-back, just below the electronic scoreboard and about in line with the left-hand post – but not so early that our legs were starting to ache by half-time; our timing was a question of where we got in, not *whether* we got in. Four years in the Second Division, twelve years without a trophy, had taken their toll on the crowds, which had fallen to as few as 13,000.

We realized it was going to be different for QPR when the bus from the city centre got stuck in traffic on the slip road leading from the motorway to the ground. More so when a few of its passengers opened the emergency exit and started to jump down on to the road and run through the traffic to get to the turnstiles quicker. And completely when we did the same, only to arrive to find a scene of absolute bedlam. There were no queues outside the Kop, just shapeless and shifting swarms in front of each turnstile. The ones in the middle, where a fence at the back of the concourse limited the room for movement, had all merged into each other to form a single heaving mass. Some of those in it who managed to click through shot past the gateman side by side with fellow fans, forced together purely by the pressure of the crowds. Among them was another student called Andy, with whom I'd later go to games and who still describes the moments before the game as the most terrifying in his life.

Darren and I joined one of the swells at the edge of the mass, ready to be buffeted, to be shoved and fall this way and that until we made it to a turnstile. All around others were arriving behind us, to the side of us and in front of us, some running from swarm to swarm in the hope one was going to be quicker than another. Soon we had to use our hands to create breathing space away from the next man's back while balancing as our torsos abruptly shifted one way and then the next as our legs remained still. We tried to move, but there was nowhere to go unless a surge took you. Every step forward was lost by several to either side. And when cheers echoed from inside as the teams took to the pitch, the pressure increased along with tempers and desperation.

Then the Kop entrances began to be closed, so the crush moved to those to the Lowfields terracing, which ran down the side of the pitch. Then they were closed too. The ground was, for the first time anyone could remember, full, with more than 31,000 fans – the biggest crowd for five years. Hundreds and hundreds more of us were locked out – a fact which is utterly unremarkable today, but then was incredible, unknown in the memory of anyone around me.

Some of us ran from entrance to entrance, all around the ground, to see if there were any still open. A few caught a glimpse of the unreachable green grass of the pitch as we jogged past the large iron access gates for the groundsman's equipment – and one or two made a hopeless attempt to force them open. The pace of the search dropped as we completed an entire circuit of the ground. Some, disappointed, drifted off home. But a couple of hundred of us were more stubborn.

We hadn't travelled out to the ground not to be part of the game – so we walked away from the Kop and the Lowfields, past the away end, crossed the main road, stood on an area of gritty wasteground and waited. And waited. Until one of the goalkeepers punted the ball upfield, and high above the pitch, where we caught a glimpse of it through a gap in the corner of the ground and cheered wildly. And then waited for the next sighting. In between we watched the electronic scoreboard above the distant Kop and sang and clapped our support – even though it was unlikely anyone could hear us. But we felt we were playing our part. And when the Kop sang back, 'Car park, car park, give us a song', we knew we were. We jumped into each other with glee when we saw the terraces erupt in celebration of the opening goal. We stood in angry silence as the scoreboard flashed up 1–1 to the muffled sound of cheering.

Then, with full-time approaching, the police, who had monitored us but not moved us on, cleared us away towards the buses back to the city and, more relevantly, away from the exit for away fans. And that is why one of the most cherished goals scored while I was at Elland Road – a thwack of a header from a perfectly timed run by centre-half Brendan Ormsby which he celebrated by continuing past the goal at the Kop end and scaling the perimeter fence to get as close to the fans as possible – was one I never even saw and which I celebrated by bouncing up and down in a seat on a stationary double-decker bus.

The memories all came back as I sat down in the Whip for the first time in years, now attracting nothing more than slight curiosity for being on my own. The brass and dark wood bar was unchanged, but the ambience was a world away from its previous spit and sawdust, and more spit. A television piped the thoughts of Sky pundits from the corner of the room, although no one seemed very interested. Among the small groups supping, there didn't seem to be anyone heading to Elland Road.

At the ground, I looked across from the old car park. The empty corner of the ground over which we watched the scoreboard had been a symbol of the club's decline. Work started to develop the area in 1975, but stopped, with only concrete foundations and piles in place, because of a lack of money. For the next sixteen years the only change was the length of the red-brown rust stains which bled from the posts until, in 1991, they were finally built upon in the first major ground improvements in almost two decades. Now it's completely overshadowed by the neighbouring development, which came within a year: the 17,000-seat East Stand. Its side cladding, topped, appropriately, by a satellite dish, blocked my view from outside.

I walked around to the match-day ticket office and joined the queue. On the left used to be the training pitches. They were where, in my childhood, the team picture used to be taken. In the background, behind Bremner, Gray, Lorimer and the rest, dapper lettering spelling out Leeds United (complete with what I always thought was the classy addition of 'AFC' afterwards) was clearly visible on the distinguished rear façade of the West Stand. It hadn't changed at all in the 1980s, when we sometimes watched a bit of the youth team – including lads called David Batty and Gary Speed – for free in their match-day-morning fixtures on the training pitch. Now, the West Stand has an ugly banqueting suite grafted on to it and the training pitches have been covered in asphalt so they can be used for more car-parking.

In the programme I read of the future plans for what were the training pitches. Chris Akers, chairman of the public limited company which owns the club, spoke of the proposal to build an arena for basketball, ice hockey and other non-football events as the way to close the financial gap to the likes of Manchester United. In the programme from my previous game a couple of weeks earlier, against Villa, he had explained how the project fitted in with his overall vision for the club: 'At the time of our successful offer for Leeds United, we described our objective as being to create one of Europe's leading vertically integrated sports, media and leisure groups. The . . . arena is a major step towards achieving that objective.' On the page opposite, I'd happened to notice, was an advert for a Rolls-Royce dealership, nearby one for a private boarding school.

Back around by the redeveloped corner, the leisure part of the group was in operation as a steady stream of fans wandered into the superstore. A routine enough scene – except that some of them were in the black and white stripes of Grimsby, the visitors in the fourth round of the cup. They scurried towards the away end, only too happy to have purchased a piece of the Premier League while they could. The store exit delivered them outside entrances to the away end, the point where tensions always used to be highest. Now, in the greatest trans-formation in a sport where shopping has replaced fighting, there was not even the merest suggestion of violence.

But neither was there any real sense of rivalry, or of a shared past – even though two weeks after the QPR game I watched when Grimsby visited Elland Road in the *league*. Still less any sense of a shared future. In 1987 the match wasn't safe until a late penalty saw us home 2–0; now, the result was pretty much a foregone conclusion. The visitors started brightly, but Leeds soon started to display an extra degree of class and Robert Molenaar, then fellow Dutchman Jimmy-Floyd Hassel-baink confirmed another 2–0 win. The same result, but from teams now really much more than just two divisions apart.

The most vivid contrast, though, was among the crowd itself. The passion of the past, the spontaneity, the humour, the culture, perhaps most of all the sense of *us*, were absent. Obviously, there were cheering and applause when the goals went in, but not a fraction of the explosion of joy – even outside the ground – at Ormsby's cup goal. There was some singing too, but at a gentler volume and less frequently, and with less variation, than that which crowds of half the size used to generate. And the crowd itself was well under the average for Premier League games. A decent cup run was unfolding again, but no one seemed very excited – apparently because it wasn't the all-encompassing Premier League. Per-haps compared to the 1980s and early 1990s, the worst I can say is that within a matter of days I didn't really remember much about it.

One thing hadn't changed, superficially at least, because at kick-off I was still standing outside the ground as the Kop turnstiles failed to feed fans through quickly enough. But there was no crush, no anarchy and probably little danger as the mostly orderly queues started to snake into one another. Even when cheers echoed from inside as the teams took to the pitch, everyone carried on queuing. I was just beginning to think that football really had changed beyond recognition when someone immediately behind roared what I'd been long expecting at the nearest steward: 'This is a bloody joke, this is. Why's kick-off not been put back? Haven't you heard of Hillsborough?'

one
spring day

The football continued to joyous shouting and singing round the rest of the ground while those crushed and trapped slowly expired.

Lord Justice Taylor's interim report, paragraph 79

On a dividing wall in an unexceptional common room of a student hall of residence in Sheffield hangs a small photograph. It is an image of a young man enjoying a social function held in the hall or at one of its similar near neighbours. Resplendent in black tie and dinner jacket, he grins, slightly out of focus, from the sort of snap by which every student remembers carefree college days. The sort that come to adorn kitchen notice-boards and photo albums as mementoes of new-found friends or partners. This one, however, is a reminder of something else.

Joe McCarthy was president of Sorby Hall, a fact recorded in the roll of honour above the picture. In 1987 and 1988 he helped welcome new students and ease them into life away from home and parents. Today he might be deploying those leadership skills, allied to a degree in business studies, in commerce or industry; he would probably be living in a leafy suburb such as the one in Sheffield where the hall stands; perhaps, like many of the friends with whom he shared those formative, independent university years, he would even have a family of his own. Except that Joe was one of the ninety-six who went to a football match just a couple of miles across the city on a glorious spring day in 1989 and never came back.

A plaque below the picture records simply: 'This room is dedicated to the memory of Joseph Daniel McCarthy, who died in the Hillsborough Stadium disaster on the 15th of April 1989, aged 21 years. R.I.P.' The tribute in what is now known as Joe's Junior Common Room has been there ever since, reminding generations of subsequent students of his death. The transitory nature of the hall's student population meant that within a couple of years there were none there who actually knew Joe; a couple more and the academics who were wardens and had helped to establish the memorial had also moved on. Now Iain Forrest, the hall manager, is alone in being able to remember the person in the picture. But still it remains. 'Of course, none of the present-day students knew Joe at all,' Iain says. 'But when the room was refurbished recently they were very keen to keep its name and leave the picture there. Even though no one knew him, they very much wanted to remember him.'

Above and to the left is another roll of honour, this one recording the supporting cast of student representatives. Again the dozens of names on it mean little to the teenagers and twenty-somethings playing pool and generally winding down beneath it now – even though one of the anonymous ex-officials was and will be forever linked with Joe. There is no indication of it, but Colin Auton, Sports Secretary 1986/7, was one of Joe's best friends. Nor is there any hint of how close he came to being remembered in words and pictures too.

At the heart of the story is a grotesque irony: Colin came within seconds of dying because of football, only to be saved by it. By student standards, he was a great player, conspicuous in kickabouts in the shadow of Sorby's tower block because of talent which matched his midfield-dynamo build and Chris Waddle haircut; by professional standards, he was promising, appearing for non-league Marine before university and later offered a trial with Doncaster. In between, in Sheffield, he was recommended to Wednesday. Twice a week he trained with the youth team at Hillsborough. And so when he came to be trapped on its terraces, gagging for breath, he was saved by the fitness developed, in large part, at the ground where one of his best friends was dying.

Before the story unfolds, perhaps I should explain how I know of the bond between Colin and Joe, or can comment on Colin's footballing prowess. I was at Sheffield, and in Sorby, with them. That notice about the trip to Leeds was scrawled on a blackboard in the corridor just outside what is now Joe's common room. In it I once half-heartedly discussed with Joe himself whether or not I would stand in the presidential election which he went on to win. In the ad-hoc games in which Colin starred, I was one of the less gifted participants.

And there is one other thing: Hillsborough was the day I tried to show some youthful journalistic initiative and ended up in the midst of a disaster.

Colin had graduated in engineering in the summer of 1988 and left Sheffield with happy memories, not least of the FA Cup semifinal at Hillsborough that year when Liverpool beat Nottingham Forest. He'd taken time off from revising for his finals to go to the match with old schoolfriends from his native Merseyside. But it was one of only a handful of games he'd managed to get to that season. And that was why one of his first buys with his wages from his first full-time job was a season ticket for the Anfield Kop.

He had moved back to Liverpool, back to those friends and back to the routine of joining them in their fortnightly pilgrimage to Anfield – a pleasure he'd forsaken as an impoverished student. He went with his oldest friend, Paul Brady, and a couple of others. 'I just wanted to get a job back home and go to the match, live life to the full and enjoy myself with them, sort of catching up on what I missed out on when I was a student,' he said in his soft Scouse lilt.

Come January and the yearly contrast between the warm optimism of the early stages of the FA Cup and the bitterness of the winter weather, there was no question but that they would be at every tie. For the most distant fixtures, they were in Liverpool's travel club. But for the closer away games Paul's job as a driver for a refrigeration company gave them cheap, if chilly, transport courtesy of his works van. They used both methods to follow a run which took them to distant places such as Carlisle and Hull and, in between, a dangerous one, Millwall ('That's how keen we were'). In contrast, the short hop over the Pennines to Hillsborough for the semifinal should have been easy and safe.

Colin had more reason to look forward to the trip than the others. He had arranged to meet about half a dozen friends still in Sheffield for lunch. Among them was Joe, a Liverpool fan despite coming from London, who was, thanks to the ticket Colin had got for him, also going to the match. Their rendezvous was a pub especially popular with students on account of its head-swimmingly strong beer. Colin and his friends from home, though, were tender after a Friday night out and just ordered shandies.

At the sun-drenched stadium the first members of the 54,000 sell-out crowd were starting to take up their places. The terrace-dwellers among the Forest support eased through one of forty-two turnstiles and spread themselves across the vast 21,000-capacity Kop. But the 10,100 Liverpool standing fans, served by just seven turnstiles, were unable to do the same at the opposite, Leppings Lane, end of the ground because of changes introduced after an accident eight years earlier. Then, thirty-eight fans at another semifinal, between Spurs and Wolves, were injured in a surge caused by late-arriving fans. Now, sideways movement was restricted by fences which ran from top to bottom of the terrace and anyone who followed the obvious route on to it found themselves in the central two of the pens created by the fencing – and confined to them.

At 2.15 a Tannoy announcement asked those in the central pens to move forward to make room for others still coming in. But far fewer than expected were doing so as confusion outside the turnstiles became congestion. Some fans got to a grille in one of the three blocks – two for the 14,100 fans in the seats, the other for those on the terraces – and found their confusingly labelled ticket was for one of the other two. A few other fans without tickets tried to pay their way in and a few more with Kop tickets attempted to use them at Leppings Lane. All were redirected across the increasingly packed concourse or turned away back into it. Individual queues had already gone.

All the while more and more fans were streaming in through the bottleneck at the entrance to the area, past the arc of gateposts and gates which marked the outer limits of the ground when they were closed on non-match days. On the left, a corner shop was the barrier defining one edge of the crowd; on the right, a fence which stopped fans from spilling down a bank to a brook below. The headcount in between, in a space about the size of the penalty area on the Hillsborough pitch, was already in the thousands. And all the while more and more fans were arriving.

By 2.30 the crush was such that police officers positioned outside the turnstiles to search every fan no longer had the space to do so. Colleagues on horseback were finding it increasingly difficult to manoeuvre. At the front of the crowd, the pressure was further slowing the rate at which fans were getting in as some became jammed in the doors or the turnstiles themselves. Further back, the backlog was starting to spill into the road and into the paths of buses and cars. The officer in charge of policing the area, Superintendent Roger Marshall, radioed to have traffic stopped.

Less than 100 yards away other senior officers were also monitoring the situation via closed-circuit television. Pictures from the cameras overlooking the turnstiles were relayed into the Portakabin-style police control room which was perched above the corner of the Leppings Lane terrace and looked out across it. Watching them was Superintendent Bernard Murray, who assessed the situation, and the overall match commander, Chief Superintendent David Duckenfield, who agreed with his colleague's advice that all those still outside would be in by kick-off. He also reaffirmed the policy on delaying kick-off: only if there was some major outside factor, such as a crash on the motorway; not if fans just turned up late.

On the concourse, Superintendent Marshall climbed on to a parapet to try to get a better view of what was happening. A fan tried to push him off. Another threw a beer can at one of the mounted officers. But most were far more concerned about getting in well before the looming kick-off – and relieving pressure so intense that one of the horses was lifted into the air and a fan who put his hand in his pocket to check that his ticket was still there found he was unable to pull either out again. Some women and children were fainting. A few of the more athletic supporters managed to climb on to the roof of the turnstile block and jumped inside the ground, showing their tickets to police and stewards before heading to the terraces. Others started to rattle the concertina gates at the side of the turnstile blocks which would be opened to allow fans out of the ground after the match.

At 2.40 there were more than 5,000 fans crammed on the concourse. For those at the head of the phalanx, closest to the turnstiles, it had become difficult to breathe. The lucky few who did pass through staggered out the other side, into the ground, winded and dripping with sweat. Most of them complained to the police inside and demanded something be done to ease the crush. Then caught their breath and headed towards the tunnel which led to the central pens.

Superintendent Marshall realized that the crowd was unmanageable. He radioed to ask for reinforcements, a Tannoy announcement to ask fans to stop pushing and a vehicle with a loudspeaker to deliver the same message. A PC in a Land Rover arrived and made the amplified request for restraint, but it had no impact; most people couldn't move, let alone move back or away to create space. The PC radioed back his failure and suggested that kick-off be postponed. The request was rejected – even though the crowd was so big that it would have required at least forty minutes to pass through the turnstiles even in perfect conditions.

At 2.50 Superintendent Marshall radioed control with a request that the concertina gates be opened, warning that otherwise someone was going to be killed; he had already asked twice in the preceding three minutes. Finally Chief Superintendent Duckenfield approved the order: 'Open the gates.' There were three, one for each turnstile block. But Gate C – the one for the terraces – was opened by far the longest and allowed in by far the largest number of fans. In five minutes more than 2,000 streamed through, most of them heading for the central pens.

The previous year's semifinal, between the same two teams, had also been played at Hillsborough and also saw the central pens full before kick-off. Then, police officers stood at the tunnel entrance and directed fans around to the sides. But the debriefing contained no mention of it and so it formed no part of the planning for 1989. Chief Superintendent Duckenfield was also ignorant of the crush in 1981 and inexperienced in big-match policing at Hillsborough: he had been in his job just twenty-one days before the match and the only match played in that period had been a far smaller one – and even then he had left control to his deputies. Worried about a possible pitch invasion, he did order officers to monitor fans heading for the stand, displaying the conditioning which saw all fans marked down as potential hooligans. But he did nothing about those heading for the terraces; they were fenced in, controlled.

All of them were faced by the sign above the tunnel as soon as they entered the ground. 'Standing', it said, and 'B' – the letter corresponding to that on their tickets. There were two other routes, both to the outside pens, but both involved ignoring the sign and walking around the sides of the stand (one was via a gate through a brick wall), and they were little known even to regulars. Plans to install a better system had been shelved because of the cost. So the vast majority of the 2,000 went down the tunnel, towards the central pens, which were already over-full according to the capacity guesstimated by Sheffield Wednesday's engineer, over-full according to safety regulations, which assumed proper crush barriers were in place – which they weren't; and well over-full, most obviously, according to the faces, draining of colour, of those already in deep distress in them.

Colin's group – him, a distant relative, Mick O'Keefe, Joe and Paul – arrived a couple of minutes after the gate was opened, cutting it a bit fine after lingering over lunch with their friends, but confident that they weren't going to be late thanks to Colin's local knowledge from his twice-weekly trips to the ground. They'd even budgeted for being held up for a couple of minutes, as they had been the year before, at police ticket checkpoints. But there were none. Instead they walked straight up to the turnstiles, but then through the large concertina exit gate, which was open alongside. Any questions about why it was open were overwhelmed by the need to get in as quickly as possible. No one checked their tickets. They too headed for the tunnel and the central pens. Colin said, 'I knew

Hillsborough quite well, from training, and I didn't even know there were other ways to the terraces.'

They emerged from the darkness into a trapped pack of humanity. Joe and Paul, the taller ones of the group, could see something they didn't like in front, so they all eased themselves further to the right, towards the far fence of the right-hand pen and, they thought, away from danger. Around them other fans were starting to make their escape into the stand above, climbing up the wall which flanked either side of the mouth of the tunnel or the fences and being pulled up by those above. At the sides others were clambering over the fences into the comparatively deserted neighbouring pens.

At 3.04 a Peter Beardsley shot rattled the Forest bar at the Kop end. Fans at the rear of the Liverpool end surged forward in excitement; those closer to the pitch, not even watching the match as they fought to keep breathing, were crushed further. Usually a surge would see fans tumble forward and then ebb back. But the weight of numbers in the central pens meant there was no receding. Anyone whose breath had been knocked from them now had about four minutes to live. One fan later said, 'There was no cheering around me, just screaming.'[1] And hidden by the noise, by the shouting and the crying, was the creak of metal, corroded metal, being reshaped and then snapped as a steel barrier in the right-hand pen succumbed to the pressure being exerted on it.[2]

Those standing behind it fell forward. Others standing behind them toppled on top. Some of the force pulsed down to the front of the terrace, where the earliest arrivals were pressed into the wire mesh of the perimeter fencing. But much was simply absorbed by the pile-up of bodies where the barrier had been. And in the middle of it were Colin and the others.

The police control room had first spotted that something was wrong when one of the emergency exit gates in the perimeter fencing, then another, sprang open just before kick-off and a few fans staggered out. The surge when Beardsley hit the bar forced a few out through the narrow gap. Others were scaling the fencing. Senior officers called for reinforcements – to deal with a pitch invasion. The rank and file arrived to be confronted by the truth: piles of bodies, especially at the exit gates where fans had tried to escape, some alive, some only just, and many dead, faces blue, eyes staring.

Superintendent Roger Greenwood, the senior officer at pitch level, had also become concerned when he saw fans spilling from the terraces. He walked from his position at the players' tunnel to the Liverpool end and immediately realized that there was a severe crush inside. At first he thought it could be eased and he stood on the low wall in front of the fencing, waving his arms to urge fans to move backwards. Other officers joined him. But at five and a half minutes past three he turned away, ran on to the pitch and told the referee to stop the match.

A little over a mile away Darren and I were loafing around the house we had shared after leaving Sorby, him in the kitchen watching *Grandstand*, me upstairs in my bedroom, reading the paper rather than revising. When the snooker gave way to first news of some sort of trouble at the semifinal, he called me down. He had the experience which would have given him a good idea of what had happened. Two years earlier he had been among the Leeds fans who visited Hillsborough to see a semifinal and experienced difficulties getting in and then a crush in the central pens, but also a delayed kick-off. Watching the game on television, I had realized how packed it was when I spotted him jammed right at the front of the terrace, far away from our usual position. When Leeds scored, it seemed that the surge which engulfed him would have swept him on to the pitch but for the perimeter fencing.

I knew nothing of the dangers of a big match, though.

When *Grandstand* switched back to snooker, I decided to see if the national papers in London wanted a 'stringer' – albeit one with no experience beyond student journalism – to cover what appeared to be the latest outbreak of violence. Even if they had staff in the North, I thought, they would have to travel from Manchester or Leeds. I could be at the ground in minutes. I grabbed a pad of Basildon Bond writing paper and a pen. From a phone box at the end of the road I called the *Sunday Times* and was told to get to the ground quickly.

Writing now, I have that pad in front of me, and a complete ticket for the Leppings Lane terrace. I can't remember which of the fans I interviewed as I headed towards the ground gave it to me. It might have been a Chris Grogan, the first supporter I questioned, about a quarter of a mile from Hillsborough, and leaving because he was 'scared shitless'. He was the first to indicate hooliganism was not the story: 'People went on the pitch not to cause disruption but to get help.' And the appalling scale of the story: 'There's people dead on the pitch.'

Or perhaps a John Kinsan, among the far greater numbers walking away once I'd got just a few hundred yards further on, who identified the basic problem and voiced a fear: 'There was too many people in too small a space. Everyone's worried now that the fans are going to get the blame. It's not our fault.'

Or it could have been an Anthony Coleman, on Leppings Lane itself, who was the first with the key fact: 'The police opened the gates. Hundreds got through. It was about eight minutes to three. The radio reports are saying the gates were forced, but I wish I had a camera. I'd lay the total blame on the police. If the fans were at fault, I'd condemn them, but they weren't.'

None of this ever appeared in the *Sunday Times*. Its report alluded to 'claims that police and turnstile staff waved through crowds of Liverpool supporters' but added the phrase 'without tickets'. Further down a fan named Peter McGuiness was quoted: 'Moments before the kick-off a steward opened the gates outside the ground to let us in . . .' But it came after Wednesday secretary Graham Mackrell's quote: 'The disaster was caused by a surge. Forest were in the ground early, Liverpool were not.' Yet the ticket I have in front of me clearly states: 'You are requested to take up your position 15 mins. before kick-off.' And below the appeal is the signature of Graham Mackrell.

As I heard the real story from Liverpool fans leaving the scene, my willingness to do the job I'd talked my way into, to get a cherished by-line, was fading rapidly anyway. It was clear that this was more than the pitch invasion or hooliganism I'd been expecting. It was also worryingly apparent that some fans were so furious that one comment or confrontation could yet spark some violence. But most of all, it was bloody obvious that there were people dead.

One instant finally extinguished the last embers of my enthusiasm. A lad about my age saw me taking notes as I talked to other supporters and headed towards me wearing a look of child-like bewilderment and animal fury. His eyes were blazing with malice, but flooded with tears. He walked straight at me and kicked my makeshift notebook from my hands as he told me to fuck off, and then to fuck off again as he stood waiting to see if I did. His mates pulled him back before he could kick any more, if that's what he wanted to do, told him to calm down and even apologized on his behalf: 'He's upset. You know?'

Him and thousand upon thousand of others. Fans leaving through Gate C, some missing their shoes, many missing friends or relatives, were desperately scanning the crowd for familiar faces. Others, sitting on the pavement and slumped against walls, were weeping uncontrollably – their emotions in complete contrast to the occasional embrace as families or friends were reunited. Some sat hunched, very still and very quiet, and didn't move. Others loudly tried to make complaints to the police. One man shouted, 'You should all be up in court for this.' Soon afterwards the Tannoy made its first announcement of consequence: 'Unfortunately, the game has been abandoned. Please stay calm.' It was just over an hour after the players first left the pitch.

Try as I might to remember, the next couple of hours have long been confined to the deepest recesses of my mind. I know I ended up in the press box, where I had been told to meet the *Sunday Times* match reporter. But how I got there is almost blank. There is the vaguest of recollections of somehow getting into the ground through Gate C, walking around to the right – one of the ways fans should have been directed – and cutting across the corner of the terrace to get into the main stand. Past the once solid metal of that crush barrier, now grotesquely twisted out of shape. Past the few Liverpool scarves hanging from some of the other barriers. Past the perimeter fencing now half peeled away after doomed efforts to rip it clean off. And finally past the perimeter track, where the advertising boards which had been requisitioned as ad-hoc stretchers had been dumped, next to a series of plastic bags, one containing watches, another glasses, a third predominantly red and white T-shirts, hats and scarves, and another shoes from boy's sizes upwards. Past all the details captured in photographs and absent from my mind.

In the press box the journalists who should have been filing match reports and finishing their day's work by getting the post-match quotes were having to keep their offices informed not of a simple scoreline but of the mounting death toll. At first it was merely confirmation that there had been fatalities, then numbers: twenty, then fifty-three, seventy-four, eighty-four and finally ninety-five – figures which were being compiled in what had been a gymnasium in the bowels of the stand, but had become a makeshift mortuary. And with each upward correction, the mood of resigned desolation, but professional efficiency, among the reporters seemed to lurch further towards just plain despair at a playing field becoming a killing field.

As the real reporters went about their work, I sat in silence having filed my limited, and unused, contribution to the story. They had watched as Beardsley's shot against the bar at one end was soon followed by the sight of a Liverpool supporter seemingly trying to demolish the goal-frame at the other. Some of the crowd voiced their anger at the apparent hooligan. In fact he had been hoisted on a policeman's shoulders to take down the net, which was hindering the rescue efforts. Within minutes, with the mood in tune with the awful reality, there was a ripple of applause as a man lying prone on the pitch responded to mouth-to-mouth resuscitation with a twitch of his feet. It died as he did.

By the early evening I had slipped away and was sitting on the pavement in the eerie, deserted streets around Hillsborough, pulling on another cigarette from a pack which was emptying rapidly – especially for a non-smoker. There was a silence at odds with the aftermath of an FA Cup semifinal.

From a phone box, I managed, after several attempts, to contact Darren and arrange to see him and some other friends. We met in a student pub called the Broomhill Tavern, where many from the nearby halls, including Sorby, went drinking. And where the night before, I learned later, two other students, Richard Jones, aged twenty-five and Tracey Cox, aged twenty-three, had enjoyed a drink and celebrated their good fortune in swapping seat tickets for the semifinal for ones for the terraces. Where they both died.

From the pub I, like many others, tried to call home to reassure relatives that I hadn't, somehow, got a ticket and gone to the match, but it was impossible. The switchboards were jammed taking calls to and from Liverpool. Among those ringing and redialling, and ringing and redialling again, were Colin's parents, and Paul's, completely unaware that Mick had gone temporarily blind through trauma, Colin was in a coma and Joe and Paul were both dead.

A couple of days later and the entrance gates across the bottle-neck were closed. Hanging from them were the colours of dozens of teams. There was the red and white of Liverpool, of course, and Forest, the blue and white of Wednesday too, but Barnsley and Leeds, Rotherham and Sheffield United, and clubs from far further afield were all represented. At ground level scores of bunches of flowers gave off a fragrance which calmly drifted over the area where there had been such confusion.

The day Liverpool's cup run began at Carlisle three months earlier, Darren and I had walked this way to watch from the Leppings Lane terrace as Wednesday disposed of Torquay United in another third-round tie. With Leeds far away at Brighton, we decided to wander along to support the lower-division underdogs just for something to do. We, and other friends, returned on the Monday or Tuesday after the semifinal to add Leeds colours and some flowers to the tribute.

The silence matched the hollowness inside every soul, the incomprehension in every mind. Everyone was moved by the display by fans of so many clubs, united by the knowledge that, in only slightly different circumstances, it could have been them. Maybe at other Hillsborough semifinals – Spurs–Wolves in 1981 or Coventry–Leeds in 1987. Or perhaps at Spurs–Newcastle in 1987, when fans in overcrowded pens were pinned against the fences, or Cardiff–Sunderland in 1980, where bedlam outside the away end was eased only by a sensibly delayed kick-off.[3] Or in any number of other near-misses which took on new relevance in the light of Hillsborough.

For the ninety-five who died – Tony Bland became the ninety-sixth after almost four years in a coma – were just like the crowd at every game. They were mostly men, with only seven women victims; they were mostly young, with almost forty under twenty, the same again between twenty and twenty-nine and just three over fifty; about one in six had supped a couple of pints or more, but most, including all of the women, who hadn't drunk at all, had not. In short, they were like the blokes you stood next to. Like the blokes you went with. Like you.

Coming on for a decade later, Colin was talking about the events of that day for the first time. We were sitting in a small café-bar close to his home, back in Liverpool, where his wife, Jacqui, was putting their baby daughter, Ellie, to bed. With a calm which belied the horror of the day, he recounted his story in one subdued outpouring, questions only necessary to clarify the fine detail. But he too had a caveat: 'I don't remember any of it. The last thing I can remember is going over Snake Pass listening to the Waterboys.'

All of his story has been reassembled from the friends who were with him, fellow fans who saw him outside the ground and what the doctors told him. The telling of it above has also been augmented by facts from the report compiled by Lord Justice Taylor, but it is just one of the official versions of the disaster which Colin has avoided. He has not looked at pictures, watched television coverage – not even Jimmy McGovern's acclaimed drama-documentary – or had anything to do with the families' support group. 'I've always avoided all of that, just in case any of it triggered something,' he said.

He can't remember the crush, how he was pulled from it or how he survived it – apart from what the doctors told him. 'I just kept breathing until I couldn't any more. Later at hospital they found I'd vomited up a meat and potato pie which I'd had for lunch on the way, but I'd sucked it back into my lungs because I was desperately trying to breathe. They told me if I hadn't been so fit I wouldn't have survived. My lungs would have just exploded.'

He can recall nothing of the despair of Saturday night or of his subsequent three-day coma. Paul's brother Mike, whom they had met earlier at the city-centre pub, had gone back to Merseyside, certain they would be waiting for him. He'd struggled to get in, even though he'd left the pub about thirty minutes before they were planning to and reasoned that the rest of them wouldn't even have made it to the turnstiles, certainly not past them. But in Liverpool there was no sign of them. When hours passed with no word from them either, both the Brady and the Auton parents decided to drive to Sheffield.

Paul's parents called at the first police station they found, were told which hospital to visit and there were informed that their son had died in an ambulance taking him to casualty. Colin's parents struggled to find him at all. His clothes had been removed by medics treating him when he started having convulsions, starving his brain of oxygen, and mislaid in the bedlam. His student friends, who were also desperately hunting for him, could ask all they liked for Colin Auton, but his name was not on any list because no one knew it. Eventually, at about 10 p.m., one of them was ushered on to a ward to look at the last unidentified patient and was able to reunite him with his name.

What he can remember is his recovery, particularly the unusual elements such as the visit of Labour leader Neil Kinnock (even though it occurred when he was still unconscious). Then there was the Princess of Wales, who provoked smiles rarely seen on the ward that week by saying, 'Men are awful in bed, aren't they?' before adding, 'No, I mean when they're ill.' Bob Paisley called around too, the Forest players as well and, of course, their Liverpool counterparts. Alan Hansen, who had been told by one of the first fans who spilled on to the pitch, 'There's people dying in there', was so distraught that he was sick in a sink.

Colin had finally awoken on Tuesday, the day before Paul

Brady's funeral – only to be told he couldn't go. 'That morning I was so frustrated – I couldn't even pay respects to my best mate.' Instead he was confined to sitting in bed staring in utter disbelief at the *Sun*, with its infamous front-page headline, 'The Truth', and reading the first story seeking to shift the focus of the disaster on to drunken fans. The report claimed that some from Liverpool had 'punched, kicked and urinated upon' rescue workers, that others had 'rifled the pockets' of the injured lying unconscious on the pitch and that one group which had seen that a dead girl's blouse had ridden up to expose her breasts shouted to police, 'Throw her up here and we will **** her.'

The sources for the story were unnamed police officers, with support, if not collaborating evidence, provided by a representative of the 'union' for the lower ranks and a local Conservative MP. South Yorkshire Police later pursued the theory – if not the *Sun*'s sensation specifics – of drunk and ticketless Liverpool fans being responsible both in evidence to Taylor, who summarily dismissed it, and then again anyway at the inquests into the deaths too. The theme was subsequently taken up by those from whom you expected no better, such as ex-Prime Minister Margaret Thatcher's ex-press officer Sir Bernard Ingham, and those from whom you did, such as Brian Clough.

'The smear campaign had started,' Colin said. 'There was "The Truth", of course, but I particularly remember reading a piece by John Junor, who said the fans were just a bunch of yobs who'd obviously been drinking. I just remember being so bloody angry with him. He didn't know what he was talking about – like a lot of them. The comments were so out of touch and generalized. At the time I thought I'd write to him, but, of course, I never did, because there were other, more important, things to try to deal with.'

Such as Joe's funeral. By then Colin had been discharged. His physical injuries were on the mend, but mental ones were only just starting to surface as he realized the scale of his escape, and most of all as he spoke to Joe's mourning family with a nagging sense of guilt for surviving. It returned a few weeks later when he went to a Liverpool game as a guest of the club and saw a schoolboy who had also lost oxygen to the brain – but who had suffered the brain damage which he escaped. 'I thought that could have been me. Another ten seconds, thirty seconds, a minute or whatever and it could have been me.'

It was six months before his emotions engulfed him and he broke down: 'Because of the coma I missed most of the grieving around me and I suppose I didn't really believe what had happened. I never had the chance to grieve and I was always thinking that I'd pop into the pub and Paul would be there or I'd bump into him in the street or I'd see Joe again in Sheffield. People were even coming up to me and saying they'd seen me outside the ground, but I couldn't remember and still didn't really believe any of it. The first time I cried was six months after, when my girlfriend at the time referred to a conversation she'd been having with her friends. It was the first time I actually heard someone say, "Paul is dead" and it sunk in. I just broke down and couldn't stop crying.'

Today Colin, like hundreds and hundreds of other victims and their families, is still living with the legacy of Hillsborough. There is a slight lingering fear of crowds and confined spaces. There is, more positively, a new career, in marketing, which came after he quit engineering in the wake of the disaster and after he returned from a subsequent backpacking expedition. The postgraduate retraining course for his new profession accounted for the few thousand pounds' compensation he received for his injuries and the deaths of two friends. But he stressed that money is irrelevant – except when he reads reports of police officers on duty that day receiving more than twenty times as much. It provokes a flash of quiet fury at odds with the ebullient character he always was. The guilt, too, remains: 'I often think, why did I survive and the others didn't, and wonder what Paul and Joe would have been doing now.'

Probably going to Anfield again, just as Colin is. He never stopped completely, attending the post-Hillsborough FA Cup Final and then managing perhaps a game a season. Three or four years ago he started going to games a little bit more regularly, but now he has a season ticket, a present from Jacqui after the application was speeded through by the club. The same group who followed that 1989 cup run still meet up for matches – but there is more than just Paul missing: 'Football's all changed. I used to go and stand on the Kop with my mates. Now it's all-seated and the prices have gone up so that some of them can't afford to go.'

Of course, 'You'll Never Walk Alone' still echoes around the ground as it ever did, but it is another song which Colin notices: 'There's still people singing "Justice" – but it's getting less and less, I think. You can imagine that it's hard work to keep the campaign going, but there's got to be someone still doing it. All they want is justice and for people not to forget those who died and why they did. They want someone to be held accountable for what happened. It doesn't seem like a lot to ask. I suppose I feel no different to anyone else who was there: very angry. But I'm afraid I can never ever see there being justice. It's been a cover-up from the start. I just hope that I'm wrong.'

You might think you know all about Trevor Hicks, one of those who sees that the campaign does keep going. How he went to a football match with his wife and two teenage daughters and returned home with a soon-to-be ex-wife, a bin bag holding the belongings of Vicki, aged fifteen, and the leather jacket of Sarah, aged nineteen. How he was told, 'Shut your fucking prattle', as he voiced his concerns to a senior policeman as they watched the crush developing on the

Leppings Lane terrace. How he found both his daughters prone on the pitch and tried, unsuccessfully, to save their lives, accompanying Vicki to hospital but forced to leave Sarah on the grass.

You might have read reports of his evidence to the Taylor inquiry – 'an impressive witness and, despite his grievous loss, remarkably stoical' – or others including his reasoned reaction, in his capacity as chairman of the families' support group, to the latest twist in the ongoing Hillsborough story. You'll probably have heard or seen him calmly debating the campaign for justice, usually with the Chief Constable of South Yorkshire Police, Richard Wells. Most likely, you will have seen him brought to life, with uncanny accuracy, by actor Christopher Eccleston as the central character in Jimmy McGovern's drama-documentary about the disaster. Trevor Hicks is, of all the victims, the personification of their loss; the most public face of what is, thanks to where it occurred, the most public of all disasters.

What remains well hidden, however, is his anger. How he called the Chief Constable a lying bastard in a stand-up row on discovering that not one officer on duty at Hillsborough would face disciplinary measures. How he would take his air rifle into the back garden of the family home and fire at a photocopy of a newspaper picture of David Duckenfield. And how, using his knowledge as an engineer who helped build industrial installations, he devised a plan to petrol-bomb Hillsborough. 'The problem with petrol bombs is that people throw them when they're lit,' he said. 'What you need to do is throw them unlit and allow the vapour to spread and then ignite it. I designed this bazooka which would fire pop bottles full of petrol into the admin-block windows. They would crack and the vapour would spread, then you'd fire in a lit one and "Boom".'

Sitting in his office of the small engineering company he owns in the small Yorkshire town of Keighley, he laughed as he remembered the idea. On a shelf there was an aerosol of Bullshit Repellent – 'which should be sprayed on any affected area such as lies, deceit, exaggerated claims, tall stories or any others dubious statements, including innuendo concerning political rhetoric'. Critics might say its use would be about the closest to direct action the justice campaign has got.

The bazooka never made it off the drawing board. Despite everything, Trevor still has an underlying faith – although perhaps not one to which he would readily admit – that the system which has tormented the families just as much as the deaths ever did will eventually come to their aid. But the very thought of the weapon illustrates how far a man who admits that before Hillsborough he was a pillar of the establishment – a Freeman of the City of London who scolded his daughters when they followed the 1980s fashion of calling the police 'pigs' – was driven by the disaster. It also helps humanize the man whose serene public persona sometimes seems at odds with the pain of 15 April 1989.

No one can quantify loss, say one person's suffering is worse than the next's. But Trevor's story was among the first the media latched on to to illustrate the human cost of Hillsborough – and the one to which it returns most often. His was not the only family to endure two deaths, though: Linda Howard, from Cheshire, lost her estranged husband and four-teen-year-old son; brothers Christopher and Martin Traynor, aged twenty-six and sixteen respectively, died together; and so did another set of siblings, Carl and Nicholas Hewitt, aged eighteen and sixteen. The pair, from Leicestershire, had refused to take the young children of a neighbour to the match in case they got hurt.

The difference with the Hickses was that they were almost unique, not just at Hillsborough but in football as a whole at the time: a family of fans. In many ways they were the prototype of today's new audience: middle class at least by income if not roots; London-based followers of a team from a city with which they had no links beyond football fandom; and over-whelmingly female. Trevor and Jenny, who were both born in the North-East, started following Liverpool, from their armchairs, thanks to her best friend's boyfriend, who was an active fan. They began attending occasional games and then, as Sarah and Vicki grew into fans, bought season tickets and went to matches, home and away, as a group. 'Football was the thing we did as a family,' Trevor said.

But they were exceptional. Friends in the same strata of Home Counties commuter belt were astounded to hear that the Hickses spent their Saturdays driving to Liverpool, or Birmingham, Manchester or Sheffield, to watch *football*: 'People used to think we were mad going up and down the motorways all day. They just couldn't understand the attrac-tion, especially given the game's reputation. Very different to today.'

In fact, the atmosphere and antagonism around matches had taken a toll. Away games were deemed off limits at the start of the 1988/9 season, partly because of the comments two pretty teenaged girls on the terraces were beginning to attract, but mostly because of one particular incident the pre-vious season at QPR: 'Sarah was pulled out of the crowd by the police. A lad she knew was supposed to have said some-thing and was pulled out, and she tried to defend him and then she was too. Vicki went as well, because the rule was that they had to stay together. Afterwards, we argued all the way home. They were saying how badly they'd been treated and I was saying that the police wouldn't have done anything unless you'd done something. I was taking the police's side against theirs – which was ironic, in hindsight.'

The lure of the semifinal, though, was too much and the Hickses headed for their first away game in months. With Jenny in the seats, Trevor took up a position standing on his own in one of the side pens after watching the girls head off into the central pens. A couple of feet above his head was the police control box in which closed-circuit television cameras were monitoring the crowd. But even with his bare eyes, Trevor could see enough to concern him behind the goal: a man of sixty or so whose grey hair was framing an ever-greyer face. He shouted at two officers on the steps to the control box: 'Can't you see what's going on, for Christ's sake? There's a problem.'

Within half an hour, he was on the pitch, leaning over the bodies of his daughters, sucking vomit from Vicki's mouth, trying to clear her windpipe for resuscitation. A fellow fan who was a doctor helped him. But the official medical team – thirty St John Ambulance volunteers, including five children – was understandably overwhelmed. Its efforts were best characterized by the keen teenager who was trying to help but whose brand-new white satchel contained no first aid equipment. The only ambulance at the ground was a brigade one. When another responding to the emergency call arrived on the pitch, Trevor and Vicki were driven away in it as, in the stands, Jenny helplessly wondered where her family was. Trevor was promised that the next ambulance on to the pitch would take Sarah. But there were no more.

So it was that at about the time they might have been expecting to get home after the match, Trevor was reunited with Jenny, both by then knowing they would never be reunited with Vicki. When Vicki would have been getting ready for bed, her parents were being told by a policeman that they couldn't see her body because it was 'now the property of the coroner'; when they should have been looking back at the memories of a great day out, they were examining Polaroids of the faces of dead bodies on a board outside the makeshift mortuary to see if Sarah was among them – she was number 64, Vicki, 89; and when they might have been settling down for a nightcap, Trevor and Jenny were being asked how much the girls had drunk before the game and if they had had tickets.

Taylor dismissed the police 'conspiracy theory' – that the late, and allegedly drunken, arrival of fans was a deliberate ploy to ensure the ticketless gained entry – in the first of his two reports, the one which dealt with the specifics of Hillsborough. He concluded, 'The main reason for the disaster was the failure of police control'. And of the efforts to smear fans, he added, 'It is a matter of regret that ... the South Yorkshire Police were not prepared to concede they were in any respect at fault in what occurred ... It would have been more seemly and encouraging for the future if responsibility had been faced.'

His judgements delighted the families and fans, whose worst fear was that the conspiracy theory would be believed. But for the former, it also proved to be the highpoint of their campaign. At the subsequent inquests the police presented the conspiracy theory again, with greater success. The Director of Public Prosecutions ruled that there was no evidence to charge the police, Sheffield Wednesday, its engineer or the city council, which monitored safety, with any offence, and insufficient evidence to prosecute any of one hundred individual officers. Most controversially, Chief Superintendent Duckenfield was allowed to retire on the grounds of ill-health, ending the disciplinary proceedings against him and having a knock-on effect on the similar case, the only other one which remained against any police officer, against Superintendent Murray.

The morning after the disaster Trevor uttered his first public words of the countless number aired in interviews over the last decade. The facts were told as simply and stoically as they would later be to Taylor, but it was one quote which stood out: 'Football was the one thing we did as a family and now we're not a family any more.' In his office he used almost identical words to me, which couldn't help but reinforce the feeling that the families' campaign has changed as little; perhaps, too, that it has achieved as much as it ever could – and in the face of the massed ranks of the officialdom and the legal system, maybe that was never going to be an awful lot – and should wind down. Such opinions will be aired aplenty around and after the tenth anniversary of the disaster.

But they were theories I felt reluctant to raise. How do you ask a man who lost both his daughters if it's not time to move on? One who still remembers his fury when he was offered £206 in compensation for losing Sarah – £200 for her death and £6 for her ticket? And one who is still overwhelmingly devoted to the cause. He cleared his diary for more than two hours to talk to me, made a matey but efficient telephone call to the support group office in Liverpool to ask them to fax a cutting and promised to send me photocopies of others. He couldn't have done more. So when I asked if the group might disband, he, of course, took it in his stride.

'There are people who think we should shut up and go away. It's all right for them to say that, and, believe me, there are many times I wish we could all put it behind us, so that we could get on with building our new lives, but we are part of a major miscarriage of justice and we can't stop fighting. Everybody says all sorts of things were wrong – the inquest system, which wasn't designed for disasters; and the police disciplinary system, which failed us; the Director of Public Prosecutions taking the soft option so no one was held accountable. No one lost a day's wages – except the families; no one's lost anything – except the families. People think it's about money, but it isn't. It's about recognition of what happened and it's about fairness. Justice.'

Perhaps, I suggested, the campaign might become more radical, less well behaved, less like Trevor. And he admitted, 'We've had this argument within the group. But the reason we still have the public respect and support we do is that we've behaved reasonably. There are times when you could do differ-ent things, but where would they get us? We could chain ourselves to railings or whatever, but again where would it get us? I'd rather we conduct ourselves with dignity, but with passion too.'

Then again, as he points out, if he had gone through with the bazooka attack he'd probably be on parole by now.

Four months after the final Taylor report outlined the scale and scope of the revolution to come, I helped bid farewell to one of the first of the homes of the *ancien régime* to go.

No one would have pretended that Fellows Park, Walsall, needed anything other than knocking down. Indeed the club's board had made the decision – a pioneering decision then – to relocate long before Taylor, long before Hillsborough. Even though many grounds were, like Fellows Park, outdated relics which wore their age and ad-hoc development badly, the last one to be replaced had been in 1955. Post-Taylor it was reckoned that up to twenty would be demolished, like Fellows Park, redeveloped as housing or supermarkets and the funds used to create modern stadiums featuring such avant-garde features as a roof which offered cover to all, toilets which worked and ample car parking.

Even so the last night at Fellows Park, after ninety-four years and more than 1,500 games, was a sombre one. I'd been there only once before with my brother, who was at school in Walsall, and some of his classmates. We'd experienced the greatest day in the club's league history, when it won a pro-motion play-off for a place in the old Second Division, and the joy was so immense that you began to wonder if the rickety old ground could stand it. The emotions on my second visit were as heartfelt, with a palpable sense of sorrow drifting across the ground after the final whistle when players, past and present, joined arms in the centre circle to lead a chorus of 'Auld Lang Syne'. On the terraces too there was a sense of sadness for the living museum being lost. When the players departed, many of the crowd wandered mournfully on to the pitch, leaving behind others prising toilets and other signs off the walls for souvenirs.

I ambled on to the grass too and took a last look around at the soon-to-go view: the hotchpotch of dated, ugly accommodation; terracing with cracks criss-crossing it; and the two train lines and main road hemming the ground in, precluding car or coach parking and any redevelopment. There was also the uncovered away end, matched by sections of the home terrace likewise open to the elements. Taylor could have been talking of Fellows Park when he wrote, 'Inside . . . grounds decay and dilapidation are often extensive.' It was as clear as the summer's night that if grounds like this had to go because of his recommendations, it would be no bad thing.

There was much else to be welcomed in his final report too. He demanded the removal of the cages containing fans on the terraces. He recognized that prisoner-of-war policing of supporters, especially away supporters, had to cease and called for police to cultivate better relations with fans. He acknowledged the invidious presence of ticket touts and called for their trade to be made illegal. He also recommended the creation of other new laws prohibiting the chanting of racist abuse, throwing a missile and going on the pitch without a reasonable excuse. He appealed for new measures to deal with hooliganism, including electronic tagging and the use of orders keeping convicted hooligans away from grounds when matches were played.

A whole new culture of safety and customer relations was outlined, with emphasis on the leaders of the game – from the FA to directors of individual clubs – to actually provide the leadership which had been lacking in the past. He concluded:

I hope . . . I have made it clear that the years of patching up grounds, of having periodic disasters and narrowly avoiding many others by muddling through on a wing and a prayer must be over. A totally new approach across the whole field of football requires higher standards both in bricks and mortar and in human relationships.

And he identified one of the relationships he wished to flourish: 'By consulting with supporters they [the clubs] could enlist the goodwill and help of the decent majority to isolate and rebuff misbehaviour from the minority rather than imitate it.'

Most welcome, though, was his rejection of government plans for the introduction of an identity card scheme. Now it's hard to believe that football had fallen so low that it was on the point of being made a private members' club, marginalized from the mainstream of society. Every one of the estimated 6 million supporters would have had to fill out an application detailing their team, a second team and a national allegiance; provide photographs; pay £10; and then go through the whole process again every two years. The necessary legislation had already been passed – and remains on the statute book – but Taylor torpedoed its implementation.

It appeared to be a victory for the new consensus he demanded. The FA, the Football League and the clubs had campaigned against ID cards but in doing so had, for the first time, also joined with fans. They united with the Football Supporters' Association (FSA) – a group born, like ID cards, of Heysel, to act as a 'trade union' for fans – to oppose the plans. The FSA's founders' aim was simple: to give fans a say in the game. In the long term, the hope was to gain representation in its administration, bridging the gaping chasm of alienation between fans on the terraces and those in charge of the game. Its alliance with the football authorities appeared to be a first step. When Taylor granted the FSA the same legal rights at his hearings as the authorities, it appeared to be a second. A new role for fans had seemingly been born. Asked if such cooperation might be one of the positive aspects of the abandonment of ID cards, the secretary of the Football

League, Andy Williamson, even said, 'I think Hillsborough did that.'[4]

Except that Taylor's main recommendation proved otherwise. Reluctance among fans to the idea of all-seaters was overwhelming. Less than 10 per cent agreed with the suggestion that they were necessary to improve safety; almost 80 per cent disagreed. Even when given assurances that seats would be 'fairly priced', those in favour only just outnumbered those against.[5] Most felt safer on the terraces, where they thought escape from an emergency would be easier than from seats. Taylor admitted, 'There is no panacea that will achieve total safely and cure all problems of behaviour and crowd control.' Then he added, 'But I am satisfied that seating does more to achieve these objectives than any other measure.'

In fact the advent of all-seater stadiums was signalled before Taylor was even appointed. Graham Kelly, chief executive of the FA, went on a wake-like *Match of the Day* on the night of the disaster to say that fans had to 'move away from the ritual of standing on the terraces'. Two days later Home Secretary Douglas Hurd, announcing Taylor's appointment, confirmed that the government wanted to see all-seaters. Liverpool's chief executive, Peter Robinson, also admitted, 'I have thought for a long time that the introduction of seats is the only way that a crowd can be controlled.' The previous summer, though, he had hinted at the real logic, commercial as much as behavioural, behind any such move. 'It's the Kop area we're not filling – the standing area. I think the statistics prove that more people are now moving into the category of middle class. As disposable incomes have increased we have more and more people wanting to sit. Obviously, those who do not have a job are finding it more difficult.'[6]

On another May evening, four years after my visit to Walsall, I stood on the Kop at Elland Road for the last time. The final game I saw standing in my place was a 2–2 draw with,

ironically, Sheffield Wednesday. The game itself was forget-
table but provided a few last memories after the final whistle.
We stayed where we were, demanding the reappearance of
the team – a team of which only Gary Speed and Gordon
Strachan remained from the 1980s. Gary Kelly planted a corner
flag in the penalty area and hung his white shirt on it as if to
symbolize the end of an era. When the team trooped off again
the bulk of the Kop began to drift away, but some of us lingered
– just like the fans had at Walsall – mentally replaying favourite
moments.

Eventually stewards moved in and encouraged the remaining few hundred of us – some singing all the way – to move
towards the exits. For me it was the end of a way of life. I often
worked on Saturdays by then and had been seeing fewer and
fewer matches, but always from the Kop. When it became
all-seater, it was harder and harder to get in unless you had a
season ticket. And though there have been a variety of reasons
– distance when I moved to London, work and whatever other
excuses I could clutch at – the bottom line is this: I've only
ever been back on the Kop once and that was for the Grimsby
game in the cup.

I'd never been back to Leppings Lane either, perhaps subconsciously trying to forget that one spring day – and I'm not
alone. Many Liverpool fans still avoid the annual return to
Hillsborough for the game against Wednesday, afraid of
rekindling bad memories and of their reaction on revisiting the
scene of such trauma. The absence of one such fan, however, a
regular home and away supporter who had found something
more pressing to do for one Saturday afternoon, meant that I
had a ticket for the St Valentine's Day league fixture almost
nine years after the disaster.

Hillsborough has changed less than almost all other top
grounds in the last decade. The Leppings Lane end, which
some said should have been razed to the ground and rebuilt,

is largely as it was, except for the obvious: the terracing converted to seating, the perimeter fences absent. The entrance off the road and the concourse around the turnstiles have also been stripped of the clutter of gates and railings. But the general layout and features – most notably the tunnel – remain the same.

A few strides away, fixed on an outside concrete pillar, was a small, understated plaque, not immediately obvious but worth further investigation once spotted. I read: 'Fifty per cent of the total cost of this West Stand opened for the World Cup series 1966 was donated by the 1s per week subscriptions to the SWFC development fund. Thank you. September 1966.' And of the appalling disaster with which Hillsborough will always be synonymous, there was nothing.

The victims' families have lobbied for years for a memorial at the ground. At first they wanted a small area at the front of the new seats left vacant so that there was a permanent, visible reminder of those who died, but backed down having accepted that it might impede safety. Instead they hoped for a plaque. But Trevor Hicks said, 'The secretary at Wednesday doesn't want it, the chairman doesn't want it and the directors don't want it, so we can't do anything because Sheffield Wednesday don't want to know. They just say it would be too distressing for their staff to have to pass it every day.'

Such sensitivity was rather unevenly applied, however, on another crisp, sunny day – not unlike 15 April 1989 – which featured a Michael Owen hat trick in a pulsating 3–3 draw – and a staggering new insult. It was delivered courtesy of a bland address before kick-off. Already some of the away fans were upset that they had been told they couldn't bring commemorative bunches of flowers inside the ground. Instead a trestle table was provided at the turnstiles. But even that seemed as nothing when the Tannoy boomed out the identity of the match sponsor: the *Sun*.

On the way out ninety minutes later one of the cards attached to a bunch of flowers left outside fluttered in the wind, its author not knowing how wrong they'd been proved. 'You will never walk alone,' it said, 'and never be forgotten.'

A short stroll across Sheffield city centre from where Taylor gathered most of his evidence into the state of the game a similar exercise was taking place again. The Football Task Force was in town, its members being informed of where Taylor has been proved wrong.

Where he wrote, 'It should be possible to plan a price structure [for all-seater stadiums] which suits the cheapest seats to the pockets of those who presently pay to stand', the Task Force heard from a supporter who said, 'I feel very strongly that corporate hospitality is pushing me out from watching my team. I can stay at home and watch on Sky now and have a meal at the same time all for less than the price of a ticket. I'm being priced out of live football.'

Where he wrote, 'I am not convinced that the cherished culture of the terraces is wholly lost when fans are seated. I have noted no absence of concerted singing, chanting, clapping or gesticulating in unison', the Task Force was entertained by the brass band which has been formed by Wednesday fans to counter the dearth of atmosphere.

And where he noted, critically, 'The football supporters' organizations complain that supporters have not hitherto been much consulted about … anything … affecting their well-being and enjoyment', a group of Doncaster Rovers fans described how the club's board had tried to sell the ground – which it didn't even own – threatened to introduce ID cards unilaterally and thrown the supporters' club out of the ground. How, too, no one at the FA had taken any interest in the situation.

In several areas Taylor's recommendations have also been ignored. Electronic tagging for hooligans, like his call for the advent of new superstadiums shared by clubs, has never got any further than his words. He suggested a levy on transfer fees to fund ground improvements and the formation of an independent stadiums design council to advise on ground development and rebuilding; the former was quietly ignored, the latter lasted less than three years before the FA and Football League decided that the £80,000 a year it cost them to run it – less than a tenth of 1 per cent of the £90 million being spent on ground improvements at the time[7] – was too much. So, while we now have some of the most modern stadiums in the world, we also have some of the least inspiring.

When I opened my copy of the final Taylor report to look up those quotes, a yellowing cutting, from *Today*, fell out:

The bosses of British soccer were finally damned yesterday as the culprits behind the game's violence, seediness . . . and death. They were condemned for subjecting fans to gross indignities as if they were prisoners of war. When the bosses guzzled champagne in their boxes, the crowded terraces were insanitary, dangerous and seething with racial abuse. Lord Justice Taylor pinned the blame on the Football Association, Football League, the directors of the big clubs and the players. They encouraged hooliganism and the cult of excessive drinking by the way they have mismanaged the soccer industry. These same men turn a blind eye to dilapidation and decay inside their grounds . . .

On the inside spread there are pictures of the 'guilty bosses of football', the twenty chairmen of the then First Division clubs who had treated fans as 'scum of the earth'. Doug Ellis of Aston Villa, whose stake of £500,000 in 1982 is now worth around £30 million. Ken Bates, whose infamous £1 has multiplied into a personal stake of £50 million. And Manchester United's Martin Edwards, who invested £600,000 in 1978, has cashed in shares worth £33 million and still has another £64 million worth.[8] There's also Irving Scholar, formerly of Spurs, now at Nottingham Forest, and Sam Hammam of Wimbledon.

And a quote from Taylor which leapt from the page: 'The fast buck stops here.'

Ten years after Hillsborough, the real truth about football is that everything has changed and nothing has changed.

winners

As for the clubs, in some instances it is legitimate to wonder whether the directors are genuinely interested in the welfare of grass-roots supporters. Boardroom struggles for power, wheeler-dealing in the buying and selling of shares and indeed of whole clubs sometimes suggest that those involved are more interested in the personal financial benefits or social status of being a director than of directing the club in the interest of its supporter customers.
Lord Justice Taylor's final report, paragraph 53

It was only a ticket and for a routine fifth-round FA Cup tie at that. But it told of so much more. Once it would have carried the name of one of the most famous terraces in English football, the Stretford End. Of late, it had also included the new name of that part of Old Trafford, the West Stand – a renaming necessary for safety and security reasons, according to Manchester United officials. Now its design had been changed again to feature a 3-D image directing holders to the West Stand/Megastore. The Stretford End, physically long-gone, was expunged, left to live just in history books and the memories of those who had stood there.

Who knows how many of them were among the tens of thousands who rose early on a grey Saturday morning a month later, in mid-March, to make their way to the new Old Trafford.

There was no wake for the Stretford End, no obituary apart from a mournful mention of the disappearance of its name in a fanzine, its final official passing – six years after the terracing which shaped its character was replaced – unlamented. There were more immediate and obvious issues to worry about: the looming match against a rampant Arsenal which was billed as, and became, the Premier League title decider, then, in four days' time, the visit of French champions Monaco in the second leg of the European Cup quarterfinals. Victories would likely bring United more success, more trophies, more fans and more money; defeats failure, a fallow year in which the trophy cabinet went without major addition, disillusionment among the faithful and the loss of tens of millions of pounds.

Handfuls of fans began forming into a column heading for the ground at the metro stop a mile or so away. As it was swollen by the occupants of the cars parked along the kerbs of an adjoining industrial estate, there was a debate on the perceived weaknesses of United's young team. As the cars became BMWs, Jaguars and other executive saloons using paid-for parking spaces nearer the ground, the atmosphere rose a degree as the image of one of those youths, David Beckham, began to appear on the flags being hawked by the first pavement vendors. Finally, as a line of traffic including two Bentleys, one with a scarf incongruously draped out of the window, waited for permission from a red light to move towards Sir Matt Busby Way and the official stadium car parks, the first shouts came: 'Any spares, any spares.' Old Trafford was, as usual, a 55,000 sell-out; the most noise was coming from the touts.

The muted atmosphere may have been due to the unfamiliar hour. The burger bars at the top of the stadium approach named after United's modern founding father were busy, but offering brunch before a kick-off brought forward to 11.15. Otherwise it was a typical match day and business as usual. The dozens of fanzine sellers gave way to the face painter, who was succeeded by a long line of stalls selling badges and flags, T-shirts and scarves, which stretched all along the right-hand side of the road running past the rear of the stadium. Behind them, billboards spelt out the forthcoming attractions at the United museum and invited visitors to spend 'A Day in the Heart of United'. Over the road, in the shadow of the ground, one of the attractions being advertised – the club's shops – was so busy that a queue was winding from its doors.

Those in a rush picked up the Manchester United Direct catalogue, which included one of the latest additions to the merchandising range: the recently launched fourth strip, specially designed to be worn in just European Cup matches. In the brochure's introduction, manager Alex Ferguson praised the contribution of the shopping supporters to the success of his side:

Teamwork! That's the key to the amazing success we've experienced here at Manchester United over the past few years. Success that's been achieved not only by the team's efforts on the pitch but by the efforts of everyone behind the scenes too. The part you, the supporters, have played has been incalculable, with a display of vocal and financial support that is in a league of its own. There is little doubt that the passion of the fans has helped us drive on to such incredible heights. Naturally you want to show your colours, which is why Manchester United Direct can help, by bringing you official merchandise of style, quality and value that's fit to carry the club's name. Merchandise you can really wear with pride, knowing that not only will it look great but the profits will go back into the club, to strengthen the team and improve facilities at Old Trafford.

Happy to have played a part – having contributed to the more than £1 million banked from every home match, having helped United generate more income in one day than twenty-two of its ninety-one nominal league rivals manage in a season – scores of fans hurried from the store clutching plastic bags carrying the club crest, once just a motif, now an integral part of United's global brand identity. And immediately faced the statue symbolizing the other half of the split personality which characterizes almost all top clubs now, but United more than any. The bags were a sign of the commercial power; the frozen features of ex-manager Sir Matt Busby a reminder of the playing glory. Behind him was the memorial to the acclaimed players who died in the Munich air disaster of 1958; behind and above, the red neon lettering spelling out the name of the club that he, they and the likes of George Best and Bobby Charlton combined to make famous around the world. And stored inside the statue is the evidence of how much it all meant to fans, the true heart of United: scores of scarves which were left as tributes after his death in 1994.

Some of the shopping supporters peeled off to the left to walk through the wide tunnel under the main stand to reach the family enclosure. From the walls of the darkened passage the faces of various United players, accompanied by one word, stared out in a series of in-house adverts which seemed to proclaim the strengths of the club as much as the individuals pictured. May, Cole, Gary Neville, Giggs, Beckham and Keane; drive, determination, dedication, inspiration, cheek and power.

I followed, flicking through a programme which carried an almost pointless page of ticket news: 'Monaco – All tickets have now been sold; Wimbledon – All tickets have now been sold; Blackburn, away – All tickets have now been sold; Liverpool – All tickets have now been sold.' Sold to the lucky few of the estimated 4 million United fans – representing one in five of all fans – throughout the country, most of whom have obviously, mathematically, never even been to Old Trafford. The ground is filled by 40,000 season-ticket holders – some still using the name of a long-dead friend or relative whose demise has gone unreported to the club for fear of having to give up the pass; the successful 10,000 members of 150,000 who are entered in a lottery staged for each game; more than

2,000 who enjoy the view from corporate hospitality boxes or sponsors' seats; and 3,000 away fans.

I walked on and took up my seat – secured via a friend of a friend and that's all I can say without exposing him to the risk of losing his season ticket for breaking the ground rules – in what was the Stretford End. There I read another Ferguson exhortation, for a different sort of support, in his programme notes on the two crunch games.

They are crucial and they are also games which our support can win for us! I'm thinking of the wall of noise that flooded from the stands when we played Juventus and Dortmund. Not everyone can handle that kind of cacophony and I would like to hear Old Trafford on Wednesday as a cauldron again. It is a special occasion and the prize of a place in the semifinals is an incentive for us all, for the team and hopefully for the fans as well! You all know what is at stake and I urge you, both today and then on Wednesday, to get behind the team and will them to win the two games which, as I say, will determine our destiny this season. Sometimes our fans have a tendency to sit back and wait for something to happen, for the team to do something special before they start to become involved. I am not saying this in a critical way because the reasons are many and at the end of the day it is just something that has evolved over the years. In the main, the supporters have shared our hopes and ambitions, and they have certainly been right behind our successes of recent years, but, as I say, from time to time they have given me the impression that before they cheer they want to be shown something worth cheering. You cannot argue too much about the fairness of that; after all, if you pay good money to be entertained, that's what should happen, and it's right to expect value for cash. But football is not like ordinary business and there is far greater opportunity for the customers to play a key role in achieving our common goal of success.

As Marc Overmars ran United ragged before scoring a long-threatened goal which proved to be the only one, the words fell as flat as the atmosphere. In the East Stand several hundred United fans were out of their seats and singing at kick-off, but, as the visitors began to gain the advantage, the chants faded. In the West Stand/Megastore there was silence broken only occasionally. In the monolithic, triple-decked North Stand and the Main Stand opposite it, less passion still. More than 55,000 supporters were watching the league-title decider and the most memorable noise was the metallic echo which bounced around Old Trafford's structure when one fan clapped his hands to urge on his team, and his fellow supporters. And then later the synthetic rustle of plastic bags being gathered at the final whistle.

The route to the megastore began roughly twenty miles away, but 120 years ago, when two Scotsmen, named Fergus Suter and James Lover, arrived in the Lancashire mill town of Darwen. Both had been Partick Thistle players when Darwen went north on tour. Both moved south soon afterwards and starred as their little-known new side stunned the football world by taking the Old Etonians, one of the founding fathers of the game, to two replays in an 1879 FA Cup tie. And both were being paid, illegally, to play.

Until then football was an amateur, gentleman's game which had been formulated into an organized sport, governed by the FA, by representatives from the Oxbridge universities and the public schools. When its first competition, the FA Cup, was established in 1872, its opponents' chief objection was that the desire to lift the 'little tin idol' would become the primary motive of teams. The character of the game was the taking part, not the winning – and certainly not winning by flouting the rules. Darwen's two draws in London confirmed both the overwhelming attraction of competition and a new willingness to use whatever means necessary for success – and that football was becoming more than a sport.

The FA bowed to the inevitable and legalized professional-

ism in 1885 – and one of the first clubs to take advantage
was Newton Heath, a side formed by railway workers in
Manchester. Otherwise, though, the FA wanted as little as
possible to do with professional football. So three years later
the professional sides came together to launch a new competition, the Football League, and again Newton Heath
were among the early pioneers, joining four years after the
original twelve-club competition started, but lasting only until
1902.

For the obvious corollary of professionalism was commercialism and when crowds fell to as few as 500, and with the
players pawning their suits in lieu of wages, Newton Heath
FC was no longer viable, economically. But there was a second
consequence of professionalism, the emergence of wealthy
benefactors wanting to buy into football, and one of them
proved to be the club's saviour. A brewer called John Davis
acquired it from the liquidators and decided that a new name
was needed: Manchester United. He oversaw the rechristened
club's first league title in 1908, its first FA Cup win the following year and then uprooted it to five acres of land he had
bought on an industrial area near Old Trafford cricket ground
and to a stadium which was soon acknowledged to be as grand
as the team. It staged an FA Cup Final replay, then the final
itself.

But the prosperity of the Davis era was brought to an end,
by economics again, as the Great Depression sent a chill
through sport as society. Crowds slumped, debts rose and
another new benefactor appeared, a clothing magnate named
James Gibson, who paid off the banks and began work on his
vision for the club. There were further ground improvements
and even discussions about increasing its capacity to 120,000.
He also issued new shares in the club to steady its finances
and appealed to supporters to invest. And it was these shares
which would pave the way for Old Trafford's third, and most
important, patron to take over.

Louis Edwards, a meat trader, became a director the day after the Munich disaster. For four years his stake in the club was tiny. Then his placemen began to trawl the backstreets of Manchester buying up a couple of shares here, a cluster there, from those who had bailed the club out in the 1930s and their descendants, until he was the largest single shareholder. When Gibson's son also sold out to him, Edwards owned United – despite an earlier agreement between the directors not to allow one man to control the club. When he died in 1980, his son, Martin, took over.

A similar history unfolded at Arsenal. Munitions workers in Woolwich formed the club, adopting the name Royal Arsenal after a first game played on a less than regal pitch with an open sewer running through it. The club's first crisis came when the Boer War meant crowds fell and debts rose and so, despite the founders' wish that the club should never become 'a proprietary or capitalist'[1] one, local businessmen were invited to invest. A second slump, in 1910, resulted in a new owner and a new home at Highbury. The difference from United was the boardroom stability under the aristocratic, patrician Hill-Wood family, first Sir Samuel, then his son Denis and then his son Peter.

In 1983, as another change in FA rules allowed Martin Edwards to become one of the first football club chief executives to be paid, a slightly bemused Peter Hill-Wood welcomed a new director, David Dein, and his £300,000 investment. 'I'm delighted,' Hill-Wood said, 'but I still think he's crazy. To all intents and purposes it's dead money.' But he was just another Old Etonian about to witness the all-encompassing march of professionalism. And this time the FA was at the heart of it.

Leeds were the last champions of the old First Division. I mention this not because United were the team we beat into second place, prolonging their twenty-five-year wait for the league title for one last year, but because it helps explain why the establishment of the Premier League in 1992 rather passed me by.

When the debate was raging over its formation, over the FA endorsing a breakaway of the leading clubs from the Football League, I was more concerned with our confident early season form; when a players' strike was mooted in protest at their cut of the earnings from the new league, I was revelling in a sublime 4–1 victory at, of all places, Villa; and when the league finally became reality, six months before it actually kicked off, I was still savouring a televised 6–1 win at Sheffield Wednesday – little realizing that such free broadcasts of top league action were about to become a thing of the past.

The Premier League was where the game had been heading throughout the 1980s. A century before, when the Football League was formed, there was a recognition that the competition had to be kept competitive; that the biggest, wealthiest teams – those with the largest catchment areas and biggest gates – shouldn't be allowed to dominate. Rules were introduced to help the smaller sides: gate money was shared between home and away teams; there was also a levy on all receipts which was split equally between all the clubs at the end of the season. Later, much later, in the 1950s, when television first started to pay to screen matches and highlights, that too was shared equally.

But during the 1980s the cooperative spirit evaporated. Gate receipts were made the sole reward of the home club in 1983; the First Division clubs were allowed to keep half of the television money in 1986, when the levy was also cut; and their share of the TV cash was upped again, to 75 per cent, in the new deal agreed in 1988. In the middle of the decade, during an impasse over money, Martin Edwards had indicated his thoughts on the future when he said, 'The smaller clubs are bleeding the game dry. For the sake of the game they should be put to sleep.'[2]

Edwards and Dein were both at a dinner in late 1990, along with representatives of the other three of the so-called 'Big Five', Everton, Liverpool and Spurs, at which the previous threats of a breakaway league began to harden into something more concrete. The theory underpinning all the talk was that of 'event' football, in which United against Arsenal, for example, was an event which television viewers would watch in droves, whereas United against one of the smaller First Division teams – Luton or Notts County – was of little interest. And anything not involving the Big Five at all was of no real interest to anyone beyond the fans of the two teams involved. Games such as Sheffield Wednesday 1, Leeds 6, for example.

A Premier League of eighteen clubs, as was first intended, would cut away the dead wood, the smaller clubs for which Edwards had no time; a Premier League, authorized by the FA, would be free of the Football League strictures on splitting the television money; and a Premier League was what television executives wanted and were prepared to reward handsomely, according to the host of that end-of-year, end-of-an-era dinner, Greg Dyke of ITV.

When that league became reality, however, he saw a baby he helped conceive snatched from under his nose by the struggling, but fiercely determined, satellite broadcaster Sky, which offered £40 million more than ITV for the television rights to it. Dein and Edwards voted against Sky's bid, but overall they had what they wanted: a new league, more money and no need to share it with Fulham or Rochdale.

Gerry Boon has played a small, but significant, role in the phenomenal success of United since then. Not in the same way as Alex Ferguson, the manager who is now mentioned in the same breath as Busby or Liverpool's Bill Shankly, or players such as Cantona, Giggs or Schmeichel, the stars who won four out of the first five Premier League titles, but as an accountant.

United's glory and growing bank account since the launch of the Premier League have been based on three elements: the formation and development of the league itself; the side's immense playing accomplishments in it and in other competitions; and, of least general interest but most importance for the development of the club and the game, its flotation on the stock market.

The share offer in 1991 was, in fact, little short of a disaster. Even though United were fresh from a second successive Wembley appearance (the FA Cup in 1990, the League Cup in 1991), European triumph over Barcelona in the Cup-Winners' Cup, had the biggest ground in the country and the most fans, only half of the shares offered to the public were sold. The remainder had to be bought by reluctant financial institutions – and then the price fell by almost a fifth on the first day of trading. The scepticism in the City about football appeared to be well founded if even the country's biggest club was such an unattractive investment.

Gerry advised the United board after flotation. When it prepared its annual results, he recommended it valued its players on the balance sheet – a move which showed the City that United were prepared to treat the game as a proper business and also gave the media an inviting, sexy news angle for the usually dull financial pages. The love affair between football and the City, generously lubricated by the money from Sky which was flooding into the game, was away. Then United shares could be snapped up for just 50p; when I went to see Gerry – the twenty-first most important man in football, according to one magazine, because of advice which now extends from Aberdeen to AC Milan – they were selling for more than £7 each.

The rationale behind flotation was threefold: to raise almost £7 million to redevelop the Stretford End; to widen the ownership of the club by encouraging fans and financial institutions alike to invest; and to allow the existing shareholders 'increased liquidity', which meant they could sell shares and pocket cash. But most importantly, according to Gerry, it brought a whole new ethos to the way the club was run.

'United have had to become answerable to a whole host of external parties who have forced them to develop business at a faster pace than Liverpool, for example,' he said. 'If you look at the two businesses they are very different in character. Liverpool have been answerable solely to themselves. Some people will say, "Well, which club would you rather have? One which has preserved, as far as possible, its traditional values and attitudes or one which has pressed on?" You can have a personal view of whichever you want, but you can't change what's happening in the wider world, whether you like it or not, and that's business involvement in sport. You have to accept that.'

The Stretford End was rebuilt, thousands of supporters were among the 20,000 small investors who bought a stake in the club and Martin Edwards sold shares and pocketed a huge amount of money: £6 million on flotation when he sold about a quarter of his family stake, another £27 million later. In fact Edwards had been looking to cash in his shares for years. In 1984 he discussed selling the club to newspaper tycoon Robert Maxwell for £10 million, but the deal collapsed. Five years later he agreed to sell his 50 per cent stake to property developer Michael Knighton for the same £10 million asking price, but the deal was doomed as soon as the slightly portly, be-kitted Knighton strode towards the Stretford End and lashed home a shot to the delight of fans – and the horror of his backers. His commercial vision of a marketed and merchandising United, though, lived on.

In a commandeered conference room at the modern chrome and glass tower which houses his office, and those of the rest of Deloitte and Touche's football unit, Gerry explained that the secret of United's success again revolved around the concept of football being an event. 'The key is don't make it just a game, make it an event. A game is where you turn up and are happy if you win, pissed off if you lose and either way just go back home again. With an event the result doesn't matter to an extent: you've had a day at Old Trafford. And you are far more likely to return if you have an enjoyable day regardless of the result.'

The rich financial results are there for all to see in the annual report of the plc, the parent company of which the team is now a subsidiary. Record profits of £27.6 million before tax – up 79 per cent year-on-year – based on sources of income such as TV fees (up by 121 per cent to £12.6 million) and sponsorship and royalties (up by 90 per cent to £11.1 million, thanks to a new kit deal) as well as the turnstiles (up by 54 per cent to £30.1 million with the opening of the new North Stand). It is little wonder that other chairmen and directors talk of 'doing a United'; no surprise a score of clubs, mostly in the Premier League, have followed United to the City.

In fact all of the clubs in the Premier League have enjoyed similar, if less spectacular, financial success. In the first five years the average club saw turnover more than double and operating profits triple. But over the same period the average club in the lower divisions has seen losses double; the average one in Division Three now loses three times as much money as it did. The consequences are clear, Gerry said: 'People say we have travelling support here, which other countries don't, which makes a difference to the economics, but it isn't enough. I think the league will go down to sixty or seventy full-time clubs. Basically the governing bodies in sport assume that just because something has been there for a hundred years – leagues or clubs – they will be there for another hundred and that's no longer true.'

He would say that, you might think, he's a Man United fan; he doesn't care about the likes of Bury or Brighton. Indeed, in the widest sense Gerry is a United 'supporter', a suit-and-tied devotee and disciple of the money-related revolution. But he's not a United fan. From the age of seven he was taken to see his local side, Oldham Athletic, by his father. As a young man he watched nearly every game, home and away. Such was his devotion that he made a promise to forsake Wembley until the Latics played there (for the first time). He still remains proud of the fact that his membership of Oasis – Oldham Athletic Supporters in the South – (from his days in London) is of such long-standing that his card was the ninth issued.

So there was one final, rather obvious question: what will happen to the likes of Oldham Athletic – founder members of the Premier League, now adrift in the Second Division – and lifelong fans such as Gerry Boon? 'I will always maintain my affiliation to Oldham and will always want to see them win, but it won't change what will happen with clubs faced by market forces. I think what will happen is that a lot of people will maintain that affiliation to their local team, but will develop a much broader interest in the game.' Which sounds ominously like we're all Man United fans now.

On the first day of the fourth season of the Premier League, I was at Villa Park to see the home side take on United. What I also witnessed, however, was the game which provoked one of the most infamous quotes of football in the 1990s *and* was the prelude to one of the most comic episodes thrown up by its commercialization.

Villa won, surprisingly, 3–1, provoking Alan Hansen to inform *Match of the Day* viewers, 'You don't win anything wi' kids.' The youthful United, containing Beckham, Butt, the Nevilles and Scholes, of course, went on to win the double. But not in the kit they wore that day – the infamous two-grey away strip which looked like it had been inspired by bin liners. The players pulled it on another six times, but with increasing reluctance as they never won in it and began to doubt, as only superstitious sportsmen could, that they ever would. Its last outing was at Southampton, where the lowly home side promptly took a 3–0 lead before half-time. When United re-emerged after the break they were wearing their blue and white third strip.

More than a hundred miles away, Simon Marsh's mobile phone rang as he watched Hyde against Northwich in the FA Trophy, sponsored by his employers, Umbro. 'There had been rumblings before the game that they weren't happy,' he remembered. 'We were talking in the stand when the score from the Dell was announced. I knew that they had also packed the third strip and I said, "Bloody hell, just watch them change at half-time." But I didn't really think they would. The kit had become a bit of a psychological barrier to the club, to the players and the manager as well. A lot of footballers are very superstitious too, but there's nothing we could do about that. We just had to respond to what had happened for whatever reason it happened.'

A highly embarrassing episode for the firm, but a richly entertaining one for fans who had complained for years at the increasing number, and increasingly outlandish design, of strips. It prompted an emergency meeting at Umbro head-quarters at 7 the next morning, a Sunday, and the launch of a temporary white away strip which retailed for just £10. But also front-page stories in the papers, a weekend of laughter at United and their inability to suffer defeat gracefully, even a book compiling such lame sporting excuses. And it also confirmed that kit manufacture – the most obvious example of the commercial imperative in football – must be one of the most thankless tasks in the game.

Umbro have been in the business for seventy-five years. Matt Busby wore an Umbro jersey when he played in the winning Manchester City side in the 1934 FA Cup Final. Stanley Matthews wore Umbro in his eponymous final in 1953. Danny Blanchflower and Dave Mackay wore Umbro as Spurs

won the first double of the twentieth century in 1961. England's
red in 1966 was Umbro, as were the strips of all but one of
the sixteen finalists. When Bobby Moore and Pelé embraced
after the following World Cup's classic confrontation between
England and Brazil, each was holding a sweat-soaked Umbro
jersey. A photograph of that moment still hangs on the wall
at the company's headquarters on a slightly shabby trading
estate on the outskirts of Manchester.

The difference, of course, was that no one could buy replicas
of any of the shirts. Not any more. In United's range alone
there's the home strip (red with a grey collar, as if it's been
washed with some black jeans), the away (white with black
and red), the third (blue with black trim) and the European
one (red again, but with the pre-washing-machine incident
white collar restored) – all best-sellers in a kit business which
is now worth £200 million a year in the UK alone.

When I saw Simon, Umbro's marketing manager, he was
preparing for the launch of the new home strip (red, with a
zip down the front), costing a record £47; earlier that week two
Newcastle directors had been secretly taped claimed replica
shirts cost £5 to make. Rubbish, said Simon, but without
providing the real figure because of commercial confiden-
tiality. Instead he made a general defence of the price: 'We
recognize they are expensive, but there is an awful lot that
goes into the design. What makes a BMW worth £21,000, or
whatever, is not just the components that go into making it,
but the fact that someone is sitting there designing it and he's
got to be paid. There's someone working out how to get the
components made and he's got to be paid. There's someone
else working out how the components will be assembled and
he's got to be paid, and so on and so on. It's the same with
us.'

Prices will only go on increasing, perhaps faster still, he
admitted, as clubs demand to maximize their earnings from
replica kit – mostly paid as an advance for the right to produce

a strip – and manufacturers look to recoup the money. 'It's a highly competitive industry. All the major brands are fighting for the same properties and that's good news for the clubs, as it drives the earnings up for them. We will pay, of course, to secure the properties we want, but the knock-on effect is we can pay only what we can afford to pay, and that means what we can recoup. There's been some large sums passed to clubs, but the demands are always for more and more money, which in turn feeds back to the prices in the shops.'

That means more designs too, more chameleon kit and more innovations, such as minidresses for girls – the latest innovation for United – but, Simon said proudly, no more third strips – perhaps the most hated and pointless of the kit makers' armoury. Even Simon called them 'superfluous'. But then he went on, 'We took on board the adverse publicity third kits were getting, but also had to ask ourselves how can we still meet a side's needs? So what we've decided is that from this season each of the clubs will have a particular training kit, which will then be used as the third strip if necessary. Chelsea's, for example, will be white.' And, of course, it will be on sale.

Martin Edwards doesn't give interviews. He is in the fortunate position of having enormous wealth and immense power without an awful lot of accountability – beyond the City. I was lucky, though, that he had a new deputy, Peter Kenyon, recruited from Umbro, who was willing to talk, to tell me about future plans at, and emanating from, Old Trafford. And that means, to a large extent, about the future of football.

An enormous security guard accompanied me from the reception in the North Stand to the second floor, which is the commercial heart of the redeveloped ground with the new £4 million museum at one end and the extensive Red Café restaurant at the other. We walked between the two and knocked on the door of one of the boxes overlooking the pitch

– and interrupted one of the business meetings which keep the United machine moving forward. Peter apologized at the double-booking and rearranged our appointment. But it wasn't a wasted journey as I did what 500,000 visitors a year now do: pay a visit to the museum (adults £4.50, children and senior citizens £3; open every day except Christmas Day).

In its first three weeks there had been more visitors than Liverpool's similar new centre had managed in three months. Soon it will be in the top-twenty tourist attractions in the country, the club hope, and few of the 500,000 will go away disappointed. There was the history of the club since its foundation as Newton Heath and state-of-the-art touch-screen terminals offering comprehensive records, including video clips and photographs, of every United player. There was a potted history of the kit, from the original green and gold of Newton Heath to its reincarnation as a 1990s away strip and details of off-field activities from the first commercial boxes to even the hooliganism of the Stretford End in the 1970s.

When I finally saw Peter, a more square-jawed, taller and toned version of Knighton, but without the moustache, he explained the reasoning behind the huge investment: 'When you look at the Old Trafford experience, the next best thing to coming to a game is coming to the ground. We did some research and we found the museum was very high on the list of attractions. We've also made sure it's for the next generation too – it's not just stuffed display cases. It's something we see as core to building a relationship between the club and fans.'

So too, he said, will the other possible initiatives he outlined: most directly another 10,000 to 12,000 seats at Old Trafford, but also a hundred-bed hotel within chanting distance of the ground, in which United have invested £500,000 and will receive in return a royalty every time a room is let, and the opening of megastores and Red Cafés throughout the country. 'They wouldn't work in Liverpool or Newcastle, but in Bristol, for example, which hasn't got its own member of the Premier League and has a significant United fan base, it would do.'

Already three-quarters of United's 4 million fanbase lives outside the North-West. I wondered what gave the club such appeal? 'It's success over a long period of time. It's heritage, being around since 1878. It's the Munich air crash, which put the club on the world map, then the next ten years, which led to the European Cup. At the same time it created the first football superstars in Best, Law and Charlton. Even today if you go into China or Malaysia people who don't even have TV will still know about Charlton and Best. We are the team of the 1990s too.'

The mention of overseas markets was significant. On Peter's desk, in a surprisingly humble office overlooking the forecourt and superstore, was a commemorative shield from the supporters' club in Malaysia, presented during a pre-season tour to a region where live screenings of United games attract crowds of several thousand. Plans were being finalized for a summer tour to Norway, where at some games supporters of the home side were outnumbered by compatriots supporting United by four to one. Even so less than 3 per cent of United's turnover is generated from overseas; megastores and Red Cafés there too will soon address that. United's rolling programme is aimed at recruiting fans from Swindon and Sweden rather than Swinton – because it has to: 'We are a plc and we have to build the business, both the revenue and profits. That's what the shareholders demand of us.' But, he stressed, with no question of forgetting the football: 'Success is the best marketing tool.'

United were also about to launch another – an in-house television channel, the first of its sort in the world. The initial content of MUTV was unlikely to cause concern among executives at the traditional broadcasters: the Man U Menu and other gentle lifestyle programmes, fans engaged in darts competitions and United-related quizzes. But much else about it would: the media firms recruited as partners, including Sky, and the presence of the new director overseeing United's media development – Greg Dyke, ex-ITV and Premier League pioneer. The rumours of experiments in the broadcasting of matches on a Pay Per View (PPV) basis and of United examining the possibilities which will be available when the current Premier League television deal with Sky runs out were not surprising.

But Peter insisted that the television station was just another way of building the relationship with fans, devised after more research which revealed they wanted to see behind the scenes at Old Trafford. PPV was an option, he admitted, but only as an experiment within the existing television deal: 'From our point of view, let's give it a go, but we are concerned about what it will do to attendances, particularly for clubs not at capacity – although if you look at what has happened since the introduction of Sky, attendances have been going up when more football is shown. The key is that if you are giving added value at the ground, if the options are better and the quality of the product generally continues to improve, the crowds will continue to come.'

Likewise, talk of a European Super League – with familiar faces such as David Dein of Arsenal among the keenest advocates – and the enthusiasm of television executives were dead-batted: 'Our view is that we're not interested and that we don't see the benefits, because it's already being done so well with the Champions' League. In my opinion that's fending off the need for a Super League in the short term. You've also only got to look at some of the crowds in the latter stages of the Champions' League, when there have been only 10,000 people, to see there's not scope for a lot more. We don't know enough yet and with the advent of PPV the long-term position of television is unclear. I'm not sceptical, but we've got to keep working hard week in, week out at home as a priority.'

Within a matter of weeks leaks began about the planned launch of a European league for next season, which about summed up my hour with Peter. There was nothing of real note that he could tell me. The ground expansion plans and the megastore and Red Café empire were both vague, lacking in detail or dates. Anything more significant would be heard first in one place and one place alone: the City.

Perhaps the only area where Peter could talk completely frankly was the one in which United have no interest: the fate of the rest of the league. I asked if he thought smaller clubs might fold. He said, 'I think it has to come. The Premier League breakaway became the division between the twenty and the seventy-two which is now so great. That division now also exists between Divisions One and Three. The economics of the game today don't work. I think it's inevitable there will be consolidation. We know cornershops have gone and that everyone now shops at supermarkets. It's happened across every industry. It will happen across football.'

Given that, I wondered, perhaps naively, if there was any sense of responsibility beyond the bottom line. 'Manchester United does a lot in terms of charity and in community schemes,' Peter replied. 'I think we conduct our business all the time in terms of how we can give value back.' Which may be true, but one disadvantage of being a public company is that the financial efforts, if not every altruistic initiative, are recorded in the accounts. Back at home, I couldn't resist flicking through the annual report to discover that Manchester United plc – turnover £87.9 million (up from £53.3 million), pre-tax profits £27.6 million (up from £15.4 million) – donated £8,476 to charity. Down from £29,721.

On the glossy pamphlet advertising 'A Day in the Heart of United', lavishly illustrated by a drawing of the Theatre of Dreams and its various attractions, there was another slogan dreamt up in the marketing department. In fact, there were

many – 'The Glorious Past, Present and Future' for the
museum, 'Follow in Your Heroes' Footsteps' for the stadium
tour, 'Feed Your Passion' for the Red Café, of course, and
'Wear Your Colours with Pride' for the megastore – but this
one stood out: 'More a Way of Life than a Football Club.'

Andy Walsh is one of those for whom the slogan is a fact,
not a copyline. Manchester born and bred, and with the nasally
urban burr to prove it, he is what was a traditional United fan;
now he is an exception, some might say an endangered species.
He went to his first game, away at Burnley, as a five-year-old in
the season which culminated with Busby lifting the European
Cup. By the time he graduated from four or five games a season
with Dad to meeting up with schoolfriends for every home
game, United were still playing in the shadow of Busby's
success. Today, well into his fourth decade of support, he still
goes to Old Trafford with the same four schoolfriends, revelling
in the parade of league trophies he had begun to despair of
ever seeing.

But unhappy that he's doing so with only his schoolfriends
and not his children too. They are the same age as he was
when he first fell for football, and United; the difference is the
difficulty of getting them into Old Trafford. He said, 'My
oldest's been to just three first-team games – although plenty
more youth and reserve ones – because I have to wait for a
spare to come up somehow. Then I've got to swap that with
one of the lads I go with so my son can sit with me. Officially,
I'm not even meant to do that, and it's against the ground
rules because tickets are non-transferable. In the old days
he'd just have stood with me on the terraces, but not any
more.'

For the revolution at Old Trafford, as elsewhere, has come
at a price. Traditional fans have been priced out of the ground
as it has been redeveloped. New, wealthier fans, from anywhere but Manchester, have replaced them; only half of the
season-ticket holders at Old Trafford are born within twenty

miles of the ground, by far the lowest figure for any Premier League team. Some in the city attribute the startlingly high crowds at City, even in the Second Division, to the fact they have become Manchester's club, an unlikely refuge for former reds.

When the Stretford End was redeveloped tickets went up from £10 to £16 (while a large part of it was also given over to an exclusive and expensive 'club class' section). That was on top of an earlier threefold rise in prices between 1988 and 1993. There are those only in their thirties who remember fondly when it cost less than £1 to get in, but there are fewer and fewer of them. And the worry is where this leaves the fans of the future, such as Andy Walsh's children. 'There was, and is,' he said, 'a feeling that the club has been dragged away from its roots. We recognize that it has to be a broad church – not everyone who goes to games is from a working-class background – but that broad church shouldn't exclude the old, traditional fans. Now the crowd's getting older and older. You hardly see any lads in their early twenties on their own or with their mates like there used to be.'

The tensions arising from change have resulted in confrontation. At an earlier crunch game against Arsenal, in March 1995, some United fans stood up when their side attacked – and stayed standing, supporting as they felt most comfortable, when the moment passed. A Tannoy announcement asked them to sit down, and immediately scores more stood up in defiance. After the match there was a more lasting result as a dozen fans who feared their relationship with the club – already undermined by the demise of the terraces and the flotation – was under further threat decided to act. A few days later they held a meeting, somewhat ironically at the Free Trade Hall, for others concerned at the direction the club was taking and formed a group, the Independent Manchester United Supporters' Association (Imusa). Andy was one of the dozen.

There was a shaky start as one of the other founders' off-the-record comments about the sale of players such as Paul Ince were reported in articles aimed at unseating Alex Ferguson. But the spat was quickly resolved; Ferguson has attended an Imusa meeting and regularly sends along his players. Andy said, 'We don't want to run the club, but we do want the supporters' view represented and heard by the club and to play our part. What we had to do was establish our credibility and our ability to represent the view of Manchester United supporters.' The benefits for the club were apparent early on when Imusa organized a flag day for a game against Juventus, helping to ensure an atmosphere as stirring as any from famous European nights of the past.

The relationship with the club has improved. Andy said, 'Since we started I think the club have accepted us more and more. When we started we would get one-line answers to our letters to Martin Edwards; now we get considered responses. We can even pick up the phone and call the club secretary and he will return the call. We still don't get anywhere near as much as we'd like, but there are areas, such as travel for European games, where action has been taken which wouldn't have been without us.' But on other occasions, most significantly with the introduction of a singing section, action has been promised and then failed to materialize.

Direct access to the board has remained through one route only, though: the annual general meeting of the plc. One of Imusa's first actions was to form a share club in which members contributed to a fund which bought a stake in the club. It allowed them to ask questions at the AGM, and perhaps even a direct, if small, say in the future – especially as there had been persistent talk of a takeover for two years. The share club members could help decide who owned United. In the absence of any firm bid, Imusa's stance was neutral. New owners might pump funds into the club and replace the still-disliked Martin Edwards, perhaps even open real channels of dialogue with fans; or skim off profits, keep a tight control of the transfer budget in line with the interests of the overall business and replace Edwards with someone worse still, possibly even a London-based company which would move the AGM away from Manchester.

Andy discussed the pros and cons, but with just a hint of weariness. The key to any takeover was that United remained a football club – a way of life, if you like – not a business, aware of its fans, he said, but without any great sense he believed it would happen. Perhaps it was the defeat against Arsenal, or worry about the Monaco game the following night, but there was a hint of sorrow, maybe even bitterness, as he supped up in the pub where we'd met and summed up: 'Who's been sustaining football all these years? The likes of us. Now there appear to be better fans out there for the clubs and they're just not interested in us.'

The next day I was among those better fans. Not the best, admittedly, as the £300-a-head platinum package – unlimited champagne, a three-course meal, free telephone and fax facilities and luxurious airline-style seats – was sold out. The 600 places went within ten minutes of the draw. Instead I had paid a mere £155 (plus VAT, making a total of £182.13) for a corporate hospitality 'package' from one of the London ticket agencies. A package which consisted of one £19 ticket, admission to the exhibition marking the anniversary of the Munich disaster – which was free anyway – and a sub-pub-grub meal in the Red Café after the match.

As I made my way to my seat, this time in the East Stand opposite the ex-Stretford End, the Tannoy was being put to full use to whip up the atmosphere. It boomed uplifting and vaguely appropriate anthems with attitude by Mancunian bands, first the Stone Roses' 'This is the One' and then James's 'Destiny Calling'. Then came an announcement: 'The difference between winning and losing tonight could be singing. If there's people singing in the East Stand or in the West Stand, join in.' In the programme – with the back page devoted to a line-up of the official 'partners' in the Champions' League rather than of the players – Martin Edwards also appealed for 'passionate and partisan support'.

The response cut through the night air. Chants of 'Follow/ Follow/We are the Busby boys' and the jaunty refrain of 'United Calypso' cascaded from an East Stand almost entirely full of fans who stayed on their feet, bellowing their support, for the entire game. Indeed, its lead was followed by much of the rest of the ground. But not where I was sitting, squirming with more discomfort and greater feeling of fraud than natural for a Leeds fan at Old Trafford, above the corner flag in one of the corners abutting the East Stand. I was an impostor, but also one wearing, for the first time ever, the most unnatural attire in which to watch football: a suit.

A couple of seats away a United fan about my age, but dressed in jeans and with shoulder-length hair spilling over his collar, was looking even more torn. He wanted to join in with those to our right, those with United pulsing through their veins and from their voices. But he too was sitting in the posh seats. When the game started and United began to attack he jumped to his feet, as we all did, but when the forays came to nowt he stayed standing before glancing over his shoulder as all about him dropped back down into their seats and then slumping down too. At half-time, as a few mobile phones were whipped out, he surveyed the scene with the slightest hint of disdain. With fifteen minutes to go and United desperately seeking a single goal to win their most important game of the season, one of the other suit-wearers did get to his feet and opened his mouth – but only to say cheerio to his colleagues and excuse himself as he weaved past the rest of his row on his way out.

Finally a crew-cutted barrel of Mancunian pride to our left barked what my near neighbour on the right had clearly been thinking, 'C'mon, yer bastards, sing up.' Around me the other suits self-consciously got to their feet and clapped with the enthusiasm of members of a Cold War Politburo watching a parade passing the Kremlin. But it was too late. A few minutes later the only singing was from the tiny pocket of Monaco fans, delighted as their goalkeeper, Fabien Barthez, jumped into the stand just in front of us, raced past stewards and departing United fans and threw his jersey to them.

In the Red Café I found myself next to the long-haired United fan. He admitted his mixed feelings about being a corporate hospitality customer and explained how he ended up there: he had been going to Old Trafford since the late 1980s, when he was a student, but now, living in London, this was the only way he could get into games. He'd paid £130 plus VAT for the last home European game and would have been prepared to pay £180 plus VAT for the next if United had won.

Everyone else around the table was, as much of a surprise. I suppose I was expecting others in suits, businessmen doing some wining and dining. But realistically they would have been in the boxes (prices up to £50,000 a season). Instead the other four sharing a bottle of wine and the meal were ordinary fans too, just a different type of ordinary fan: all from the South-East, all clutching their branded plastic bags and with just a couple of previous trips to Old Trafford between them. There were a father and his primary-school-age son enjoying a treat for Dad's fortieth and a couple, the trip her surprise present to him for the same landmark birthday. The archetypal long-distance Man U fans lampooned by many, labelled 'tourists' by the likes of Andy Walsh and loved by few apart from the club itself.

On my right a single, long-haired relic from the past; on my left, and then all the way round until back to the relic again, some of the new fans and, in the young lad, the future, the next generation of United supporters. In between, me, a fan of a team because of television, but once a terrace die-hard when to express an interest in football was almost certifiable and now a London-based part-timer too. But also in between, somewhere, hangs the balance of the game in coming years. In the language of Taylor and his 'supporter customers', it's supporters against customers, or, put another way, fans by participation against those by association and consumption. The two different types to which Alex Ferguson was appealing in his subtly different messages. And the fundamental question for the future is how, or ultimately if, the two can coexist.

The next morning City traders took in United's exit and wiped £26 million off their value. Alex Ferguson bemoaned his inability to sign world-class players, which he felt was holding the side back from European glory – an inability widely attributed to the caution and careful fiscal approach of the plc. His attempts to recruit Chilean Marcelo Salas, for example, had crashed against the barrier of the bottom line, so that Salas eventually signed for Lazio, a team, in football finance terms, less than a quarter of United's size.

Perhaps a few of the brokers in the City hummed to themselves what has been described as the new national anthem: 'Stand Up If You Hate Man U'. A few weeks later up to 15,000 England fans sang it with gusto at Wembley during an international, prompting Gary Neville to try to explain its origins: 'I suppose they do it because they're jealous of us, but this was nothing to do with United.' But nothing in English football has nothing to do with United any more, as Peter Kenyon well knew when he admitted the source of the sentiments behind the song: 'A lot has changed. I think we have done things first and I think that does have a pay-off in that we do get the dislike.'

But heading out of Manchester for the last time, it was another song which I couldn't get out of my head. The Tannoy had blared it out before the match. Sky was fond of using it, too, as the soundtrack to its highlights packages. It's called 'Only the Strongest Will Survive'.

losers

Football is our national game. We gave it to the world. But its image in our country has been much tarnished . . . The picture revealed is of a general malaise or blight over the game due to a number of factors. Principally these are: old grounds, poor facilities, hooliganism, excessive drinking and poor leadership.

Lord Justice Taylor's final report, paragraph 26

Beckham, Scholes and the Neville brothers, all England stars, all so famous that first names are unnecessary. Their former Manchester United team-mates Keith Gillespie and Robbie Savage, both internationals, both Premier League regulars, both counted among the 200 or so heroes of the highest division. And Chris Casper and Ben Thornley, less precious gems, but gems none the less, hewn from Alex Ferguson's seam of youthful promise. All were boyish members of the same Old Trafford youth team which Ferguson described as his best – better even than its immediate predecessor in which Ryan Giggs was groomed. But all second best in their first grand public contest, the FA Youth Cup Final. All losers.

On the other hand, Rob Bowman, Kevin Sharp and Mark Tinkler, all England stars in the same under-18 side as Beckham and the others, a side which won the European

Youth Championship. Their ex-Leeds team-mate Noel Whelan, whose international career – along with another Elland Road trainee, Andy Couzens – continued to under-21 level, now another of the Premier League regulars. And Jamie Forrester, a fifth Leeds member of that victorious young England squad and a player who had been groomed at the same French youth academy as Eric Cantona. All were fresh-faced victors over red-hot favourites United in that cup final, humbling them 4–1 over two legs played in front of an astonishing aggregate crowd of more than 61,000. All winners. For one night, at least.

The night was Thursday 13 May 1993, the date of the second leg at Elland Road. From before kick-off there was a buzz all around the ground. The crowd of more than 31,000, most of them struggling to identify the largely unknown players, was one of the biggest of the season and all the more welcome for being totally unexpected; in previous ties supporters had been counted in the tens rather than the tens of thousands. It was also one of the noisiest, with the large and vocal contingent of away fans ensuring a lively soundtrack to the events on the field, and the fact that it was the last game of the season adding an end-of-term party element to the atmosphere. To augment the sense of occasion, parts of the gargantuan new 17,000-seat East Stand were being used for their first big game. The future of football was around us and in front of us on the pitch.

Four weeks earlier at Old Trafford the Leeds boys had taken the merest edge off the mounting excitement as United headed for their first title in twenty-six years by recording a 2–0 win in the first leg. Forrester had scored the first, from a corner flicked on by his international team-mate Bowman, and Whelan added a second. In the first fifteen minutes of the second leg the two strikers combined for another goal as Whelan flicked on a Tinkler free-kick and Forrester executed a stunning overhead kick. A quarter of an hour later the opponents' ginger-haired striker – a Paul Scholes, according to the programme – equalized with a penalty, but Whelan's height crafted an opening for midfielder Matthew Smithard to restore a three-goal aggregate lead before half-time.

At about 9.30 referee Paul Durkin blew the final whistle and started celebrations among the now semi-familiar figures in white, whose kit seemed a bit too big, whose gawky joy was a little self-conscious and whose features failed to hide the shock of seeing the ground almost full and echoing to the songs they knew from spending match days on menial tasks behind the scenes. Eventually the players trooped off and the crowd, humming with contentment, drifted away, again eventually; later the floodlights dimmed and another foot-balling year was over.

But everyone at the game knew that it was really a beginning. In the programme Leeds captain Gordon Strachan said:

I am not getting carried away when I say there are some potentially exciting prospects on the horizon and I have really enjoyed watching them play. Already people like Rob Bowman, Jamie Forrester, Mark Tinkler and Kevin Sharp have progressed sufficiently to be given a taste of what it is like in the first team. Make no mistake, they've deserved their opportunities, because they are all good players – and if you work hard in life, like they have so far, you will get an opportunity somewhere along the line.

All of them did play for the first team. All but Forrester even appeared in European ties. Lanky centre-half Bowman had been first, making his full debut in a 0–0 draw against United as the junior cup run progressed. Even as a seventeen-year-old with virtually no reserve-team experience, he was trusted to mark United's then-wonder-winger Lee Sharpe and played in the next two Premier League games as well. Forrester, then Tinkler, Sharp and Whelan also all made their debuts between the cup ties. Mark Ford, the captain who lifted the cup, had to wait until the last game of the following season; the terrier-like Couzens the best part of another. His second full game reunited him with Whelan, but also with several other young men, in red, growing into the limelight, in a 0–0 draw at Old Trafford. A couple of months later he was called up by England under-21s for the annual summer tournament.

But five seasons after their night of triumph, as Beckham and his United colleagues played for places in the England World Cup squad, Forrester was at Scunthorpe, Sharp at Wigan, Tinkler at York and Ford at Burnley. Forrester was too small, Sharp too one-footed – and perhaps too blond. Tinkler's ability was undermined by injury and Ford was either inconsistent, unlucky or just unfancied by a new manager when Howard Wilkinson was replaced by George Graham. Whelan was the exception, paired by Strachan with Darren Huckaby in an almost unique young and English Premier League striking partnership at Coventry. Meanwhile, Rob Bowman, perhaps the greatest loss, and Andy Couzens, were at another United, Carlisle, the club Michael Knighton acquired after sparking the revolution at Old Trafford – and a city which is the definition of a football outpost and a good example of the life outside the Premier League.

For both sides in the Youth Cup Final victory promised so much more than the simple fact of it. From its inception in 1953, it had been the platform for the first flowering of the stars of tomorrow, a competition which indicated a club's present and future strengths. Manchester United won the inaugural competition – and Duncan Edwards became the first great player to be noticed appearing in it, leading the embryonic Busby Babes to a 23–0 win in one tie. Three years later they were the young heart of the side which won the league title by a record margin and began an all-too-brief era of domination, curtailed by the tragedy of Munich. In more recent times, a tubby, juvenile player called Paul Gascoigne first emerged as part of the triumphant Newcastle side in 1985.

There have never been any guarantees, though. The best teenage players are often those whose physique allows them to dominate – until the later developers, perhaps more skilful players, catch up. Injuries can rob them of their dreams before they are even close to realization, as can the catch-all diagnosis of attitude problems, personality clashes with coaches or even ebbing confidence. To succeed, any young player has always needed skill and dedication, but most of all luck. But for the young winners at Elland Road and for aspirants like them everywhere there is now another, new barrier: overseas imports.

On that one night Andy, Rob and the others were accorded hero status (including, I admit, by me and my mate Andy, watching them arrive at the players' entrance) and accepted it with a confidence born of the expectation of further adulation to come. They were stopped for autographs and congratulations. A handful of schoolgirls nudged each other and whispered names before snatching photographs. Inside the ground the crowd adored them. Andy's eyes smiled at the memory as he said, 'We just couldn't believe how many were there. We went out for the warm-up and then came back in the dressing room and sat down. We couldn't get over it. We knew it was going to be big, but . . .' And 31,037 was reduced to an incredulous shake of the head.

But we were sitting, almost five years later, in the players' lounge at Carlisle's Brunton Park, a chilly and gloomy room without the life of match day pulsing through it. Both Andy and Rob were track-suited and trainered images of professional athletes, but their deportment and personality were far removed from the type. Andy, small and dark-haired, fetched the keys to let us in; Rob, tall and blond, made me a coffee and brought it in. Both were slightly curious at being interviewed, of having to talk about their careers, of communicating outside the circle of family, friends and team-mates. The contrast to the hopes of their night of glory was as harsh as the neon strips lighting the room.

The season after the cup win should have been the springtime of their young careers. Instead it was the autumn days of two newcomers, and injuries, which first denied Rob. Ex-Arsenal veteran David O'Leary, aged thirty-five, and John Pemberton, from Sheffield United, aged twenty-eight, joined the club. There were three other centre-halves on the books too and when the following summer, 1994, saw the big-money arrival of Carlton Palmer as well as South African Lucas Radebe, both to play in the middle of the defence, competition became fiercer still. Rob said, 'It was experience before youth and that was that.'

Andy fared little better. His favoured position of right-back was filled when winger Gary Kelly was converted to an accomplished defender and then failed to miss a game for the next two and a half years. Instead Andy became a utility player, covering when injuries or suspension sidelined the expert defenders or midfielders. His full debut came at centre-half; the following week he was on the left of midfield. Words of support from manager Howard Wilkinson were rare and, in keeping with his cryptic style, even when they came, Andy laughed, 'it took you two weeks to understand what he was talking about'.

In October 1995 both enjoyed their biggest games, against PSV Eindhoven in the UEFA Cup. Andy appeared as a substitute in a 5–3 first-leg defeat at Elland Road. Rob played for the first time in more than two and a half years since the Youth Cup Final in the largely academic (and lost for good measure) second leg. But a couple of weeks later another experienced central defender, Richard Jobson, aged thirty-two, arrived from Oldham, to add to the latest summer centre-half arrival, Paul Beesley. Rob started one more game to add to two appearances as a substitute in the season. And that was his last Leeds appearance.

The arrival of new manager George Graham and two more central defenders spelt the end, in 1996. The new recruits offered value for money as well as experience. One was Dutchman Robert Molenaar, the other Norwegian utility player Gunnar Halle, an international but, at £400,000, less than half the price of the uncapped Jobson. Rob's departure was as sudden as a call from his agent saying Rotherham were interested: 'That was it really. I spoke to them and agreed to join. There wasn't any goodbyes or anything. I just got my stuff together and left. I was pretty much there one day, gone the next.' On a free transfer.

Initially Andy seemed better set under Graham. In the first minute of the new manager's first game, at Coventry, he scored his first senior goal. He played in the next eight games, culminating in Graham's first return to Highbury – and that's when Andy's Leeds career effectively ended. He was substituted at half-time with the side losing 3–0. He made an appearance, from the bench, against Sunderland the following week but that was his last. He was allowed to go on trial at Rapid Vienna, but decided he would prefer to stay in England.

Come the end of the season he too was called to Graham's office. 'He actually offered me a one-year contract, with a £250-a-week pay rise, but I was more worried about playing some first-team football. I was twenty-one. I needed to start getting into the team, but he said he couldn't promise anything. I decided I had to leave.' He signed for Carlisle for £100,000 – the last of the cup-winners to leave – and was reunited with Rob, who had moved on from Rotherham after just a couple of months following a change of manager. Four days later another defensive utility player, Norwegian Alf-Inge Haaland, arrived at Elland Road for £1.6 million.

So instead of playing in front of almost 40,000 in the Premier League at Elland Road, Andy and Rob were appearing in front of about 5,000 each week. The biggest game of the season had been a Coca-Cola Cup tie with Spurs, which Andy graced with a goal in a 3–2 defeat at White Hart Lane. The home leg drew 13,500 in the dashed hope of some giant-killing, but six months later, as the season was played out, Carlisle were fighting relegation back into the lowest division for the third time in five years. Just down the M6 Beckham and others second best in the Youth Cup were watched by millions on television every week, pin-ups on thousands of walls. Their battle was for the Premier League, the European Cup, the England squad. Interest in the Coca-Cola Cup, treated by United as a chance for a run-out for the reserves, ended with defeat in their first tie – assuming, generously, that it existed at all.

There must be some resentment of the United stars, but Andy concealed it with a cliché, 'Fair play to them', and a shrug of attempted nonchalance. 'Yeah, we beat them in the cup final, and quite convincingly, but you've got to give them credit for what they've achieved since then. They've worked hard and they deserve the success.' But an unprompted explanation followed immediately: 'The difference is that they were brought through in ones and twos into a successful team. We were brought in in twos and threes in a struggling team. They gained confidence and grew from that. We were playing in a side which only just stayed up that year after winning the league. There's pressure on young players anyway, but it's even more difficult to come into a team which isn't playing well.'

Still, they knew that they were lucky. When we finished Andy was heading back to the house he had recently bought to walk his dog. Rob reckoned he'd probably have a nap: 'People think you're lazy, but they just don't realize how much training every day takes out of you.' On other days they might pot away an hour or two with some snooker-playing friends. In the evenings they occasionally meet up with team-mates for a drink or some food, although aware that reports of every pint, every pub, every curry house will get back to the club.

And for this life of semi-leisured, semi-luxury, for being some of the best English players of their generation, they are paid about £700 a week. Meanwhile, most of the Youth Cup-winners aren't even playing professionally.

For both of them their first year at Brunton Park was a disappointment. Andy's season, perhaps his career, could be summed up by the fact he played centre-forward in his first game, right-back in the next two and then in midfield. By Christmas he was on the substitute's bench again, where he stayed for most of the rest of the year. Rob was struck by injury again at the start of the season, recovered for a run of five games at right-back, culminating in a goal at Wrexham, but then picked up another injury and didn't play again.

Their aim is to claim regular slots in the side and help it to promotion. A victorious season might produce a few good notices and win the ultimate personal prize: a place back among the élite. But they know it will be difficult. Andy said, 'We've seen the difference between clubs at the top and the bottom and I know where I'd rather be. Everyone just wants to play at the highest level, after all. The problem is you know managers are coming to look at you and thinking, "I can get a foreign player for next to nothing," sometimes nothing but his wages.'

Transfers from lower league clubs used to be football's social security, redistributing money from the affluent to the needy. The likes of Carlisle would bring on a young talent and then cash in on their asset. Forrester's Scunthorpe, for example, honed the skills of Ray Clemence and Kevin Keegan until Liverpool spotted them and took them on. The legend who signed them, Bill Shankly, was himself schooled as a player at Carlisle before moving to then-giants Preston (and later returning to Brunton Park for his first managerial post). His successor at Anfield, Bob Paisley, dipped into the lower divisions to sign Ian Rush from Chester.

Sometimes it does still happen. Two of Andy and Rob's team-mates at Brunton Park had moved on in big deals as the season progressed, both making that longed-for move into the Premier League. First full-back Rory Delap joined Derby for £500,000 and showed the two-division gap was less than insurmountable by immediately becoming a fixture in the first team. Then striker Matt Jansen turned down lucrative overtures from Manchester United to sign for Crystal Palace for £1 million. By the time Palace succumbed to relegation he was being linked with an even more lucrative move, for £4 million to Southampton.

But they are the exceptions. The arrival of overseas players – more than 150 of them – has largely stemmed the flow from the lower leagues. More noticeable now is the movement in the other direction. Even Manchester United, the home of home-grown talent, have started to buy foreign talent – Blomqvist, Stam and Yorke – and sell members of their own Youth Cup team, Thornley and O'Kane. Likewise Arsenal have bought cheaply from abroad, prompting Arsène Wenger to warn of the consequences for the England side. And its coach Glenn Hoddle has in turn admitted that he will increasingly have to scout outside the Premier League to find his players of the future. The Catch-22 is that some of those clubs, starved of transfer funds, will not even exist.

When the creation of the Premier League was finally confirmed after months of wrangling, David Dein welcomed it as a 'historic day for football . . . The evolution and management of the game have been in neutral for the last hundred years, but today's decision has sent it into overdrive, which should reward all clubs great and small.' Five years ago almost two-thirds of the losses incurred by Division Three clubs were covered by the proceeds of player sales; now it is a fifth – and the losses themselves have doubled. Across the league as a whole the situation is even worse: transfer income doesn't even cover a penny of the losses incurred by clubs; bank loans and other borrowings are subsidizing transfers. And in the last five years league clubs have lost a total of £118 million.

All that is keeping many clubs afloat are their creditors – not the banks, who have become far more choosy supporters[1] as they've realized the risk of lower league football, but the other traditional source of funds: directors. But as the gap between the Premier League (average club profit: £4.3 million) and the rest (average club loss: £400,000) grows and the costs of running a club continue to mount, benefactors are going to have to be richer than ever to get involved. It's one thing to have to spend £500,000 for a small stake in a profitable Premier League club, but that's now about how much anyone wanting to invest in a loss-making lower division one might have to pay – and quite possibly lose. In a year.

The irony is that the fight for survival is being played out against a backdrop of booming attendances – and even record amounts of money from television. Last season more than 13.5 million spectators, the largest total for twenty-six years, watched football in the three lower divisions. The year-on-year increase of more than 13 per cent was the twelfth consecutive rise since the low point of 1985/6 and meant that crowds have almost doubled since then.[2] The extra money taken at the turnstiles has been matched by bulging receipts from television too. The Football League clubs now share a record £25 million a year from Sky – and because of it they saw their annual turnover increase by an average of 19 per cent.

But still the gap is growing. Every indicator tells the same story. The attendance boom is more comprehensive in the Premier League, where eight out of ten seats are taken, than in the Football League, where grounds remain under half full. Fans watching top-flight games spend more on tickets, and on merchandising and catering, handing over an average of up to £1,500 a season to their clubs; supporters in the lower divisions pay as little as £190.[3] And the income derived from those watching at home is equally skewed: Sky pays almost

£200 million a year to the twenty clubs of the Premier League compared to that £25 million shared between seventy-two in the Football League, but with First Division clubs getting more than Second, who get more than Third.

The question is, who would miss a lower league club like Carlisle anyway? The weekend in April I saw Andy trot on to the pitch at Brunton Park (Rob was injured, again) armchair fans had the following choice: Chelsea against Middlesbrough in the Coca-Cola Cup Final, live on Sky; *Match of the Day* featuring highlights of an incredible Premier League fixture between a Barnsley side reduced to eight men and Liverpool; or Wolves versus Portsmouth, again live on Sky. Or West Indies–England one-day cricket, a semifinal of rugby league's Silk Cut Challenge Cup or Formula One from the Brazilian Grand Prix, all live. In contrast, Carlisle against Bournemouth was almost the definition of non-event football.

The devoted 5,000 at the ground, of course, would despair. But they'd find something else to do, someone else to support, perhaps, just like most of the 27,500 who once crowded into the ground have done. Even one young lad who was there clearly wanted to be somewhere else, his Manchester United shirt betraying him. Away to his left the cracked concrete and towering clumps of grass and weed of the derelict Waterworks End were as far from the Theatre of Dreams as it's possible to get.

Equally bereft might be ground-hoppers keen to sample the peculiarities of Brunton Park: its unique isolation, fifty-eight miles from its nearest rival, Newcastle; its location next to sheep-filled fields and rugby pitches; even its unique flood-lights, with bulbs running up the limbs of each pylon like fairy lights rather than clustered at the top. Perhaps some football historians as well, fond of recalling the landmarks of the game – again the floodlights, the first to be used in a competitive match between league sides, or the site of Shankly's managerial apprenticeship. But the bereaved would still be counted in the thousands as opposed to the millions of Premier League fans.

In a few years the vast majority of fans probably wouldn't even register that the name was once that of a league club and, as recently as the 1970s, a First Division club. Carlisle would slip into the same non-league obscurity as Cumbria's other two ex-professional sides – Barrow, deselected in 1972, and Workington, deselected five years later. Or quietly fade away like Accrington Stanley, died 1962, reborn in a lower, amateur league; Aldershot, died March 1992, later reborn in a lower, amateur league; or even Maidstone United, died the day after the first Sky broadcast of a Premier League game, August 1992, but never reborn.

An evening in Bournemouth almost a year earlier had shown me the answer to the question. In particular, a fan called Trevor Watkins and dozens like him who fought to save their club; who were determined to preserve a small part of English football's rich history and gave it a future; and who made a 0–0 draw with Stockport the greatest night in the club's history.

Bournemouth, it has to be said, are not AC Milan. Their red and black stripes, though, tell of the ambition to be. In the early 1970s a visionary commercial manager named Dickie Dowsett copied the kit of the Italian *rosseneri* as part of his dream of transforming the sleepy retirement resort's side. It also acquired an AFC prefix and a new European-inspired crest – and indeed just over a decade later did humble Manchester United. But knocking the holders out of the FA Cup in a third-round tie in 1984 was an isolated success for a club which had then never risen beyond Division Three in sixty-one years in the league. The giant-killing remains its most famous result – and was, by happy coincidence, its most lucrative, grossing almost £34,000.

Yet that modest past contains everything that football, and

indeed any sport, is about: ambition and uncertainty. At the heart of every athlete and every club beats a simple desire to win, to be the best; and if not the best, the best possible. At the crux of any game is a doubt over its outcome – the chance that Bournemouth can beat United and the possible drama any such result holds. It doesn't matter that compilers of record books have been little troubled by the Cherries, whose sole honour is the 1987 Division Three title, while there is still an appetite for glory and the prospect of a run like that thirty years earlier. In the FA Cup Wolves, third in Division One, then Spurs, lying second, were beaten on the way to the quarterfinals; then the league leaders, Busby's Babes, went 1–0 down at Bournemouth's homely Dean Court ground, before recovering to win 2–1. And that's why the scoreless draw with Stockport, on 1 April 1997, was so important – because it was the game when Bournemouth were saved to dream of beating United again.

Before the evening kick-off Trevor walked on to the pitch among a party of suits and microphones which cast lengthening shadows and lifted the shades from the club. The 5,476 faces collected underneath the tall trees which decorate the skyline around the stands listened intently, some with concern still lining their features, until Trevor came to the punchline of his announcement from the centre circle: 'This club will survive. We have got to sort out the bits and pieces, but we have got a bright future. The sun is setting on the past.' A couple of minutes beforehand he had stressed to me the importance of the crowd in this real-life fantasy football – the launch of Europe's first community-owned club: 'It's all about making people feel part of the club and its future.'

At the time, though, it was hard to suppress cynicism, especially when the scale of the task was writ large in the balance sheet. A matter of weeks earlier Bournemouth were almost £5 million in debt, with another £50,000 a month vanishing into the red hole in its bank balance. For years it had sold its youth to survive, with the departure of Jamie Redknapp, the son of ex-manager Harry, to Liverpool the most celebrated example and Joe Parkinson's £800,000 move, to the rival, blue part of Merseyside, the most lucrative. But its bankers had begun to realize that such subsidies were no longer enough. Crowds, hovering around the 4,000 mark, were well below the break-even mark. Ominously, the main asset was Dean Court itself, handily located by historical chance on the fringe of a lush urban park and so ideal for redevelopment as housing.

Lloyds Bank precipitated what could have been the final chapter in the club's history, but what ironically became its new beginning. After years of mounting losses and extended overdrafts to cover them, its patience – £4 million of it in the form of a loan which it wanted repaying – ran out and the receivers were called in. Dismay washed over the town in a greater wave than an outsider might say the size of the club, the size of its recent support, merited. Over a small corner of an office in the City too, where Trevor, a solicitor but also a fan since his first game as a schoolboy in 1974, worked. Desperate to help save the club, he sent the board a letter offering his legal advice. It went unanswered. He followed it up with an unreturned telephone call. Then, as five of the seven-strong board resigned as the crisis entered its end game, he was finally summoned by the remaining two directors. What he heard of their plan – a daring, but futile, showdown with the bank – horrified him, but started the chain of events which would lead to a more realistic solution.

The following morning he was asked on to a local radio show to report on the situation as a representative of the remaining directors. Other fans who called the station to discuss the way forward asked for a face-to-face meeting and it was arranged for the next night. There it was decided to call a full public meeting at the town's Winter Gardens to rally support and raise cash, which would help the club trade in the black – a condition imposed by the receiver. The buckets which went round collected the first coins and notes of more than £130,000 donated as an atmosphere of defiance replaced thoughts of defeat. The money was literally loose change given the size of the debts, but it was a lifeline, however flimsy.

Even so, there was nothing to suggest Bournemouth was anything more than another of the small fry teetering on the edge of oblivion while potential new owners quibbled with the receivers and the sitting board over the price – and with their intentions for the club unknown. One of the bidders was a director who hadn't seen the club play for three and a half years; the only rival, a businessman whose plans to sell the ground for housing were exposed purely by chance at a motorway service station when Harry Redknapp got chatting to a demolition contractor who had been asked to quote for the Dean Court demolition job. But by then Trevor and the other supporters behind the Winter Gardens meeting had gone public with a third bid: a revolutionary buy-out by the club's most loyal backers, the supporters.

Such an emotive effort from the grass roots should, you might think, have been agreed swiftly and easily, but no. For three months – both six weeks before and six weeks after the Stockport match, at which the deal was announced in principle – the final reel still seemed certain to contain images well-known from elsewhere: stadium gates padlocked and an asterisk under the league table noting points won and lost against a deceased side had been wiped from the record. The Football League insisted that arcane rules by which creditors were paid first were followed to the letter, thereby giving the directors who had overseen the decline of the club an effective veto on its club's future.

A year after all the outstanding issues were resolved and the deal done, Trevor's normally mild manners still bristled at the mere mention of the bureaucracy. 'The league were scared shitless by what we were trying to do,' he said. 'They just didn't know what to make of it. Some individuals there were extremely helpful, I must say, but as an organization it was hamstrung by its attitudes and rules. It sat on the fence, unwilling to be seen to help. We reckon that the delays cost us about £300,000 and we ended up with a deal the same as the original one put forward in February. I think in future the league has to be prepared to offer more leeway and take a longer view.'

That year witnessed a remarkable turnaround. Bournemouth and Boscombe Athletic Community Football Club Limited, the People's Football Club, was debt-free and banking about £10,000 a month in profits. The board, chaired by Trevor, was on the point of buying a Premier League player, Mark Stein, from Chelsea, but just as importantly was able to keep the likes of captain Ian Cox, the sort of player once exported to bigger clubs. Average attendances had jumped by a quarter to 5,000. And to cap it all they were about to make their first Wembley appearance, in the final of the Auto Windscreens Shield, watched by 40,000 of their fans, and to bank record receipts of £80,000. The single released to mark the occasion was an apt cover version of the Bee Gees' 'Stayin' Alive'.

The healthy figures tripped happily off Trevor's tongue when we met at Waterloo Station before one of his rarer meetings in the City. He had just gone part-time and started working from home in Bournemouth so that he could devote more time to the club. As we queued for coffee, he talked enthusiastically of the prospect of securing the services of a new French player from under the noses of several bigger teams. He was excited by new initiatives aimed at helping to cement the club's place in the community: a kit deal which would offer a discount to local children and free tickets to try to prevent the youngest from falling for Manchester United or any other Premier League giant. He was excited by the rising attendances, which he viewed as essential to catapult the club to First Division security – and perhaps even greater achievements. In short, he was just excited.

The club is more healthy than it has been for years, possibly ever. The trust fund established after the Winter Gardens meeting has a controlling 51 per cent of the shares. Its trustees make up the board, some of them doubling as investors among the eighteen who invested £300,000 in £1 shares as part of the restructuring. In the future the club might follow the trend to flotation to raise cash for ground redevelopment, but the trust's 'golden share' will remain – and anyway none of the directors could be accused of favouring the route to the City for 'fat cat' benefits: none of them takes a salary, all but one pay for their season tickets – as does the receiver, who liked the club so much that he became a fan – and that one exception is manager Mel Machin. The ambition is now a place in the First Division.

No one in the coffee bar at Waterloo would have guessed the studious-looking thirty-something professional sipping his pick-me-up was either a football club chairman or a revolutionary. In his smart suit and round glasses, with slightly receding hair tidily trimmed, there was no hint of the self-importance and pomp of many of the old-style oligarchs. But the one characteristic he shared with them was quickly clear: civic pride – the belief that a football club matters more than for its financial contribution. Trevor said, 'It brings people together in a way that a theatre or an orchestra cannot do. It's talked about in the working men's clubs and in boardrooms. It becomes the lifeblood of the community. And in our case, if the club had gone it would also have been another example of the list of things the town had lost. That's why we had to fight.'

Why not, though, just accept fate and come back, like Accrington or Aldershot, as a more modest non-league club? 'What's the point of that? There would still have been a part of me missing. Every time I looked at my programme collection, I would have realized there was something which I used to do, which I used to enjoy enormously, which I've enjoyed enormously all my life and which all of a sudden I was no longer able to do in the way I did.'

There was someone else I had to see in Carlisle, perhaps the most famous man in the border town, not that I was looking forward to meeting him. I quickly realized that I wasn't alone.

Soon after he sat down at a table in the darkest corner of the pub where I'd been told to expect him, a barmaid approached with a mixture of weary resignation and justified trepidation. She started to gather the emptied pint pots from the gloom, but knew her job demanded more. I tried to smile reassuringly at her, but she was staring at him as he craned his head back and up to catch the climax of a televised horse race – as he rolled himself a joint. She sighed and said, 'You're not gonna light that in here, are yer?', a disapproving plea more than a question.

Paul Dodd, England's most notorious, or self-publicizing, or, therefore, stupid, or all three, football hooligan looked around, speed-ogled this unexpected and attractive authority figure and puffed himself up. 'I'll,' he said, far louder than necessary, rolling the joint between forefinger and thumb, cocking his chin towards her and beyond to the rest of his gang at the pool table, 'do what I fuckin' like, when I fuckin' like and where I fuckin' like. All right?'

There was an instant of silence. Some of the posse gave exaggerated, laddy laughs. Some just smirked to themselves in between pulling on cigarettes or supping. Dodd himself wore the arrogant grin of an untouchable; the barmaid, unsure what to say or do next, a contemptuous but slightly confused frown. Silence. Then he spoke again, more quietly, perhaps even with the slightest hint of shame. 'I'm just joking. I'll see what I can do, just for you, eh?'

Beery bravado, twinned with violence rather than flirty apologies, is Paul Dodd's speciality and has been for years. At fourteen he was expelled from school for head-butting. At fifteen he was fighting with Carlisle's hardcore hooligans, the Border City Firm. At sixteen he was sent for a two-month 'short sharp shock' at a young offenders' boot camp for attacking a policeman who was holding him back from charging into battle against Bolton fans. At seventeen he was part of a twenty-strong pack armed with knives and staves which ambushed Scottish fans at services on the M6 in what the judge who sentenced him to two and a half years called 'gang violence of the most appalling kind'. One of the victims had to have his cheek stapled back together.

Dodd explained how he was caught as if the episode was as routine as collecting his dole money: 'We went to Lancaster after, to hospital, 'cos one of our lads had been stabbed off one of them. One of their vans rammed right at us too and knocked one of our lads out the way. He had twelve stitches in his arse. And then another lad had been slashed on the arm, so we had to go to hospital and they obviously phoned the Old Bill. You know, twenty lads all trooping in with fuckin' cut eyes and all – there's obviously something wrong. We got back on to the M6 but the police pulled us. They shut the next service station down to the public and they boxed us in our van and nicked us all.'

Not that all his violence has been focused on football. Five years later, in 1993, he gatecrashed an engagement party at a golf club, head-butted the cake, punched a guest to the floor and stamped on his face. He has also admitted to following pub quiz-winners outside and 'kicking their fucking heads in'. But football has been the backdrop for most of his outrages. In 1994 he led a pitch invasion in a play-off game at Brunton Park, running towards the away end screaming, 'Come on, you bastards, come on.' Three days later he led the charge on to the pitch again in the return match. His subsequent conviction saw him banned from every ground in the country. He now has thirty-odd convictions, half for hooliganism, according to comprehensive newspaper cuttings.

In person, though, there was nothing to mark him out from thousands of other lads all too similar to him. He wore the same designer labels, Stone Island and Ralph Lauren, with the same swagger as many. He chatted easily enough – about Carlisle's form, perhaps surprisingly, and about having a laugh with his mates – and even let slip a few unlikely background details such as his schoolboy career as a rugby scrum-half and his CSE in English Literature. Only his habit of punctuating his sentences with relentless obscenities as well as regional tics – an 'aye' to start, an 'eh?' to finish – betrayed the ugliness inside. And while no one would suggest he was overly bright, he has a shard of wit and some self-awareness of his ridiculous fame. Separated from his cronies, he even admitted that his reputation 'bothers me mother' with a wry smile. But give him a few pints, perhaps, a bit of blow, maybe some coke too and watch out.

I first came across him at the same time as the nation at large – after England's game in Dublin four years ago was abandoned because of a riot inside the ground. He was among twenty-six England supporters arrested as the friendly fixture mutated into the most disgraceful outbreak of hooliganism for a decade. A downpour of seats and lumps of wood from the upper tier of the stand housing the visiting fans crashed on to Irish supporters below, fighting spilled on to the pitchside and all the while the night air resonated with either the visceral roar of violence or vile chants.

Dodd was named in the papers as one of the ringleaders of the riot. Others of the twenty-six were also blamed for specific incidents which fuelled the fighting. Others not arrested, but identified by the papers, were revealed to have played significant roles too. But Dodd stood out. For me it was because when he walked from a Dublin court after being fined and given a three-month suspended sentence he tried to cover his face with a copy of the *Daily Mail* which featured a front-page story about the riot which I had written. For other reporters

it was because of his recidivist's record, by far the worst of
any of those arrested. For the public at large it was as an
illustration of the impotence of the authorities against the
thugs when it emerged that he should have been in court at
home to face hooliganism charges rather than in Dublin.

In fact Dodd was no ringleader. He was already in custody
when the riot flared in the stadium. He had been detained
outside the ground for launching an unprovoked attack on
Irish fans. He had immediately drifted back into the crowd,
trying to avoid arrest, but was easily spotted: 'I had the lad's
blood on us.'

In his cell, he was scared. 'I was trembling, me, like. Imagine
getting locked up over there – in Ireland. Unreal. We were all
in the cell together, like, but they took us all up one at a time
and we're all like, "Fuckin' hell", 'cos usually they just put
you on a plane and deport you, eh? But it was different over
there. I had visions of the IRA bastards getting hold of us –
and I've got No Surrender tattooed here,' he said, pointing to
where most of us have a heart. 'I could've found meself in the
showers and got shot or stabbed. But I didn't go to jail. We
was lucky. I got a fifty-quid fine in the end and told never to
return to Ireland. I've got a jail sentence waiting for us if I ever
go back.'

When he got home he found there was plenty more waiting
for him. There was hate mail. There was his mother, who
disowned him. And there was fame, although he didn't know
it, and the press which gave it him. Not the local paper, which
had charted his juvenile progress through the courts, but the
regional news agencies which supply the nationals with stories
and reported the court appearances he missed while he was
in Dublin. Then a staff reporter from one of the nationals,
Today, arrived in person to investigate 'what makes the pond
life tick?' and to chronicle the life of 'a waste of space' behind
the 'carefully orchestrated acts of violence' at England games.

The centre-spread, 'Diary of an England Soccer Yob',

revealed that Dodd and his gang ate fish and chips, bought margarine from his local Spar and drank Scotch bitter. It witnessed one of his appearances at the local magistrates' court and recounted the already-known details of others. In fact it was of little note except for being Dodd's first interview, the start of a career, and for one passing reference to Paul Scarrott – a name, and a life, which have faded into obscurity but were at the time notorious. Scarrott was the first media hooligan, the first to exploit his criminality by appearing in the papers and on television, the first whose amoral willingness to talk – not to mention the clinching detail of having the word 'Forest', as in Nottingham, tattooed inside his lip – made him the ideal interviewee for any piece on hooliganism. Dodd was reported to consider himself 'the new Paul Scarrott', the new number one hooligan. And so he was.

Scarrott first appeared in the newspapers in 1984, when he was jailed for six months for throwing a beer bottle on to the pitch in a UEFA Cup semifinal between Forest and Anderlecht. Three years later he was serving his thirteenth prison term after, armed with a Stanley knife, he led a fifty-strong gang of England fans in a brawl at Hampden Park. Among those jailed with him was Dodd. The following year Scarrott was deported from Germany before the European Championships were even under way, but not before proclaiming himself 'King of the hooligans', shouting 'God Save the Queen' and urinating on shop windows in one of Berlin's upmarket streets. At home he predicted 'blood on the streets' in a series of interviews which sparked a rumour that a tabloid was willing to pay him to return to Germany.

The World Cup in Italy proved to be his little-lamented farewell. He threatened that 500 English hooligans would 'wage war' against the Dutch. 'We have CS gas and, believe me, we will use it. We plan to give the Dutch a right good kicking. After all, this is war,' he said, before he was arrested in Rome and sent home. Six years later he was dead, a down-

and-out alcoholic killed by drink in Barcelona, where he had moved to escape his own publicity. But in Rome, as England faced Italy in their crucial World Cup qualifier eighteen months later, his spirit lived on in Dodd and a good many others, as it does every time England travel abroad.

No one with any sense of shame enjoys England away. Not even the keenest fans I met in the late 1980s were willing to subject themselves to the beer-swilling, glass-breaking and, if it was Poland, Auschwitz-visiting reality of a foreign trip to follow the national team; still now, few of them are. Even those whose desire to support their side overcomes the reservations know only too well that the most likely sight and sound at the end of every evening abroad will be blue lights illuminating city streets and the wail of police sirens.

The final World Cup qualifier in Rome was my first experience of it – and was all I'd expected, and more. On the eve of the match – well, actually until dawn on the day of the match – I was kept awake by a gang of fans in another room of a *pensione* on the outskirts of the city drunkenly singing club chants, 'Ing-er-lund' and, most often, the hooligans' battle anthem, 'No Surrender'. 'Give me joy in my heart, keep me English,' they leered, defiling the hymn and the quiet night. 'Give me joy in my heart I pray. Give me joy in my heart, keep me English. No surrender to the IRA.' Then barking, 'Noooh surrender, noooh surrender, noooooh surrender to the IRA. SCUM.' And repeating their efforts over and over again as the unfortunate Italian owners tried to sleep downstairs.

The first skirmishes had been earlier that evening. I'd seen a few glasses thrown in the city centre, some plastic bar furniture lobbed around and a couple of parked cars kicked and rammed by wheelie bins. All the usual sights if you try to enjoy a meal sitting outside a restaurant – with waiters serving you with one eye watching the end of the street to see what might come around the corner – when England are in town. All the abrupt crashes which clatter over the relentless echoes of 'Ing-er-lund' and choruses of 'No Surrender'. On match day there were incidents too – a bar smashed up near the Spanish Steps, some running scuffles with police – but none to match the violence at the ground itself; none as dramatic as the riot police confronting the England fans in the stands; and none as widely watched as the television pictures of the blue helmets of the police bobbing up and down in time with their flailing batons.

Before kick-off, the first insults were being hurled between English and Italian fans alongside each other in one end of the ground. At the bottom of the section for visiting fans dozens of flags had been set down, the colours of St George spilling out from the confine, marking out English territory; nearby, an Italian banner proclaimed 'Victory to the IRA'. A few yards from the flags a small group of English fans marched up and down the lower half of the side of the section and started taunting the Italians visible through, but penned apart by, a Plexiglas fence.

As the match started, the threats which flew across the divide inevitably became missiles – first bottles, coins and cigarette lighters, then seats ripped from the stand. At first the green and blue line of riot police positioned on the English side of the divide did nothing but watched, the floodlights glinting off their helmets and visors and exaggerating the worrying decoration of their brilliant white belts and holsters. Then they began to advance, batons drawn, to clear English fans away from the Italians. Some English started moving back, pushing into others behind them, all trying to retreat in the face of the first blows. But then some advanced too. Perhaps 200 fought back, charging at body armour and helmets, fists flailing, feet kicking. The roar went up, the cries of 'C'mon England.' No surrender in action.

As the match went on, all eyes, bar those of the players, switched to the drama at the base of the away end. Police who had been in the home end poured through gaps in the Plexiglas at the top and bottom of the section and stood shoulder to shoulder as the reinforced line swept into the fighters, then everyone else in their path too. And still a few of the English struck out. Every couple of minutes the fighting stopped, the police seemingly back in control. Then another missile or punch would be thrown, another flurry of Anglo-Saxon shouting and furious gestures would become a charge and it all started up again until, after half a dozen charges throughout the first half, an uneasy calm settled as the players trooped off at the interval.

There had been equally serious clashes with armed police before the game. There were a few more episodes afterwards too, but being kept in the ground for up to four hours after the final whistle extinguished enthusiasm for everything, from fighting to celebrating the 0–0 draw which confirmed English qualification for the World Cup. Most of the English were bused out and flown home. Those staying in the city found it closed after the game. Taxis were not picking up the English and almost every bar was shut. The few buses which were running were being watched by scores of riot police. The very few bars which were open would allow just one or two English in and then only with the greatest suspicion. And the streets were flooded with blue lights and sirens.

Once that would have been that. The story would have been simple, the headlines in the papers littered with words such as disgrace, the articles bemoaning 'the national disease', the airwaves full of politicians and football administrators mouthing the well-rehearsed words of weary condemnation.

In fact there was some of that. But Rome was the first outing of New England, the first away trip which included an enormous number of the fans who have discovered or rediscovered football in recent years. The post-Euro 96, Three Lions-singing crowd. In fact Frank Skinner and David Baddiel were due to perform in Rome at a pre-match concert, but it fell victim to administrative problems. Plenty of other fans, though, sang their jaunty song and wore the modern replica shirts of the red in which England won the World Cup. In the ground they sang along to the innovation of an England band playing the theme to *The Great Escape*. And then some of them got baton-charged and beaten up too, locked in the ground for hours afterwards and treated with the hostility and suspicion which should have been reserved for the hooligans.

The next morning, in the lobby of a plush hotel on the Via Veneto, the upmarket thoroughfare where the glamour of *La Dolce Vita* was once reality, the 'Rotts' – the Rottweilers, the newshounds, the reporters on 'hoolie watch' – swapped notes on the story. Some of the tabloids had sightings of one of the most notorious England hooligans, one of the Chelsea Headhunters, in the midst of the fighting; a later rumour that Dodd had been arrested also proved to be true. But there was the other side of the story too: the fans with professional jobs – lawyers, the City staff, newspaper executives even – who were outraged at how they'd been treated, how their cigarette lighters and belts had been confiscated and how they'd almost missed flights home because of being kept in the ground for so long.

I was one of them, both a witness to the ill-treatment and a reporter on my first proper hoolie watch. I'd been on one before – for Manchester United's trip to Dortmund in the semifinal of the European Cup six months earlier, in April 1997 – but there was no trouble. No story, as trouble is the only story as far as newsdesks are concerned. But Rome was always going to provide one, from the moment the Rotts were summoned to an office tucked away off a dark side street just south of the Thames in central London five days before the game.

Inside the headquarters of the National Criminal Intelligence Service (NCIS), past the guards in the gatehouse of the small, modern, low-rise development, past security on reception of the anonymous office itself, Peter Chapman, a blunt Yorkshireman, gave a typically blunt message. Almost 700 known hooligans were heading for Rome, about a tenth of them convicted of hooliganism in the past and prepared to start it, even organize it, again: in tabloid terms, 'the generals of hate'. The remainder, most of whom had also been convicted of football-related violence, would happily join in any fighting once it was under way: the category Bs, as opposed to the generals, cat Cs, and the peaceful cat As.

None of us could believe what we were hearing. No one could remember NCIS ever issuing such an explicit warning. The next day the FSA publicly voiced its concern at the comment and how it would affect the policing of the game. Some at the FA were also unhappy, Peter admits now, even though it was they who prompted the press conference. He said, 'David Mellor had gone on his radio show and in the press saying that all English fans were going to be treated like animals and stoking the fires up, and David Davies [the FA's chief press spokesman] phoned me up and said, "We're going to have to reply. Will you go on the programme?", so I did, and said this is the scenario: fans will be searched, anything which could be considered an offensive weapon will be confiscated, the best advice to all decent England fans is travel light, take as little as possible. We got so many press inquiries that we decided to hold the press conference. I didn't say anything at it which I hadn't told the Italian police already, but it did generate some lurid headlines, which, with all due respect, were bollocks. Afterwards I got a call off David Davies and I said I was only telling the truth, and he said, "That's not always the best way." But imagine if I'd said nothing and there had been problems. We would have looked like we didn't have a clue.'

In fact, the treatment Mellor warned of was largely absent – and applied so unevenly that it fuelled the violence. But it was just one of the ingredients of the violence in the stadium.

There were the ticket touts who were loitering outside it in the days before the game, openly selling to the English. There were the semi-official touts, the travel firms who were bringing in English fans independent of the FA's England Members' Club (EMC). There was the stewarding which saw EMC members directed from the official England section at one end of the ground to the unofficial at the other. And it was in there, where those with tickets for another part of the ground, those with touted tickets and several hundred without tickets but allowed in anyway were mixed together, that the fighting occurred. But the real story started below, away from the cameras.

The promised thorough security checks on the approach to the ground were cursory, allowing fans through too quickly – only to face full searches at the foot of the one stairwell to the seats themselves. The frisking fed a pile of confiscated lighters and belts, loose change and water bottles, collected on a black tarpaulin. But it also led to a crush developing at the base of the stairs. More and more fans were arriving, fewer and fewer were getting through the small gap in the metal barriers funnelling them towards the stairs – and past another, unused set. Armed police guarded it and watched developments in front of them impassively. Some of the fans started waving their tickets above their heads to try to show that they had what was needed to pass. But progress got no quicker.

Those being crushed tighter as new arrivals joined the back of the throng, now several hundred strong, began pointing at the second entrance and shouting for it to be opened. One or two managed to squeeze themselves over the barriers to try to race up the unused stairs, but were quickly coshed back. Then one too many tried it, or the crush became too great, or perhaps the officers at the front of the crush just lost patience, but whatever the reason the batons were drawn in real anger, raised and thumped down on skulls and arms raised to shield the blows.

For what seemed like an age, but was a matter of seconds, the concourse between the turnstiles through which we'd all passed and the stairwell became isolated from everything around us – the Italian fans wandering by outside the perimeter fence, the stairs leading into the ground, even any thought of the match itself. Everything was focused on avoiding a beating, and all the others who were rushing away too. Those at the rear retreated easily; those in the middle had to push each other as they turned and ran; those at the front had no time and nowhere to go. If you stayed within reach you were hit. Just ask the father and his seven-year-old son.

When the movement stopped and the police were back behind the barriers, nothing had changed, superficially. The crowd re-formed, although some who had witnessed the police action – and the arrival of reinforcements with guns – walked away despite their expensively acquired tickets. Fans trickled through again and the whole process was repeated: crush, pleas, baton charge. And again. The only differences came eventually when the second stairwell – the route into what was supposed to be a neutral zone alongside the Plexiglas division – was opened and that there were a lot of bloodied and bitter England fans going up it.

The fighting in the unofficial England section started soon afterwards. I watched from the top of the stairwell as the fighters were pushed back from the Italians. As they retreated, though, they were sending a surge through the rest of the crowd. Fans not involved in any of the fighting were falling over as the pressure pulsed through the crowd. When the police advance quickened, even more found themselves tripping, sometimes into the path of a beating if they didn't bounce straight back on to their feet. And all the while the crowd was being pressed towards the Plexiglas at the other side of the section, where there would be no escape.

The next morning in the lobby meeting one of the other reporters had a quote which seemed to sum up the night.

'Downstairs, we thought it was going to be like Hillsborough and then upstairs it looked like it was going to be Heysel.' And I thought none of this was supposed to happen any more.

The presence of Dodd in Rome was, in a very small way, a cause of it, but more so a symptom of it. He was again arrested, again, like in Dublin, before the main fighting started. Police detained him in the early hours of the morning of the match as he got off the overnight train from Milan. Alongside the officers were the victims of an assault on the train who pointed out their attackers, who were taken off to a high-security prison. Dodd was put into solitary confinement, where he watched the game on television. Three days later he walked out after being convicted of attacking a sixty-three-year-old Italian man and his son. But the three days inside were the extent of his punishment. He said as he left, 'I was told to go and that's it.'

He was, of course, innocent. 'I didn't even do owt, not a fuckin' thing,' he said, pulling on his roll-up in the Carlisle pub. 'We were on the sleeper coming through from Milan to Rome for the game and there's a few Eyties getting on, obviously. There's a bit of fuckin' frisk on the train, you know, fighting and that. But I wasn't involved. I was in the carriage asleep. We got to Rome and there's these fuckin' Italian fellas there with cut eyes and what have you pointing people out and he pointed me out! I get home and it's all over the tabloids that I battered an old fella when I never threw a punch. Unbelievable. The fellas who done it got away fuckin' laughing their heads off.'

His friend Gordon Bradshaw, a Grant Mitchell lookalike who was one of the two arrested with him, also denied involvement: 'I saw it happen and it was vicious, but it weren't us. You know how some fights are just a bit of slappin'? Well, this was really vicious, kicking him on the ground and all that. It started when the Italian lad butted an English lad and the dad must have got some as the fight broke out. But the lads who did it just legged it. When the train got in, the police pulled me straight away – I mean, with how I look they're just gonna pick us anyway, aren't they? Paul was hanging back 'cos he had the coke, but they pointed him out too and a couple of others.'

And perhaps, given the brazen admission of other crimes, they were indeed innocent. But in fact only, not in intent. Asked if he was in Rome for trouble, Dodd said, 'Well, aye, of course. That's what I went for.' And to shoplift and steal, as usual: 'I like to go for a pilfer and a rob, you know what I mean, and abroad they're not clued up. It's about sitting in the pubs like this and going down the town and robbing yourself some new clothes. Make a few quid out of it. Jump the trains abroad. Have a piss-up with your mates and a good look round the red-light district – it's a good excuse for the women, eh? It's brilliant, especially when these daft cunts think it's all on the Giro, you know what I mean, eh? It's just a piss-up with the lads, that's all. Football is just what everyone's interested in in England, innit? There's hundreds like me for who getting into the game is a bonus. It's just the beer and the crack. You could have been battling with some of them the year before at home, but abroad it's all forgotten. There might be a few jokes or if you've really got a grumble you might get into them, like – we had some frisk with Villa in Poland – but mostly it's all forgotten. You're all England, eh?'

In his own words, Dodd is 'nothing special. There's lads much worse than me, but they haven't had the coverage.' Peter Chapman had another description of him: 'Small fry, a bit of a joke really. I'm not saying he's not a vicious so-and-so, but he's not very important in the grand scheme of things. He's not an organizer. He talks a lot and gets himself in the papers, but whenever he goes abroad he does our job for us because he always gets himself nicked.' Although Dodd's a cat C because of his record, his heart, mind and drinking habits are that of cat B; he gets drunk enough to have a fight but too drunk to organize one or, especially with his profile, avoid arrest.

But he does cut to the heart of the hooligan problem – just because he can still get himself arrested. The other half of the act which would have introduced ID cards in 1989 included laws on tackling trouble. Magistrates were given the power to ban hooligans from travelling to matches abroad. They could impose restriction orders on those convicted of football violence, forcing them to report to a police station when games were being played; the punishment for breaching them is jail. But Dodd – who served twenty-two months for the service station attack, was jailed in Dublin and in Rome and was once banned from every ground in the country – has never been subject to one. Of about 40,000 fans arrested at football in the past decade, thirty-five had received restriction orders.[4] Peter said, 'We've got the legislation, it's just nobody uses it.'

Instead, Dodd has been free to make a name for himself – and then exploit it. He even hoped it would make him a rich man. For hooliganism has also become a good business. The best-seller lists feature books about it, memoirs of the drinking and fighting. Who better to write the definitive account than England's Number One, the putative title? He'd already featured in a video, but thought he'd been ripped off: 'I was the main thing on the video. It sold I dunno how many copies, 100,000 or summat, and they gave me fuckin' £600. The lads who done it were meant to have made more than a million quid. If I'd had a head about us I should have asked for a percentage.'

For the book, being touted around by Gordon, he was expecting real wealth: 'I'd be happy with £50,000, but I've been told to expect more. What's that one called – The Football Factory, that's it – it's sold 200,000 copies or summat and it's fuckin' shite. There's no humour in it or fuck-all. It's all just blah, blah, blah, repeat, repeat. Mine's got a bit of humour in it.' So what would he do with £50,000? For the first time he raised his voice again, triumphant: 'Piss it up against a wall, put it up me nose, find prostitutes and go to the sun. What do you think I'm gonna do with it? Spend it, spend it good, spend it as quick as possible. I can't wait.' Not bad for a jobless lowlife from Carlisle whose ambitions begin and end with a bellyful of beer, a nose full of coke, some petty crime and a fight, hopefully against foreigners.

He might have no job and no prospects. His girlfriend, and mother of the younger of his two children, might have thrown him out after Rome. He might be banned from every nightclub and most pubs in Carlisle. But Paul Dodd has been to Rome and Poland and all over. Reporters from as far away as Australia and Japan visit Carlisle to see him. That week he was trying, unsuccessfully, to forge a £15,000 deal with the *News of the World* for a story about how he'd got a ticket for one of England's World Cup games. And that made him somebody.

Perhaps it was the self-aggrandizing talk of the book, perhaps it was the beer and spliff, but Dodd was becoming more restless. Perhaps a bit bored of talking, he was looking for some action. We adjourned to another pub and stood outside with his mates where they could leer at any passing women, teenagers mostly, but often weaving past with pushchairs.

The rest of the gang had made themselves scarce before, but now I started to notice them. The wiry ex-kick-boxing champion nodded a greeting when introduced, but said little. A smaller but harder-looking lad was distracted, trying to work out what day it was – a feat he finally accomplished by remembering the date of his next court appearance and counting back. The biggest and quietest of the group cradled his pint and observed, as if he wasn't quite used to company. Dodd explained, 'He's just come out from nick for killing his girlfriend. Drink-driving.' Suddenly I felt it was time to go.

A couple of minutes earlier a policeman who was the local spotter – the officer whose job it is to recognize the hooligans

at his club and report to NCIS – had walked by. He said to
Dodd, 'See you in France?' England's Number One grinned:
'Yeah. It's gonna be mad. Everyone's fuckin' going.'

Just over a month before Carlisle played Bournemouth, Burnley visited Brunton Park. After the match a fight erupted on
wasteground close to the ground. Police arrested several fans,
including a Richard Butcher, aged twenty-five, who was spotted punching another fan in the face. The magistrates who
heard his case agreed with his lawyer's claims that Butcher
had 'nowhere to go' when the fight began. They accepted he
was in 'the wrong place at the wrong time', fined him £200
and declined to impose any order preventing his attendance
at matches. I read about the case in Carlisle's evening paper.

On the same day as Carlisle–Bournemouth, Fulham visited
Gillingham. After the match a fight erupted just outside the
ground. Police arrested several fans, a couple for an attack on
Matthew Fox, aged twenty-four, who was hit in the face. He
fell to the ground and didn't get up again, the first fan to be
killed at football for four years. The same day fans at Barnsley
and Everton tried to attack the respective referees and suddenly the tabloids were discussing 'Soccer's Day of Shame',
every broadsheet musing on the return of hooliganism and
some at the FA even talking about putting perimeter fences
back up.

In truth hooliganism never went away. Its devotees have
largely been priced out of the Premier League and policed
more effectively across football, but never banished or even
prevented from returning when caught. In fact in the lower
divisions the arrest rates at the turn of the decade were lower
than those now.[5] The difference is that then the story in the
lower divisions may have mattered, now it's of increasingly
little interest. The all-conquering Premier League over-
shadows all else, obscuring the rest, what has been left, con-
cealing the state it's still in.

I went to Carlisle to discover parts of it, but I could have gone to many worse places. In fact the club itself is one of the healthiest, financially, in the lower divisions and the third fastest-growing in the league.[6] A new £2.5 million stand runs down one side of Brunton Park, a development which would be the envy of many clubs of a similar size and shows some new hope. But the rest of the ground – the unchanged home terrace, the derelict and disintegrating away ones – is perhaps a better indicator of the general well-being of the lower divisions.

Taylor visited fourteen English league grounds to come up with his conclusion about the 'general malaise or blight' over the game. Three of them have now been replaced by new stadiums – Middlesbrough, Millwall and Sunderland – and almost all of the others are unrecognizable from what he found. But that's not surprising as all but two were in the top two divisions, two-thirds of them in the first. The picture revealed at them may be very different now, utterly transformed indeed. But the picture revealed elsewhere is a pretty familiar one of general malaise due to many old grounds, still, often poor facilities, still, hooliganism, less overall (perhaps now as a small-town pastime as opposed to one for big gangs at the big clubs) but still, a desperate lack of money and, perhaps worst of all, only one remaining ambition: survival.

bigots

No one could expect that verbal exchanges on the terraces would be as polite as those at a vicarage tea party. But shouting or chanting gross obscenities or racialist abuse ought not to be permitted. If one starts, others join in, and to the majority of reasonable supporters, as well as to those abused, the sound of such chants from numbers in unison is offensive and provocative.

Lord Justice Taylor's final report, paragraph 289

I've tried to be honest. I've tried to remember events as they occurred, to report how it was then and how it has been since. But now I have a confession to make: I lied to you earlier. I could try to justify it by saying it was a white lie – except that would hardly be appropriate. And I would still be guilty of obscuring exactly how it was.

The abiding memory of my first games at Elland Road was nothing to do with that word, camaraderie, but of hatred. The strongest first impression was nothing to do with inclusion and community, but of exclusion and bigotry. And the searing irony, which was never fully or satisfactorily resolved, was that I'd waited years to move from being an armchair to an active supporter only to be so disgusted by what I found at my first game that I would rather have been almost anywhere else.

I wasn't, of course, expecting polite applause for opponents or reasoned appreciation of their skills. I was under no illusions that anything other than a hostile, sometimes ferocious, atmosphere would greet both visiting players and their supporters. But I also wasn't expecting the torrent of racist abuse which cascaded from the terraces.

Over the years I had read the stories: how Luther Blissett became the first black player to score for England and received a postbag full of hate mail; how some England fans who witnessed John Barnes pirouette through the entire Brazilian defence to score one of the greatest ever goals refused to count it, let alone admire it, because of his race; and how Barnes, Viv Anderson and Mark Chamberlain had to listen as fans who were somehow also on the flight back from that South American tour relentlessly harangued the FA chairman over the composition of the team. 'You fucking wanker,' they shouted. 'You prefer sambos to us.'[1]

Radio, and to a lesser extent television, was also a warning of what to expect. In the background of featured matches there were sometimes grunted ape impersonations which told who had the ball, or at least the colour of his skin, before the commentators could. Occasionally allusions were made to the noises or to other chants directed at black players, but always couched in terms which hid the true nature of the abuse. Even more rarely a reference might be made to the bananas which routinely landed at the feet of Anderson, Barnes and others as opponents of their clubs, and their colour, indulged in crude symbolism aimed at reminding them they were nothing more than monkeys.

None of it, though, was a preparation for Leeds. Perhaps I was naive not to have appreciated that the intimidating atmosphere at Fortress Elland Road must have had specific targets. And perhaps my support for the club had subconsciously shut out facts which were well known to the rest of the world. Whatever the reason, though, I was astonished when I stood on the Kop and heard the hatred. The vehemence and volume of it buffeted the senses, but the most shocking aspect was really just the fact of it, the unashamed, unpunished, almost unremarkable mass public display. And the revelling in it.

In particular there was a song which I'd never heard, or heard of, before. It began when a disembodied baritone rose above the background crowd noise. 'Trigger. Trigger. Trigger,' it bellowed, with an edge of obvious relish.

'Shoot that nigger,' hundreds, maybe thousands, of other voices barked back.

'Which fucking nigger?'

'That fucking nigger.' And fingers pointed, jabbing over the shoulders of those in front with such aggression that there was a ripple of momentum towards the intended target. As everyone adjusted to the surge and regained their balance, some screamed extra expletives at the black man playing a game, doing his job, a stone's throw away; others just grinned in satisfaction.

Whenever such vitriol, or violence, belches out, there are inevitable claims that only a fraction of the crowd are involved. Often it's true that a vocal, or violent, minority can tarnish the silent, or peaceful, majority. But at Elland Road then no such defence was possible. All around me were fans who joined in. The obvious crew-cutted bad lads, but many others too. Not everyone by any means, but a lot.

The first players I saw subjected to the abuse were from Crystal Palace, Tony Finnigan and an up-and-coming striker called Ian Wright. The week after it was Portsmouth's Vince Hilaire and Noel Blake – a no-nonsense hulk of a defender whom none of the racists would have dared to confront in the street. Then, on his own, was Shrewsbury's centre-forward, an obscure young player whose name failed to register. He was just another black man who left Elland Road, like many did, no doubt incandescent with rage and/or humiliation, and desperate to do something. Score the winner in front of the Kop, maybe, which Wright came back to do regularly (and it was hard not to enjoy his goals, his revenge). Perhaps get some mates together and pick off some of the mob sometime, but only in a fantasy. Or maybe quit the game.

In the thirteen years since then I've been lucky enough to have met, briefly, some world-famous players. I've chatted to a shell-suited Sir Stanley Matthews about the old days, I've shaken hands with Alan Shearer – and almost got a smile too – and, as you will find out, I've had Michel Platini jabbing his finger at me. But in all that time there's been one player above all others whom I wanted to meet: that Shrewsbury centre-forward. Just so he knew that we weren't all like those who abused him. To find out what happened to him. I suppose, really, to say sorry – and ask if anyone else ever did.

Finding a name wasn't difficult, thanks to football's annually published bible, *Rothmans Football Yearbook*. Mickey Brown was the only black face in the 1986/7 Shrewsbury team picture. And it turned out to be easier still to find him in person. The receptionist who answered the telephone at Gay Meadow was confused for a second when I asked about a Mickey Brown from thirteen years ago, but recovered to state what was obvious to her: 'Mickey Brown? He's here now.'

Mickey is in his third spell at Town. He's recognized and cheerily greeted as a local celebrity by young lads and middle-aged ladies alike when he walks through the town centre. He's been away – to Bolton, Preston and Rochdale – but come back twice. He's played, so far, more than 350 games in all three lower divisions and trotted out at dozens of grounds. But his one appearance in Leeds still sticks in his mind – even though it was only his third full game in his first season. Smiling ruefully, he said, 'You just don't forget that.'

It was no secret that bigotry had contaminated Elland Road. Racist songs and Fascist salutes were reported in the local

press when Portsmouth visited in 1984. When the city's
National Front (NF) was infiltrated and exposed eighteen
months later, the two reporters responsible made first contact
with the group outside the ground. Some of those who were
locked out for the QPR cup tie in 1987 sang anti-Semitic
songs about the board.

Mickey had been warned exactly what to expect too, thanks
to Palace manager Steve Coppell, whose side visited Gay
Meadow the week after Leeds, and the week before Shrewsbury were due to travel north. Coppell spoke to Town manager
Chic Bates about the reception his eighteen-year-old striker
might receive. Mickey recalled, 'He said that the crowd had
given their black guys some real harsh stick and they didn't
really deal with it all that well. Our manager told me about it
and asked if I was willing to play. I said, "Yeah, I don't mind.
I'm looking forward to it." I mean, obviously I didn't know
what it was going to be like. I knew there was racism going
on 'cos every time a black guy got the ball in a match on telly
you could hear it, but I didn't really know how bad it would
be. And anyway you can't really say, "I don't want to play." I
was a young player. I wanted to be in the team.'

Only when the team coach drew to a halt outside the players'
entrance at Elland Road did he fully appreciate the likely scale
of the ordeal he was about to face. 'There were a few supporters
waiting around, to get autographs and whatever. When I got
off the coach I overheard a couple of them say, "Looks like
we'll be having some fun today." And what was shocking was
that they were middle-aged, that's what really surprised me.
If it had been young lads you wouldn't have taken much
notice, but these two were respectable-looking older men. A
couple of the lads in the team heard what they'd said and one
of them put his arm around me, you know, as if to say, "It'll
be all right." '

At the pre-match meal Bates made a final check that Mickey
wanted to play. He got changed as normal, pulling on kit and

lacing up his boots before clattering out of the dressing room for the warm-up, nervous anyway – Elland Road was the biggest ground he'd ever visited as a player – but with an extra edge as he strode along the players' tunnel towards the light and muffled sound from outside. He trotted into daylight and immediately the noise levels multiplied. 'As soon as I ran out, there was booing and jeering, loads of it. It just seemed like everyone in the crowd was shouting and I thought perhaps it's just because I'm the opposition, you know. Then I heard "Shoot That Nigger" the first time and I knew it was more than that.'

The warm-up, for Mickey and his tormentors, completed, he returned to the dressing room. Nothing was said. The sides came out for the match and the abuse started all over again. Nothing was said. In the early minutes he appeared to be slightly cowed, almost reluctant to run towards the goal at the Kop end which Town were attacking. Nothing was said. 'No one on the pitch or on either team said anything to me about it at all, they just left me to get on with it or deal with it or whatever. Every time I got the ball there were monkey chants and all the rest, but I just tried to play.'

Then, just after half an hour, he picked up the ball on the half-way line, perhaps far enough away not to think of the hostility behind the goal, and did what came naturally – headed for it. He beat one defender, then two and finally a third before hitting a drive which beat the goalkeeper and clipped off the bar. Everything changed. 'I don't know if it's because I was concentrating on playing then, but it all seemed to drop off after that. I got some good touches and just got on with the game. In the players' bar afterwards some of the Leeds fans patted me on the back and said, "Well done, lad. You had a great game." But no one said anything about the chants. It was really strange. It was like no one else had heard anything.'

None of the Leeds players in the bar mentioned it, nor did any of the club officials either. None of his own team-mates talked about it after the match or on the coach home, nor did the management. It was, after all, what was expected – and accepted: 'It was, wasn't it, just accepted? But I accepted it as well. I didn't complain about it – I suppose because what would anyone have done? You just had to concentrate on your game and get on with it. You just couldn't let it affect you – even though that was so difficult.'

The rematch at Shrewsbury's Gay Meadow was one of the last games of the season, Mickey's first season as a professional footballer. His proud mum and sister regularly used to travel across from the family home in Birmingham to watch him play. But not when Leeds visited; he told them to stay away because he didn't want them to see and hear what he had to face – and perhaps even have to face some of it themselves.

Hitler was a Leeds fan. That was the simple, sinister message carried in graffiti on a city-centre wall. And while it might not have been strictly true of the Führer himself, it was for a number of his latter-day devotees.

Before the club's most important game in five years – the promotion play-off replay against Charlton in 1987 – one of the known ringleaders of the racism at Elland Road was spotted selling copies of *Mein Kampf*. At other games Nazi-style salutes were all part of the intimidation – and not just from those on the terraces. Watford and England's Blissett complained, 'Normally the abuse is from the terraces, but at one Leeds game whole groups in the stand were doing Nazi salutes and shouting, "*Sieg Heil.*" '[2]

The city itself had long been a centre for far-right political activity, dating back to the 1930s, when its large Jewish community was the target. Ethnic-minority footballers had also been subjected to racism from the first days they ran on to a pitch. The first black outfield player, Arthur Tull, was subjected to such abuse playing for Spurs at Bristol City in 1909 that his form collapsed and he was transferred. The difference in the

1970s and 1980s was that football and organized Fascism were combined, the sport used as a platform to promote politics and recruit members. At Elland Road, a Nazi group called the National Democratic Freedom Movement arrived in the early 1970s; soon after the NF added its more lasting presence too.

Its newspaper sellers raised funds, and awareness of their agenda, from pitches in front of the wall which ran along one side of the ground to the entrance to the Kop turnstiles. The battered red brick, speckled with graffiti, topped with barbed wire, was a fitting backdrop for the dissemination of even more bleak and ugly ideas. But it was also, perversely, the prime location. Thousands of us who travelled from the city centre by the special buses were dropped off nearby, sometimes directly opposite. Often the first publications on sale to us were *Bulldog*, the NF's youth paper, or *The Flag*, its senior equivalent. The former printed a league of clubs whose supporters were most racist; Leeds were often number one. The latter offered supposedly more sophisticated comments, such as, 'Liverpool's phenomenal success story over the last twenty years nails the lie that English soccer needs blacks to succeed.'[3]

The stream of fans pulsing past, into the ground, was superficially largely unaffected by the presence of the paper sellers. Me and my friends just walked by, disgusted but silent. When someone in the crowd did stop to make a purchase, the flow rerouted itself around the obstacle and continued towards the turnstiles, many in it disgusted but silent. The police were similarly uninterested, merely monitoring the rate of progress into the ground and watching for fighting. On a good day the sellers sold only a few hundred, after all. A few hundred, however, which were passed around so that the readership multiplied, perhaps up to 1,000, who quickly contaminated non-readers too. In crowds of less than 15,000, that meant there was quickly a significant, and noisy, section of active and vocal racists. And the disgust and silence of most of the rest of us were even less effective weapons than they had been outside.

Even more chilling was the impact away from Elland Road. At the end of the season Mickey Brown was abused, a twenty-strong group of fans got on a train to take them home from an away game and found some of their fellow travellers were black. When the songs and threats started, their targets fled to the guard's van and were locked in for their own safety. The fans, armed with fire extinguishers, sticks and a metal rod, and chanting, 'Let's throw the black bastards on the track', were prevented from breaking down the door only by a second, off-duty, guard. He was beaten so severely that he was off work for seven weeks.

And worse still was the riot of which Hitler would have been proud.

Eddie Gray was one of the greatest players Leeds ever had, perhaps the best in terms of ability with the ball. He made more than 500 appearances through the 1960s and 1970s, the Ryan Giggs of Revie's sides. He continued playing into the 1980s, by dropping back to left-back, and carried on even when he was appointed manager in a decision which was popular with the fans.

So when he approached the away end at St Andrews, Birmingham, teeming with 10,000 fans hoping to see a promotion, he expected to be listened to, to be taken notice of. All around him police were trying to contain rioting which had engulfed both the home and away ends, trying to prevent one or other of the sets of supporters breaking free to launch a full attack on their rivals. Bottles, coins and rubble ripped from the terraces littered the edge of the pitch. Gray walked to his fans and appealed for them to calm down. And became a target for the missiles himself.

'It was absolutely terrible, appalling,' he remembered.

'Everyone just carried on fighting. You just think it's a waste of time being here. Being on the pitch is a waste of time; the game's a waste of time. That day was just awful – one of the worst incidents I've ever seen, and hopefully ever will. If you cannae go to a game of football and just watch the game from the viewpoint that we got beat but we played well, or we got beat by a better side, what's the point? That's what football's all about. It's not about people wanting to fight with one another.'

But for a large number at St Andrews, fighting was exactly what the game was about. By mid-morning the routes from Leeds were already littered with broken glass and blood as riotous coachloads of fans called at pubs in Leicestershire, Nottinghamshire and Staffordshire. In Birmingham, a 150-strong advance party forced shoppers strolling near New Street Station to take cover in doorways and against plate-glass façades as running battles erupted in the heart of the city centre. A little further out towards the ground itself a pub was gutted, every window smashed as anything not fixed to the floor was hurled outside.

At the ground the violence was underpinned by a purpose: getting in for nothing. In an atmosphere of increasing anarchy, some of the younger and more athletic scaled walls and fences around the turnstiles, then the barbed wire on top too, and jumped into the ground. Behind and below them, other fans ripped lumps from the pavement and hurled them at police. Bottles and bricks, cans and coins were also used to provide cover to keep officers at bay, while larger chunks of concrete were used as battering rams on the gates. When the padlocks and steel gave way, about 150 fans rushed in, keeping up the barrage of missiles as they streamed past police. A little further along another group also swarmed in after ripping down fifty feet of metal railings and a wall. The rubble became more ammunition.

Inside the police were forced from the terraces as debris

rained down. The mob was in charge. A wrecking crew scaled the perimeter fence and began rocking back and forth in an attempt to topple it to ease the next step – the pitch invasion. All the while missiles cleared the fence and kept the police at bay. And if anyone doubted the pre-meditation involved, why else would one visitor have brought a pickaxe? He used it to churn up the terraces to provide more ammo. Then the refreshment hut was raided too and Mars Bars, even its kettle, were hurled around in incidents which might have been almost comic but for the fact that the sinister intention behind them was soon clear: the roof of the hut was dismantled and passed forward, ready for use as a bridge over the sagging fences or a battering ram.

Throughout the first half efforts to destroy the away end continued. In the unfenced home end large numbers of fans began to gather at the front of the terrace. And at half-time battle was joined. Home fans rushed on to the pitch. Away rivals surged to meet them. Police managed to get in between. Mounted officers baton-charged both sets of hooligans to force them back into their respective ends. One of the horses was hit by a flare, while smoke bombs were fired at both ends. Some Leeds fans began to clear the debris up from the pitch – but partly to rearm themselves. And Eddie Gray was stoned.

After forty-five minutes an uneasy calm was restored and lasted long enough for the second half to be played. But at full-time there were further pitch invasions from either end. Police again kept the two sides apart, but were bombarded by advertising hoardings and seats. The Leeds fans flung concrete at the windows of the executive boxes running along the side of the pitch. The goal nets were torn down. The derelict refreshment hut was set alight. A policeman had his nose broken, even though he was wearing a helmet, as a lump of concrete smashed into his face. A woman officer was also hit and needed six stitches. Three colleagues standing close to her in the front line were stretchered away. As the official report put it, the scene 'more clearly resembled the Battle of Agincourt than a football match'.[4]

The violence spilled from the ground, fanning out to engulf a children's playground, which was destroyed by home fans – partly for fun, partly for weapons; a coach, carrying a party of Asians back from a wedding, which had its windows smashed and its passengers injured; and even a nurse trying to treat one of the injured, but who was herself kicked unconscious. A police horse was pulled to the ground.

Outside the away end some fans took shelter by a wall running between the terraces and the car park. On the other side of them the last remnants of the crowd were being driven out, past the burning refreshment stall, by police. Some witnesses said departing fans climbed over the wall; some that they were deliberately pushing it; and others that there was a crush as police cleared the terraces. Whatever the reason, the wall first bulged and then collapsed, its bricks shattering windscreens, hammering dents in bonnets, injuring twenty people and killing one: Ian Hambridge, aged fifteen, who was at his first ever match.

As the medics and the police cleared up, as the area finally cleared and a sort of peace descended, they trod NF leaflets into the ground. As the innocent Leeds fans headed home discussing the appalling afternoon, they told of the *'Sieg Heil'* chants they had heard around them. And some of them passed a Transit van carrying home others who were at the match – still wearing their Swastika armbands.

The total casualty list from the day included 500 supporters, sixty of whom were taken to hospital, and almost 150 police, twenty-one of whom were taken to hospital. A total of 125 arrests were made. Damage to property was estimated at £85,000. By any standards, it was one of the worst episodes of hooliganism ever seen in this country. But what would ordinarily have been accorded the full front- and back-page treatment was condensed and placed down-page for the simple fact that it was eclipsed as the worst football story, the worst story, of that day in 1985: the Bradford City fire.

Mr Justice Popplewell was appointed to look into both Birmingham and Bradford, and then had to expand his work to include Heysel too. He reported back on the NF leaflets, the fifty-strong group of Leeds fans who had chanted '*Sieg Heil*' first at an Asian fan in the ground and then the police, and those spotted in the Transit van. In his interim report he concluded: 'There is a good deal of evidence from responsible witnesses that political activists are involved in troubles at football grounds.' But then he played down their significance in his final report: 'The considered view of the police . . . seems to be that their [the extremists'] importance at football grounds is a self-importance and they are not a significant factor in the problems with which I am dealing.'

But they were in so far as they were a product of many of the identical ingredients which caused hooliganism: largely unchecked anger, restrained only by fences and high-profile policing; a thriving mob mentality, which could spread through a crowd in seconds; and, most of all, an atmosphere of anarchy, where 'anything goes' and individual acts of mis-behaviour were lost in a stew of law-breaking and defiance. St Andrews was just the ultimate example, of the latter in particular, a riot not caused by the presence of the NF, but quite predictable once it was as apparent and unchallenged as the other, non-political hooligans.

There was talk of Leeds being hit by the most severe punish-ment ever. There were even rumours the club would be closed down. But in the end it had to introduce a membership-card scheme for all away games and was fined £5,000. Eddie Gray and his side were free to continue as before; but so were the hooligans, and the bigots too.

*

Gordon Lunn stopped them. Not on his own, of course. Not without the help of the club and the police, eventually. And not without a fight, once. But he heard what the likes of Mickey Brown heard – and coming from those around him on the Kop – and decided to act.

A fan since the late 1960s, he'd watched the rise under Revie and the collapse to mediocrity on the pitch and malice off it after his departure. By the late 1970s he was getting used to hearing the abuse the first generation of British-born black players received. For a time in the early 1980s it eased a little – although the opposition's 'niggers' still had to suffer the mass verbal attacks, the presence of 'our black lad', centre-forward Terry Connor, seemed to diminish their force and frequency. When Connor was transferred, though, the abuse returned stronger than ever. Not that it was mentioned.

'There was a conspiracy of silence throughout football,' Gordon said. 'You'd watch games on telly and you could hear gorilla noises in the background and John Motson was just saying, "There's a lively atmosphere here today." After Heysel, it was the national game still, but it was clear that it was poisoned. We'd be standing on the terraces at Leeds and there'd be people around you reading *Bulldog*, seeing where we were in the racist league. The atmosphere was appalling, but the club just put its head in the sand and hoped it would all go away. Instead it was spreading. That's why we had to do something.'

And something was this: a one-hundred strong group headed to Elland Road early, ready to occupy the N F paper sellers' spots before anyone else arrived. They arrived in a convoy, as they would travel back, to avoid being ambushed. They were under strict orders to keep together and to stand with their backs to the wall to prevent attacks from behind. One of the other founders, Alison Pilling, said, 'We were putting ourselves on the line to be threatened with violence – and we were. They could have flattened us in seconds, to be honest, but that's why we had to take so many to start with – safety in numbers.'

The police had already been warned of the plan and were worried. The officer in charge of operations at the ground, Superintendent Jack Clapham, said, 'My worry would be that the actions of this group will provoke a reaction from the National Front. It could mean a busy day for us when we are already keeping rival fans apart.'[5] But his fears went unrealized. The newly named Leeds United Against Racism and Fascism were armed only with leaflets and stickers; their volunteers were ordered to avoid any confrontation or fighting. Another of the founding members, Paul Thomas, said, 'We wanted to make sure it was peaceful, but effective, so that no one could say we were damaging the club. We were fans. We didn't want to be accused of that.'

The group had been born when Gordon and Paul met through a city-wide campaign against the far right and discovered a shared love of Leeds and hatred of the racism at the ground. Like all of us who welcomed their presence at that first match, against Bournemouth in October 1987. All of a sudden the silent had a voice. Reaction from fans arriving for the game was overwhelmingly positive. Gordon said, 'Loads of them were coming up to us and saying, "At last. Thank God someone's doing something about it." There were clearly people there looking for a lead off the club and it never came.'

The initiative, though, was a one-off. Everything was back to normal when Villa visited Elland Road in an FA Cup tie in January. Midfielder Andy Gray and striker Garry Thompson had bananas hurled at them as they took to the pitch. The songs followed. Gray's sole consolation was that he capped a sparkling performance by scoring the winning goal. The abuse was again noted in the newspapers. And within a week Gordon was in the offices at Elland Road.

The club's view, like that of many in football, was of knowing ignorance. Silence. Pretend it's not there and it'll go away. When Gordon's first leaflet was published the club had frostily denied all knowledge of it and even threatened to sue whoever was responsible for using the club crest without permission. Local politicians exerted pressure on officials to meet the new campaigners, but even when they did they were reluctant to act. They asked for suggested action; the five-point list which came back included anti-racist statements in the programme, advertisements around the ground and using the team to promote the message. But they also asked for precise evidence of the alleged problem; the dossier which came back two months later provided it – and exactly the widespread and critical publicity the club was anxious to avoid. The conspiracy of silence was completely broken.

Terror on the Terraces recorded the racist abuse. It detailed how the ground was used to recruit members of the NF. It told of how the chants and Fascist salutes were often seen in the midst of episodes of football violence. But it wasn't new. The racist abuse could be heard by anyone at the ground and was reported, albeit irregularly, by the papers. The NF recruitment had been exposed by the *Yorkshire Post*. The link between extremism and violence had been noted by Popplewell. Gordon said, 'It's not as if we did any great undercover work. We were just reporting what had already been reported.' But obviously no one had read a thing either.

The police said they would study the dossier. The council immediately announced that any fan convicted of violence or racism would be banned not only from Elland Road – which it owned – but also from every council facility. One of three councillors who sat on the board said, 'The council and the club are well aware of this problem which is discussed at every Leeds United board meeting.'[6] But still no one from the club was at the launch of the report. Secretary David Dowse claimed he had been unaware of it, but added he would also closely scrutinize the report and consider any ideas officials might have missed. When he had time to digest it, his response was, 'Many of these things have not occurred recently.'

At the next home game 20,000 copies of a letter signed by the players and manager, Billy Bremner, were distributed to fans:

Notice to all Leeds United supporters. Firstly, may we express our thanks for your great support both home and away during 1987/8 season. Throughout the year, you have proved time and time again that you can provide, both in numbers and in volume, the best support in the land. We are delighted that no longer are the club's supporters automatically linked with crowd problems, as any such problems also have a detrimental effect on the way we play. The only remaining problem is some of the language used in some songs and chants. Please let's clean up our image totally and cut out any four-letter words, racist taunts and noises, and abuse aimed at opponents and their supporters. Please 'sing your hearts out for the lads' – but keep it clean.

Before the end of the season another anti-racist leaflet was distributed outside the ground – and Gordon got a punch off one of the NF paper sellers too. When the new season started in August a regular free fanzine was distributed – and in a changed atmosphere. Outside the ground fans had begun to turn, verbally, on the NF activists. Police made concerted efforts to move them on or disperse them. Inside, two summer signings were making an impression: Portsmouth's Vince Hilaire and Noel Blake. Gordon said, 'The rumours were that pressure was put on Bremner to sign some black players because it was thought that it would help.'

Within two years of the start of the campaign the NF was banished, its financial and political reasons for being at football taken from it, its presence no longer tolerated. Nazi salutes went with them. 'Trigger. Trigger. Trigger' disappeared at the same time. The only time bananas were spotted were in the peculiar fruit-based diet of new captain Gordon Strachan.

Gordon Lunn knew the campaign was won when he overheard a fan who looked as if he might previously have been involved in other types of abuse shout, 'You're playing like a woman!' and his mate chided him, 'You can't say that now.'

There is a quick postscript. When we'd finished talking about the campaign, admiring the award it won and reminiscing about John Sheridan, we moved on to today's football, today's Leeds, and Gordon said, 'Oh, I don't go any more. I can't afford it and I stopped enjoying it as much anyway. When we were going we were in the middle of Division Two with 14,000 there and it was great – despite everything. It's just not the same now. It was a working-class game and it's not any more. We were the people who kept the club going through its darkest years. We reclaimed the game and then the money men came in and took it over. We saved the club and now I can't even get in.'

Mark Stein timed his run just a fraction wrong. The long, angled pass from midfield found the space behind his marker, as had Stein, but just before the ball was played. Offside. He curtailed his run as the whistle went and turned to walk back. The ball rolled on and out of play a few yards further on, near the penalty area. The lull in play was filled by a middle-aged man standing between the player and still-rolling ball: 'Ahhhh. Fuck off, nigger.'

An isolated incident in the first half of Carlisle–Bournemouth, it was the only racist comment I heard at all the matches in the season. It was also the most overt abuse I'd heard for years – just because the culprit was standing so close to his target. Stein, whose family fled South Africa when he was a baby to escape apartheid, clearly heard it and fixed the guilty fan with a stare which suggested the general thrust of what he'd like to do, if not the specific method. He kept staring as he walked back. Then shook his head and got on with the game.

Once similar scenes would have been played out with a larger and more vocal cast at grounds all over the country. Everyone knows the clubs where the abuse was most acrid: Chelsea, Millwall, Newcastle, West Ham. But it was heard almost everywhere. Mickey Brown said, 'I got it more or less every other week, whenever we played away, off someone. It was just a question of how much.' Instead I was at one of just two matches where Leeds fans were accused of racism – but where the target identified in the papers, West Ham's black goalkeeper Bernard Lama, was abused not because of his colour but because he was French and, whichever way you look at it, I'm afraid that counts as progress.

An apparently even better example of it, but a demonstration of where the issue is still alive, came in Cardiff on a filthy March night.

Ninian Park was a remarkable sight and not so much for the stand, which looked as if it had been transplanted from a war zone, its lack of rear cladding exposing concrete innards to the fierce rain. Nor because of the vivid green scars of moss and algae which marked where the drainpipes had long been overwhelmed by water and corrosion. It wasn't even the toilets, although they were something else: the official one at the end of the Bob Bank was four walls of whitewashed breezeblock – and no roof; the unofficial one, out behind the back of the stand, was one wall overlooking a railway line and wild undergrowth which, in the half-time darkness of an evening kick-off in March, looked worryingly like stinging nettles.

No, the truly remarkable sight was the uncovered away end. Not only was it packed, despite the lashing rain, but it was packed with black faces. Some had flags, many were dressed in yellow, green and black, most had whistles, horns or hooters, but few had much more than good humour to shield them from the storm. When the Tannoy interrupted its playlist of reggae – surely a first at Ninian Park – and crackled into life to announce a delayed kick-off, there were no complaints. The enormous Jamaican contingent did as requested and took a couple of steps to their right to make room for even more arrivals entering through the turnstiles to the left. The massed whistles, horns and hooters fell silent for a few, shuffling seconds. Then started up again.

The chants of 'Reggae Boyz', often in Cockney-ish accents, also bounced around the Bob Bank, theoretically the home 'end' even though it's a side. In all some 10,000 Jamaican supporters had travelled to Cardiff – the vast majority from London or other big cities – to witness their country's first international on European soil. Many of them made the trek even though they had seen their side play in London, against QPR, three days earlier. Then the 'away' support was estimated at nine-tenths of the 17,000 sell-out; in Cardiff it was more than two-thirds of another sell-out crowd.

Even a dull 0–0 draw which made Wales – and Wales lacking Ryan Giggs – look like titans of international football failed to dampen enthusiasm for the third leg of the Boyz' whistle-stop tour of Britain, against Manchester City. Or, as fans trekked back to their coaches and a long ride home arranging rendezvous in France, for the World Cup itself. The chat was all about how to get tickets and who already had them; whether it was better to rely on relatives back in the Caribbean or contacts in Britain. No one was asking the price.

But the enthusiasm, the turnout, the apparently healthy integration of immigrants and their children into the national sport, was in stark contrast to the league crowds, where an average of one in a hundred Premier League fans – seven times less than the number in society as a whole – is non-white, most of them Asian[7] (and while around a quarter of all professional players are black); where one-third of Premier League fans still report witnessing racism and 23 per cent have heard racist comments directed at black players in the last season; and where no one will have ever seen an Anglo-Asian professional player because there has never been one. And the situation in the lower divisions is thought to be worse.

On the pitch, too, there was another glaring example of an area where racism is still said to be rife – or at least there would have been if Nathan Blake had been playing. The only black face in the Welsh team, he has lost out on several caps after he refused to play for his country because of comments its manager Bobby Gould made about him – or more accurately his skin colour. Other players have made similar complaints: Ian Wright, long since freed of racial abuse from the crowd, but allegedly subjected to it by Peter Schmeichel; Stan Collymore claimed he was called a coon by ex-team-mate Steve Harkness. And all of the incidents were resolved as quietly as possible, without any disciplinary action. No one heard anything, you see.

Perhaps the reluctance to act is put into perspective by other unreported, recent stories which have seeped out. For example, the FA councillor who told an England manager that 'there were too many niggers' in the team. Or the Premier League chairman whose appraisal of a leading player was, 'The monkey played well today, didn't he?' Or the manager who was telling a racist joke when one of his black players went to see him. Or the Third Division chairman who signed up for Let's Kick Racism Out of Football, the game's anti-racism initiative, only after being told he had to – and after saying he wouldn't because 'I'm a racist.'[8]

Clubs' commitment to the campaign has been questioned too. Only 15 per cent have implemented all three main recommended measures: programme statements, public address announcements and pitchside hoardings.[9] More than half have introduced none or just one – and then largely perhaps the least noticeable, the programme message. One club even wrote to researchers to say, 'The incidence of abusive behaviour towards the ethnic minorities is virtually non-existent . . . Vigorously pursuing a policy . . . may be counter-productive by creating a problem that is not there.' Which sounds rather too familiar.

Glasgow is different. Different in where the faultlines occur; different, perhaps, in the more permitted public displays of private prejudices. But exactly the same in that they run into football.

On Easter Sunday it was especially different. The Old Firm match between Rangers and Celtic was about to allow its usual airing of the sectarianism which had led to thirty years of war in Northern Ireland – as the ink was drying on the Good Friday Agreement aimed at ending the war.

But tensions around the match were unchanged. Early in the morning ferries had set out from Belfast and Larne, full of red, white and, mostly, blue from the former and green, gold and white from the latter, as the shipping firms' unofficial insurance policy of segregation was colourfully illustrated. In Glasgow itself the tube trains were still, as staff refused offers of pay bonuses to work a holy day which they feared might be again marred by un-Christian conflict. And at Ibrox technicians finalized the pre-match video clips – all of lasting instants of Rangers glory, of course – to be shown on giant screens over audio of Frankie Goes to Hollywood's 'Two Tribes': 'When two tribes go to war . . .'

The charge sheet after one match, in 1975, read two attempted murders, two cleaver attacks, one axe attack, nine stabbings and thirty-five common assaults, I'd read on the train going north.[10] I'd also learned of riots around Old Firm matches even during the Second World War, of death threats, of an attack on Catholic Rangers player Mo Johnston's father and of songs celebrating bloody Loyalist victory and the supposed martyr IRA terrorist Bobby Sands. But most of all I had read in dismay of how Rangers fans, Protestants, could spot Catholics, Celtic fans, just by looking at them, at their red hair or, more relevantly in my case, jet-black hair and pasty colouring. My mum's Irish Catholic ancestry was apparently obvious at a glance – and I was heading for the most Loyalist bar in Glasgow.

Little about the outside of the Louden Tavern, the self-proclaimed Greatest Pub in the World, indicates what awaits inside. The nondescript single-storey building stands pretty much alone, bordering a few small industrial units but largely surrounded by dereliction and a litter- and graffiti-strewn area of earthy, urban wasteground. But look more closely and the letters spray-painted on walls nearby, UVF for the paramilitary Ulster Volunteer Force, identify the territory. The bar's façade, blue paint as glossy as when it left the tin, also confirms its Loyalty. The notice in the window confidently announcing a planned ten-in-a-row party merely, and rather optimistically, confirmed it.

Inside a portrait of the Queen hung above the door. But almost every other inch of wall space was devoted to regimented rows and columns of identical picture frames containing chronological certification of league and cup honours or players, past and present. The floor was blue. The tiles were red, white and blue. There was a range of manufacturers for the tops worn by the scores of torsos tightly packed before the big screen – Nike, Adidas or Umbro, but all in blue. At the bar I looked, just for an instant, for a pump serving Guinness before realizing it was as unlikely as a portrait of the Pope.

When Rangers took the lead the vein-bulging roar shook the room, the screen wobbling under the sonic assault. The goal, by Jonas Thern, produced loud, triumphant celebrations, songs old and new, traditional and contemporary, masterful and mocking. But the scorer was largely ignored, escaping the congratulations of team-mates on the pitch to acknowledge fans who, in the Louden at least, were less interested in individual endeavour than in collective victory.

Except when Andy Goram was pictured. When he made a decent save there were generous shouts of appreciation. But even when he did nothing more than appear on the screen, taking a goal kick or making an easy collection of a loose ball, there were murmurs of approval. My guide on my Old Firm experience, undertaken in the absence of match tickets, told me why: it was here where the goalkeeper allegedly decided, four months earlier, to wear a black armband in the previous Old Firm game – five days after the notorious Loyalist terrorist Billy 'King Rat' Wright, a murderer with the blood of an estimated twenty Catholics on his hands, was himself assassinated in Belfast's Maze Prison; and three months after Goram's aunt, whose memory he claimed to be marking, died.

At half-time I noticed a laminated sheet which had been tucked inside the frame of one of the pictures. On it was a tribute to a Thomas Stewart, a name I didn't know but of which I was wary as soon as I'd spotted the red hand of Ulster on the masthead. Now I know: Thomas Stewart was a colleague of Billy Wright whose association with the killer and uncompromising violence took him further and further to the fringes of the UVF and ended in death in a bloody internal power struggle. To most, an unlamentable end to a life dedicated to the termination of others; to some, the author of the sheet included, the demise of another murderous martyr.

About a mile away is the spot where bigotry begat murder.

There seems to be nothing special about Bridgeton Cross, not its train station or the trams which rumble past the shops and pubs on either side of the main road to the city centre. Shoppers amble back and forth, even their slow, shuffling movement a dynamic contrast to the inertia of the drinkers inside the pubs. But look closer in the surrounding streets and the graffiti again reveal the sinister side. The initials are there. The red hand too.

Mark Scott was happily walking towards the station, his legs perhaps just a little bit stiff after playing rugby in the morning. Over lunch at home he had swapped his kit for casual clothes, and rugby for football, for a visit to Parkhead with two friends. Celtic had beaten Partick Thistle 2–1 and the trio were heading home, conducting the usual post-match post-mortem.

At first Rangers fans around the Cross hurled abuse, then they sprayed beer. One among them screamed his contribution and waited to make his next. Jason Campbell, aged twenty-three, was a man whose hatred was so ingrained that he often wore a bright-orange anorak to display his Loyalist leanings. He watched the group of three continue past, then sneaked up behind them, grabbed Mark from behind and slashed his throat through to the spine.

Mark staggered on for about twenty-five yards before collapsing. A passer-by among many who quickly swooped to help snatched a blanket from his baby's pram to try to stem the bleeding. But the wound had severed an artery. Underneath a Celtic shirt – itself concealed under a jumper and a coat as a precaution against both the cold and also attack – his heart stopped beating within minutes. Mark Scott, aged sixteen, schoolboy and Celtic fan, was dead.

In the silence and lingering sorrow of the sitting room of the family home, Niall Scott let out an involuntary sigh as he described the doomed attempts to save his son. 'A waste of time really,' he said. And a waste of a life.

Mark was the product of a not uncommon marriage across the sectarian divide, his father a Protestant, his mother, Judith, a Catholic. His two sets of twin brothers and sisters were educated, like him, at non-denominational schools. His friends included both Catholics and Protestants. But he was murdered by someone for whom such tolerant coexistence was impossible.

Some might say that because of the inbred bigotry of his murderer, Mark's death had nothing to do with football; it was society's problem. Indeed, Campbell was a product of sectarianism which went far beyond Celtic and Rangers, sport or sense. When he was jailed for life for the murder, he was following a route to prison taken by his father and uncle; both were part of a nine-strong UVF gang jailed for a total of 519 years for crimes ranging from bombing Catholic pubs to general arms and explosions offences.

But that wasn't the way Niall Scott saw it, with tears occasionally welling in his eyes, in the aftermath of the Old Firm match: 'There'll be attacks all over the place tonight, little wars breaking out. No doubt there will always be incidents of violence. But what we should be trying to do is preventing football from being a trigger for that violence, as it will be tonight, as it was with Mark, so that if someone is being beaten up, it's not because they are wearing a Celtic scarf or a Rangers scarf.'

And football, and those who run it, can do so much to help: 'I would love to see sectarianism ended, bigotry eradicated from our society. I know that's never going to happen, but I'd like to see it at least diminish. It will take a lot of work over a long period to make real progress, but you have to start somewhere and football is as good a place as any. The power of it can be an enormous power for good.'

The Scotts weren't devoted fans. Some of Niall's family followed Rangers, but he never really had. He only went to Celtic – but Hibernian too – with Monk. He said, 'I'd say we were supporters rather than fans. We didn't go every week; it wasn't what we planned our every weekend around.' Unsurprisingly, Niall's enthusiasm for the game has waned to the extent of two games since Mark's death – both at Celtic, both as guests of the club, once to quietly collect a significant donation to the charity[11] which has been established to help teenagers fulfil dreams like those Mark never had the chance to realize.

Celtic were swift to offer sympathy and support. One evening in the week after the stabbing there was a knock on the front door of the grey stone, and then-gloomy, family home and manager Tommy Burns introduced himself. His entire first team attended the funeral; Rangers were represented too, by manager Walter Smith, Paul Gascoigne and Brian Laudrup. Management from both clubs, in Celtic's case Burns again, also attended the launch of the charity.

For in recent years the old rivalries have been increasingly set aside. Celtic have taken the lead, with a campaign called Bhoys Against Bigotry. Chairman Fergus McCann said at its launch, 'The club's role as a major institution comes with a responsibility to work against groups or individuals who use football as a medium for promoting their extreme political and/or religious views.'

Niall welcomed the initiative, and also identified the commercial imperative which was helping to drive it. 'I have a great deal of respect for what Celtic have done,' he said. 'And I think the violence will decrease as time goes by. There has been a clear improvement over the past few years and it's because, at the end of the day, football's an entertainment business now and more and more people will want to be involved in that entertainment business – and it has to be one where there are no physical threats or violence.'

At Ibrox too past bigotries have dropped away in the face of an overwhelming desire for playing success on the pitch and commercial success off it. Mo Johnston's signing in 1989 was a clear statement of intent: we will buy the best, regardless of religion. Beforehand the manager who made it, Graeme Souness, who was married to a Catholic, had tried to buy both Ian Rush and John Sheridan, Welsh and Irish Catholics respectively. Subsequently, it was followed by the regular arrival of Catholics, often from Italy, who were treated as welcome additions as they helped the club win nine championships in a row. But, off the field, it was followed by, well, perhaps not enough.

Not when Niall Scott turned the radio on and overheard

the strains of a familiar tune in the pre-match build-up at Ibrox. The words of the well-known Loyalist song 'The Billy Boys', adapted and adopted at Manchester United and elsewhere, might have been missing in the sanitized version played over the public address. But even without them, without the celebrations of being knee-deep in Fenian blood and the chilling climax of 'Surrender or you'll die', the tune was enough for Niall.

He said, 'I couldn't believe they were playing it. I just listened in disgust. I think it's an absolutely outrageous situation for it still to be played at Ibrox. It's completely inappropriate. The association it has, the sentiment behind it . . .' And his words faded as they headed again towards the death of his son. For the Billy Boys came together in the 1920s to pursue sectarian hatred in one part of Glasgow: around Bridgeton Cross.

Niall started again: 'It would be a significant step to show that they were determined to stamp out sectarianism if they stopped playing it and explained why they were doing so.' And a step closer to the day when Mark Scott's reassuring, but premature, words to his mother come true. She was worried that the Celtic shirt he had bought – the one he wore hidden on his last day – might get him in trouble. And he laughed the idea off and said, 'Nothing like that happens now.'

spectators

One would have hoped that the upper echelons . . . would have taken a lead in securing reasonable safety and comfort for spectators and in enforcing good behaviour by precept and example. Unfortunately, these hopes have not generally been realized and indeed at times poor examples have been set.

Lord Justice Taylor's final report, paragraph 51

It was less than seven weeks before the start of the World Cup, the day after more than 20 million fans tried to call the most hopeless telephone hotline ever in a desperate attempt to buy some of the last tickets for the tournament (as they went on general sale for the first time) and Sepp Blatter, the second most important man in football, was discussing one of his pet projects: banning tackling.

In the front row of a featureless conference hall which could have been anywhere, but was in the bowels of the venue for the final itself, the Stade de France, Michel Platini, the president of France '98, squirmed as if he'd been scythed down himself. In his glorious playing days he had been the sort of midfield visionary who suffered his share of over-enthusiastic and over-the-top tackles. But the dismissive smirk he wore while restlessly listening to Blatter indicated his sceptical view of any possible rule change – although not as much as the incredulous look he shot at the Brazilian delegate some rows behind who had first raised the subject.

The inquisitor had been easy to spot. Most of the seats in the semi-lit room were empty except for a selection of glossy brochures and trade magazines. Earlier Platini had given the briefest of speeches to welcome perhaps a hundred delegates to Soccerex '98, the Business Convention for Football World-wide, many of whom seemed to be either speakers at later sessions or exhibitors in the trade fair outside the conference hall. Since then the microphone had played up and the trans-lation system for the largely British audience had squealed feedback in protest. The delegates might have expected better for up to £250, plus VAT, each. They were supposed to be gaining an insight into the future of football and the thinking behind it, although, in a way, perhaps they were: empty seats are irrelevant as long as those that are full are sold at top dollar.

All around was the baggage of the modern game. Retailers advertised everything from cakes to grotesque figurines of players. Corporate-hospitality firms promoted packages to meet the demand to see those players in the flesh. And market-ing gurus offered advice on how best to exploit the all-encompassing demand for football. The seminars themselves were largely money-related, on such topics as the profitability of stadiums, the control of players' wages and corporate invest-ment in football. And every time the delegates trooped between a seminar in the conference hall and the rather subdued semi-bustle of the trade fair, there was a reminder of the scale of the potential rewards on offer in the sleek shape of a £50,000 Jaguar XK8, somehow brought indoors and downstairs by dealers also aiming to drum up some business.

The main attraction, though, was Blatter, the dapper general secretary of football's world governing body, FIFA, second only to the elderly, and soon-to-retire, president Joao

Havelange – and a candidate to succeed him. The actual content of his speech, 'Who runs the game?', was less of a draw than the rare semi-public chance to see him in action; to watch a prime example of the species of bureaucrat which outlaws the tackle from behind and oversees the distribution system for World Cup tickets; and to realize how far the governance, the politics, of the so-called people's game is removed from both the people and the game. The speech itself, laden with the endless, easy platitudes in which all international football bureaucrats communicate, illustrated that only too well. Blatter denied that sponsorship and commercialism had gone too far, but then warned about 'rich people' trying to separate clubs from the 'football family'. The undoubted highlight, however, was this: 'Football is a team game involving everybody. The purpose is to kick the ball into the goal.'

I yawned. I had been up at 6.45 a.m. the day before, confident that trying the hotline fifteen minutes early would be the key to success – as if no one else had thought of that; it was already engaged. After thirty-five minutes a connection finally clicked down the line and a loop of Bontempi organ music began, with an encouraging French voice speaking over it. The voice changed to English: 'All the lines are already engaged. Please call later.' I hung up and hit redial, once again, while watching a BBC reporter on *Breakfast News* also call the number and, again, I'm sure like thousands of others, shouted at him to get off the line. The next item featured a man called Bodger who had turned his back on modern life. Suddenly, I felt like joining him. But I carried on calling all day until eventually, at tea time, I got a new message: try again tomorrow.

So I did – by asking Blatter himself in the question-and-answer session at the end of his appearance if the system would be changed? 'Yes, certainly if one day you realize that you are in a wrong situation, you shall not repeat it,' he replied. 'For the next World Cup as soon as the new committee is established this will be an item and we will have a clear, clean look at it. But the problem will not be the same as we have today because we play in Asia and we play in two countries. But still we will have to adapt the system individually to each World Cup. We work now here with the same system we used in '86 in Mexico, in '90 in Italy and in '94 in the United States. It worked well then; now it has not. We are victims: victims of popularity – popularity of football, popularity of the World Cup and the popularity of France.' Which must have made FIFA – a non-profit-making organization with about £50 million in the bank and a property portfolio worth more than ten times that – one of the world's more unusual victims.

And that was that, I thought, until we moved out past the Jag when the session ended and I found myself being lectured by Platini himself, pulling both on a cigarette and from the full repertoire of Gallic gestures: 'I want to complain about when you asked Mr Blatter about tickets. I want to say one thing: it's not so easy. When you are qualified for the World Cup in France, it was November '97. The committee is beginning four years before and it can say, OK, Brazil, no problem with the tickets; France, no problem with the tickets. But for Mexico–Romania in Toulouse, who will buy these tickets? For Russia–Colombia in Toulouse, who will buy the tickets?'

I wasn't going to interrupt to tell the legend in charge of the World Cup that neither of those games was scheduled; that wasn't his point. Nor that many of us would gladly have bought tickets for any venue, but hadn't had the chance; that wasn't what he wanted to hear. He continued: 'You know when you have no money by the state, your budget is ticketing and sponsoring. We have no money off the state. It is not so easy, the ticketing. It is very complicated. The most important thing is that the committee wins money, because if the committee loses money you have no World Cup in the world. It is finished.'

*

Alec McGivan would like to be the Michel Platini after next. Not the celebrated player with awards and medals providing the lasting gilt on a glittering career; age and a lack of the necessary ability have put paid to that. Nor the youthful and successful manager who confirmed his status as a national icon by taking his country's side to the finals of the European Championships. Rather the embodiment and figurehead, in fact the chief executive, of the world's greatest sporting event. The man who runs the World Cup.

For the moment, though, he is the man who is running the £10 million bid to host the World Cup. The man hoping that Football's Coming Home, Again. The man producing the advertisements for the glossy magazines littering Soccerex; managing the staff at the England 2006 stall in the trade fair; and talking up the bid to reporters in France, but also all over the world in foreign visits which form part of a global charm offensive featuring 'ambassadors' Sir Bobby Charlton, Geoff Hurst and Gary Lineker. The man pressing the flesh too, sometimes in photo-calls on the steps of 10 Downing Street, of FIFA officials and foreign ministers, prime ministers and presidents in the more public second front of the campaign. In short, playing football politics.

The central part of his day at the Stade de France was a lunch-time press conference, in a more airy, lighter, upstairs meeting room, to extol the virtues of the English bid. There was nothing new to say, but the presence of Lineker put a few bums on seats. Even then, however, the modest size of the press contingent, in line with the overall attendance at Soccerex, meant that reporters only just outnumbered the 2006 team, who in turn only just outnumbered the couple of catering staff serving drinks.

For me, it was worth it: it's not often that you get to have a one-to-one with Lineker over an orange juice. For the bid team perhaps less so, as only a crew from the BBC's *Panorama* seemed all that interested. But a few more televised moments were garnered, a little more ammunition – albeit small-arms fire – in the long-term battle, and, with one of the campaign's main rivals, South Africa, merely tending to their stand, that was good enough. For the moment.

The ill-attended press call at an ill-attended conference was significant, though, simply because it was held. The short question-and-answer session and the chat before and after it may have thrown up little in the way of new insight or meaning-ful stories, but they demonstrated something as important: the new face of the FA – and its new outlook.

McGivan was as smooth in front of the single arc light and boom microphone as he was chatting, off the record, over drinks and nibbles. Lineker too knew the lines to take, when to dead-bat or to joke rather than to try to answer questions which went well beyond his unspoken role of adding big-name backing to the bid. Neither engaged in anything as unsubtle as point-scoring over rivals; both spoke in diluted versions of the language Blatter would use – diplomatic, perhaps slightly slippery, although with a little more hard fact in the mix. Both used the lingua franca of football politics, of modern politics, of New Labour and of other made-over, reinvented 1990s institutions; of what might be called, however glibly, the New FA.

Once the FA's presence at such an event, engaging in what some of its senior figures might have regarded as murky business several times over, would have been absolutely unheard of. The inventors of the game have traditionally remained aloof from its international machinations, with administrations from the four home countries either absent or often playing an almost quasi-regal role when present.

When FIFA was formed in 1904, the British FAs refused to join. When they did sign up soon after, they resigned quickly – and then rejoined and re-resigned before the first World Cup was held, in 1930, staying out until after the Second World War (with the result that none of the home countries played in the World Cup until 1950). Even when the English took a leading role, most recently when ex-referee Sir Stanley Rous became FIFA president in 1961, it was ended by utterly alien politicking. His challenger in an election in 1974, Havelange, promised extra World Cup places for countries from the developing world, called in a favour from a friend in the airline business to fly in supporters and, just before the final vote was to be taken, worked the room while Rous sat in a corner calmly sipping a soft drink, above such last-minute deal-making – and about to suffer defeat by sixteen votes out of 120.

But McGivan was in his element. His football credentials are less impressive than Platini's: he has been a Bristol City fan for almost forty years, since he was five, and is a small shareholder too; he has worked at the FA for four years. But he can still trump the man in whose footsteps he hopes to follow – thanks to the job he secured as his side was going through its most traumatic period. While City were completing their infamous, early 1980s slide through all four divisions of the league in four seasons, he was pursuing a career in his other passion: politics. For six years after its breakaway from the very old Labour Party in 1981, he was a senior campaigner with the SDP, responsible for a series of high-profile and successful by-election campaigns. And the game in which Alec McGivan is now engaged is at least as much to do with politics as football.

As a grey-kitted Gareth Southgate clasped his hands to his head as his penalty follow-through, and English involvement in Euro '96, came to a sudden halt, Alec McGivan was perhaps slightly less downcast than most in Wembley. He had watched the fateful shoot-out from right behind the goal, a well-deserved fringe benefit for one of those responsible for what was being acclaimed as a highly successful tournament. But he already knew there was going to be a rematch, of sorts, over who was to stage the World Cup. Germany might have won through to the final; the morning after it, though, the FA would announce its bid to host the 2006 finals – in direct competition with the Germans.

Euro '96 was seen as a triumph – a peaceful, but still noisy enough, celebration of English football's final rehabilitation into Europe following Heysel and the subsequent ban. It was also the tournament which confirmed that the problems of the past had been banished: the hooliganism widely predicted before the tournament was absent, quelled not by military policing but largely by intelligence and low-key bobbies on the beat; the decrepit stadiums had been rebuilt, but with the stands still close enough to the pitch to help create the unique atmosphere of British grounds; and England even enjoyed their greatest success in the competition. Perhaps the only improvement would have been a home win to crown the reborn national game with international silverware.

Now the hope is that hosting the World Cup will provide further confirmation of the new swagger in the step of English football, add to it and offer the chance to repeat the on-pitch glory of the victory of 1966. In his nondescript office at the FA's distinguished headquarters in Lancaster Gate, west London, though, McGivan excitedly outlined a range of wider aims too. He said, 'If we are awarded it we will have six years to talk about English football and build relationships and do what in my view – and I've been watching football for more than thirty-five years – is something that the FA in particular has to do, which is modernize and go into the twenty-first century with a very important new agenda. We would have a great opportunity through the World Cup to do more than just the traditional things – to look at football's role in our country, in our society and in the world and where it's going. If you get all that right, the potential of the World Cup is enormous, even bigger than it is already.'

His evangelism, his vision for the future, was unstoppable: 'I think in the past we've rested on our laurels. I want people to realize through the World Cup how football can be used to improve society, to help young people, to tackle racism and so on. I want to take a radical agenda as far as we can, so that it's not just about the new national stadium or the games themselves, but so much more.' He even echoed, almost word for word, Niall Scott's hope when he said, 'I think football is such a powerful weapon because everyone talks about it, from shop floor to boardroom, and we should try to use it to do some good.' For an FA man, a species generally reckoned to be about as far-sighted as a mole, these were almost revolutionary words. And another example of the new thinking within Lancaster Gate.

But, perhaps not insignificantly, not actually within the four walls of the HQ itself. To reach the 2006 campaign offices you report to front reception, past the neoclassical columns and polished brass nameplate outside, and wait to be escorted through corridors initially lined with trophies and a remarkable painting recording the semi-success of Bobby Robson's 1990 World Cup team (and which looks like it might have been painted by Robson or one of the team) before dropping down to the lower floors and then out through a back door and across to a small mews block housing McGivan and his team.

There he even admitted that part of the reason for the bid was the sake of it, the value of the process itself: 'In '96, when we decided to bid, the view was probably just, "Wouldn't it be great to host the World Cup?", which is the reaction of any country capable of staging it really. Now I think the process of bidding in itself is good for the FA. It has widened its horizons, both domestically and internationally. It's brought them into much more contact with the government and the business community, especially certain sections not always associated with football, and has certainly extended contacts in international football politics.' But he was vague on who took the decision to bid and why. Some would say for good reason, for it cuts to the heart of one of the two problems, partly related, which dog the campaign.

Both centre on the former FA chairman Sir Bert Millichip, one of the old-guard, old-style be-blazered administrators whose benign patrician bearing accurately reflected his leadership style and, crucially, whose word was his bond. In early 1992 he gave it in a deal brokered by Lennart Johannson, the Anglophile Swedish president of UEFA. Johannson had played a key role in ensuring the restoration of English clubs to continental competition after the Heysel ban, but was willing to take another risk by backing the FA's efforts to host a major tournament so soon after the disgraces, and deaths, of the past. He and Millichip, together with the head of the German FA, agreed that Germany would support England's bid for Euro '96 in return for English backing for a German bid for the 2006 World Cup. Months later England got its tournament.

But after its completion, when the FA launched its bid for another, English officials denied any knowledge of the gentleman's agreement, or of another UEFA-wide understanding which indicated that there would be only one European bidder – Germany. Millichip, by then retired and portrayed by some as little more than an elderly incompetent, was left upset and angrily denying suggestions that he had failed to tell the FA of his deal or that it was a figment of his imagination. But the FA maintained its ignorance and demanded to see a formal minute. There was none, and UEFA agreed both countries could bid.

Millichip, however, left his successors with a second problem as he retired, handing over his chairmanship to Keith Wiseman, of Southampton. Pre-Euro '96, he also stood down from his position on UEFA's executive, but without informing colleagues in time for a replacement to be nominated. England lost its seat and a voice at the highest level of European football. Wiseman later stood for election, but failed humiliatingly. He, and the FA, were left with a longer-term strategy of supporting Johannson in his bid for election as the head of FIFA, which would leave a vacancy at UEFA which could be filled by Scotland's David Will, leaving his position as a FIFA vice-president[1] vacant for, it was hoped, Wiseman to fill.

In the meantime, the 2006 campaign continued, heavily based on the success of Euro '96. An advertisement in one of the brochures at Soccerex said, 'We proved that we can stage a major international tournament. It was trouble-free, well organized and had a great atmosphere. Everyone enjoyed it. Throughout the world it was recognized as the best European Championship ever.' In fact McGivan admitted, 'I think organizationally we only just got there.' The ticket system – which indirectly led to the resignation of the FA's commercial director – was little better than the French one, a fault McGivan again conceded and promised to rectify. The backdrop for several games was vast swathes of empty seats. The cultural programme supposedly built around the tournament was inadequate. The number of tourists generated by the tournament was disappointing. But it was the brochure's claim of being a trouble-free tournament which struck me most.

Within an hour of England's defeat by Germany there was a full-scale riot developing in central London. Any German fans heading for a celebration anywhere around Soho and Trafalgar Square did well to keep their voices down. Passers-by doing nothing more than driving German-made cars had their vehicles set upon. Police formed a cordon around about 1,000 England fans, but came under a hail of bottles and cans as the hooligans broke out. Reporters were attacked. A police car was set ablaze and dozens of other vehicles parked nearby had windows smashed. Several shop fronts were also shattered. Again, blue lights reflected off the broken glass which carpeted the floor.

McGivan's defence was first semantics: 'I think there is a view that it's what happens in the stadium that you talk about.'

Then stories about the scale of hooliganism in other countries: 'I've started keeping international cuttings about incidents around the world so that I can put it into perspective.' Finally, he admitted, 'I've got to play to our strengths. You wouldn't expect me to make a feature of hooliganism.' And that meant he was well aware of the main potential pitfall of the World Cup in France: 'Trouble.' He said, 'It's the biggest danger – and the worst thing about hooliganism is that you feel really helpless, because there's nothing you personally can do about it. I'm fairly optimistic that France will be basically all right, but it is a threat that's beyond our control.'

All he and his team could do, and would be doing in France, at the FIFA conference and elsewhere, was woo the twenty-four men who matter, the most unknown, but most powerful, names in football: the members of the FIFA executive. Blatter is one of them, Will another, but the aptly named American delegate perhaps best sums them up: Chuck Blazer. Later this year all twenty-four will receive the formal bid documents from the competing nations. By the end of next season they will have inspected all the venues and the following month, six years before the tournament is due to start, they will vote on its location.

By then they might have been guests at the FA Cup Final, like a group of opinion-forming overseas journalists last season. If they have been very lucky, they might have seen their national side play at Wembley, like the Saudi Arabian whose side were about to play England in a World Cup warm-up and who, conveniently, is believed to be able to convince two of his FIFA colleagues to vote however he does. They will certainly have been visited in their home countries by McGivan, Sports Minister Tony Banks and Charlton, Hurst or Lineker, willing to listen to whatever gripes they have and the potential solutions to them. McGivan said, 'I think there is a growing agenda for us to start doing overseas development work. Some countries need help from the rich nations which have done so well out of football in recent years. When you go to some countries and you say you've spent £600 million on stadiums in the last ten years they just say, "That's amazing. We're struggling for posts or nets or pitches. Can you help us?" ' A map on a wall of the office shows such countries – and those with a FIFA executive delegate.

Thinking of my next destination, I wondered if there weren't clubs at home which might need help, financial or otherwise. McGivan replied, 'The whole of national life is riddled with people having these sorts of debates on what you spend your money on and what you don't. If you go to the Treasury they have debates on social services, education, health, whatever. If you take football as a whole, £10 million is not a huge amount of money and some might say, "Look at what Ruud Gullit's earning – isn't it a shame he and the other top players don't think about the little clubs?" I think the World Cup would have a great impact at all levels of the game, from top to bottom – just like I think Euro '96 had a great impact. It stimulated the game in many ways it couldn't have been otherwise. The World Cup could stimulate the game even further. The game has got to move on. I think the World Cup here would be an amazing experience – a once-in-a-lifetime experience for many fans – and by its very presence it would help the grass roots. In order to do that we have to bid and fund that bid fully. What's the point of campaigning if you're not going to do it properly?'

But properly might also mean twice. McGivan admitted: 'If 2006 did go to South Africa, I don't think there's any question that we would bid for 2010. We would be very silly not to. A lot of the groundwork would be done. You wouldn't have to run such a high-profile campaign. You'd have some goodwill, hopefully.' And more pertinently, back at Soccerex, when Blatter arrived the first stall he visited, the only stall he visited, was that of the South African FA.

*

The only question in Doncaster was whether Rovers would exist when the World Cup kicked off in France, let alone if it was ever staged again at Wembley.

The club was a season-long joke, albeit a decidedly unamusing one for its fans and those of other clubs who recognized the script, if not the increasingly grotesque punchlines. The curtain-raiser was a 2–1 defeat at Shrewsbury on the opening day, but the end-of-the-road show began in earnest only with a 5–0 drubbing in the first game at Rovers' shabby and inappropriately named home, Belle Vue – and got worse, much worse, from there. Their first victory came only in December (after twenty matches, a new league record) and was followed by just three more. They were adrift at the bottom of Division Three from August, condemned to relegation and non-league football by Easter.

There were rare, and ever more surreal, highlights for the put-upon fans to remember: when the Chester goalkeeper threw the ball into the back of one of his defenders, leaving the simplest of tap-ins for that long-awaited first win; the charity displayed by Orient, who substituted their strikers so that a humiliating 8–0 scoreline got no nearer the age of Rovers' shell-shocked eighteen-year-old goalkeeper, and the last-minute goal at Cardiff – one of only thirty Rovers scored all season, against 113 conceded – which was celebrated as if it was the winner, not a consolation in a 7–1 defeat. By then the supporting equivalent of gallows humour had long become the only way to enjoy a match. By then, though, league football had also become a fringe pastime in a town the size of Middlesbrough; home gates had fallen below 1,000 and on one occasion below 600.

The first manager of the season, ex-England forward Kerry Dixon, resigned after three games (cumulative score: 1–15), complaining the club's self-styled benefactor Ken Richardson was insisting on picking the team. His right-hand man, general manager Mark Weaver, whose only football experience was in the commercial department at Stockport County, was put in charge, but with the proviso that Richardson would still select the side. For the game against Brighton, the only other candidates for relegation even by October, he included a new goalkeeper – who turned out to be a Sunday league player who also happened to be one of Weaver's neighbours and so became one of forty-five players used in the season, one of six goalkeepers and one of five players who made just a single appearance.

When Richardson angrily relinquished his managerial role a fortnight later, while maintaining his efforts to find a buyer for a club £1 million in debt, youth team coach Dave Cowling was appointed boss – for nine days. Like Dixon, he quit because he was being told who to play, in his case by Weaver. The next manager, Danny Bergara, lasted a month before he announced that he would be taking the title director of coaching – and not attending any more games as he was upset at fans barracking; they were furious that the only decent goalkeeper had been dropped for being late for a match because of car trouble. Weaver took the reins again, concentrating on selling the better players and finding replacements as cheaply as possible. He even registered himself as a player.

One of the newcomers was striker Padi Wilson, signed from Plymouth in January on a free transfer, whose goals, fans were told, would save the club. Two months later, after one strike in seven games, he was jailed for three months for driving while disqualified. March was the month when hope finally died for other reasons too: the players were told not to bother coming in for training because the coaching staff had been laid off; a clutch of senior players joined an exodus before transfer-deadline day; and teenagers replaced them, with up to seven in the side – as it was announced that the youth policy was scrapped. Perhaps the entire farce was best captured in one sorry image, or the lack of it: the traditional squad photograph was never taken at any point during the season.

Events off the field were as bizarre. In September supporters complained that one of Richardson's henchmen was taking photographs of the crowd to try to identify anyone leading the increasing protests against him. In October the demonstrations became so impassioned that both he and Weaver left the ground at half-time on police advice. Four days later the supporters' club was ordered to vacate its office at the ground, echoing events of the previous season when its shop was closed down without warning; supporters had to offer stock which should have been sold to raise funds for the club at knockdown prices at a car-boot sale just to recover costs. In November the club announced plans for ID cards for fans which would be withdrawn from anyone who shouted abuse. Finally, for 1997, in December the only event to which the fans had been looking forward – Richardson's trial in connection with an alleged arson attack on the main stand more than two years earlier – was postponed.

The first funeral was held in November, when pallbearers carried a black coffin to a match and mourners followed with banners lamenting the end of the club. The second was a real one, that of Billy Bremner, whose cortège slowed to a crawl as it passed the ground where, in better days, when 10,000 once travelled to an away game, he was the longest-serving manager. The third, a reprise of the first, but as sad as the second, was long-expected. An issue of the programme in November was due to carry news of it – but also fell victim to cutbacks. Instead the prophetic death notice penned by teenage columnist Lucy Burke, a fan for more than two-thirds of her life, from schoolgirl to the cusp of adulthood, was seen – in a final, commemorative programme paid for by fans – only on the day it became true, the last day of the season:

Doncaster Rovers R.I.P.
After a long illness, bravely borne,
on 2nd May, 1998, aged 119 years,
beloved team of the fans and once proud
standard bearer of Doncaster town.
'Will be sadly missed.'

Lucy, the smile on her by-line photo absent, was among the mourners at the Park Hotel, a grand, sprawling pub run by the son of inter-war Rovers star Ronnie Dodd and built about the time he was playing. She was among the youngest, one of those with the least chance of having experienced any glory, or good times, at Belle Vue. All around, though, spilling on to the forecourt, were those who had, remembering favourite moments with fellow fans or quietly reading from the various publications produced to recall happier days and to send the club into history with some fondness as well as the inevitable fury.

Only the very eldest among them might have remembered deaf winger Stan 'Dizzy' Burton, who was often spotted racing down the wing long after the whistle had gone. But all of those a generation younger talked about Alick Jeffrey, a boy wonder who made his debut at fifteen but whose career was curtailed by an injury playing for England B. Or the unlikely appearance in the FA Youth Cup Final, against Arsenal, in the 1980s and emerging talent such as brothers Glynn and Ian Snodin, who both ended up in the First Division, Ian with a winners' medal. Or the career of Brian Deane, who was sold for £30,000 – the first fee in a series which have totalled more than £6 million – and who sent a message, from his latest employer, Benfica, via the local paper: 'What has happened is an absolute tragedy. I have no idea of the politics of the situation. I only know that a smashing town and a bunch of smashing supporters suddenly have no league club to support.'

Members of the procession were falling into place, fans

at the front carrying wreaths, a nameplate identifying the deceased, black balloons and leaflets which bawled, 'Richardson out.' I stood with a respectable-looking grey-haired chap, wrapped up warm in a sensible anorak, discussing the circumstances which had brought us all to a wake in a pub car park. Ray Gilbert could remember when there were more than 37,000 in Belle Vue – for a 0–0 draw with Hull in 1948. He could even almost boast of seeing Dizzy Burton. But, as the club had been brought to its knees and he helped to form the Save the Rovers group, he had become an even greater authority on its ownership than on its playing history. He had burrowed into company records and newspaper cuttings files to try to discover its future. The conclusion was unpalatable: 'There is none. I don't think we'll play in the Conference next season. The club will fold. The ground will be sold – for a lot of money. That's been the plan all along.'

The story began, he explained, with the arrival, initially welcomed, of Richardson in 1993. The club had been withering for years, with decline obvious all around the ground. In 1985 the grandest stand was condemned after the Bradford fire. Two years later half the Popular Side terrace was demolished when it was found to be subsiding. Not that the loss of capacity really mattered, as the murder of the mining industry impacted on the well-being of the club as in all areas of the community. Richardson, the 'football consultant' to the mysterious Isle of Man-based trading company which was the new owner, seemed to promise much-needed hope.

The first doubts arose within months and from an unlikely source – an advertisement in the *Daily Telegraph*. Placed on behalf of the club, it sought a buyer for the ground, to develop it as shops and a hotel – a remarkable enough plan in itself, but doubly so when the ground was not the club's to sell: it was leased from the council, and with a covenant which demanded that football be played on the site.

Richardson's background came under scrutiny and the

doubts began to mount. In 1984 he had been given a nine-month suspended jail sentence, fined £20,000 and ordered to pay £25,000 in costs after being convicted of conspiracy to defraud in a horseracing sting in which a heavily backed – and previously hopeless – winner turned out to be a ringer. The racing authorities also took firm action, banning him from every course in the country for twenty-five years.

His football record was worrying too. Until a couple of months before he arrived at Rovers he had 98 per cent of the shares of non-league Bridlington Town. In January 1993 his stake was transferred to another anonymous offshore company. In September a new director was appointed to Town's board: one of Richardson's co-defendants from the conspiracy case, who joined another from the Crown Court dock who was already in place. In between Town had won the FA Vase – but then left their ground, which was sold for redevelopment, to share with a club seventy miles away. Rovers. Within a year Bridlington went out of business.

The new directors at Doncaster were also more than just friends of Richardson's. There was his daughter, his niece and a man who gave evidence for him at the conspiracy trial. The advertisement in the *Telegraph* began to be seen in a new light by fans, who feared that history was repeating itself: buy the club, sell the ground, close the club. The FA took an interest too, with an investigating committee meeting in December 1993 to discuss Bridlington, Doncaster and the man who linked them, Richardson.

The end was slow in coming. On the football side there were always teams just a little bit worse than Rovers to ensure that relegation was avoided. Off the pitch money drained away, so that debts were £1 million at the end of the season in 1995. The administrators were finally called in two years later, the final ingredient for the last league season. In the long wait for the first win a potential new owner made an offer to the administrators, but was thwarted when the offshore trading firm made a remarkable counter-offer to retain control. As managers and players came and went, new bidders were talked of but never materialized. In defeat after defeat, for month after month, the future trickled away.

Ray, and others like him, began to realize that all they would have left was the past, recollections such as those of one of the greatest figures in Rovers' history, manager and former acclaimed Irish international Peter Doherty. He was as innovative as a manager as he was as a player, an early enthusiast for floodlights who ensured that lowly Rovers were among the first to have them and so attracted giants such as Celtic and Newcastle to play under them. He also encouraged his two wingers to switch sides during the game to test the opposing defence – and was reprimanded by the FA for such impudence. Ray scoffed at the story, the point an obvious one: where is the FA now? 'They're not interested in us at all. It's just the Premier League they care about. It's two nations really – the rich and the rest. The question is whether or not the FA has adequate powers to resolve this type of situation – and whether they're prepared to use them. If not, what's the point of the FA exactly? What's the point of a governing body which can't, or won't, govern?'

The procession, a couple of hundred strong, moved off, snaking along the pavement to the ramshackle wreck of a ground, with the by now well-known songs of defiance to the fore: 'He burnt. Our stand. He's hated by the fans. Richardson, Richardson,' and, appropriated from 'Oh, My Darling Clementine' and amended from the previous year's protests when Brighton faced an equally bleak future, 'Build a bonfire. Build a bonfire. Put Weaver on the top. Put Richardson in the middle. Then burn the fucking lot.'

At the ground the column of protesters split up, some carrying on with the singing outside, others heading in to lay flowers at the derelict end behind one goal. Just before 3 p.m. they stood in the centre circle as 'The Last Post' drifted across the ground. Weaver had promised to stay away, realizing that fans would feel 'it would be like a murderer turning up at his victim's funeral'. But at kick-off he was in his place, opposite the Popular Side, which was where the popular protest resumed once again.

A lone figure started it, nothing special in jeans and trainers, except that he had walked from the terrace, over the perimeter cinder track, across the whitewashed threshold and on to the playing surface. He walked so calmly, so solemnly and deliberately towards the centre circle that he went unnoticed as he moved past players. Only when one of the visiting Colchester team turned and almost collided with him was he recognized for what he was. The player spread his arms wide, echoing the obvious verbal plea to leave the pitch. But the fan gave a mournful, apologetic shake of the head and just carried on. When he reached the centre spot, he allowed his legs to collapse under him and slumped down, looking at the feet which had carried him there.

For a split second it appeared that he was on his own. Then twos and threes of those looking on, then fours and fives, then scores, a stream, swelled through the gaps in the low wall in the terrace and jogged to join him. Stewards and the junior police officers stationed at the gates did nothing. A more senior officer warned, somewhat half-heartedly, 'You will be photographed and arrested and fined.' But still several hundred went on.

The players and officials, alive to the inevitability of the protest, had run for the dressing rooms almost before the first fan had settled. Some of the home fans on the opposite side, less accessible to the pitch, applauded the invasion. In the away end the Colchester fans, desperate to see a result that would put their team into the play-offs, watched in sympathy and clapped the doomed anyway. Everyone knew this was the last stand. Next to me on the now severely depleted terrace Ray, looking like the magistrate he is, sighed and said, 'What can you say? I don't blame them at all. You've got to do something, haven't you?'

The pitch invasion lasted about ten minutes before it dispersed itself peacefully. In the second half, soon after the visitors scored what turned out to be the winning goal, the last league goal at Belle Vue, there was a second invasion, less dignified, more angry. By then Weaver had left on police advice.

In the five minutes it took to clear the pitch I read the programme produced by fans in the absence of a proper, official publication. Ken Avis, secretary of the supporters' club for thirty-three years, a fan who had barely missed a home match in fifty years, whose only absence, home or away, in the past fifteen was when he had an operation, recalled the playing career of comedian Charlie Williams – and when there were 17,000 members of the supporters' club. Williams himself said, 'The other day me and Alick Jeffrey went to Belle Vue for the first time in years and couldn't believe what we saw – the place is more like a tip than the ground we once rated one of the best in the country. As things are, I can't see Rovers emulating Halifax and getting back quickly because you sense the heart has been torn out of the club – and, when you've shared the good times like I did, that makes you want to weep.' Supporters' club chairman Charles Walker added, 'Our club may well be the forerunner of many. It's true that bad owners kill football, but so also does the greed of the Premiership and Sky, helped by the inability of the game's leaders to show any real authority when it comes to the control and running of clubs.'

What had particularly puzzled Ray and others was that FA chief executive Graham Kelly had been among them two years earlier when he stood on the terrace during a game at Belle Vue. They had assumed he was taking an interest, although he wouldn't tell them, but nothing ever came of his unannounced visit. They were left thinking that he was more concerned with the Premier League and England matters. And the result of his inactivity was pretty much, and presciently, summed up in the Rovers fanzine *Popular Stand*: 'The World Cup will soon be on us. Yet the events here have turned my love of football . . . very sour. If the powers-that-be can't give a shit for little clubs like ours then I couldn't give a toss for the national side. C'mon, Argentina!'

Graham Kelly was his usual, apparently hangdog self the first time that I saw him. In the weeks before, his face had become a regular feature on television and in the papers as he voiced his thoughts on the future of the game which he ran. In the pictures he appeared to be a short, squat man, but it was a trick of the cameras. In the flesh, in a large but gloomy room behind the blackened stone façade of Sheffield Town Hall, he was bulky, but tall too, the build of the keeper he once had been, although without the presence of the best of the breed. He was slightly hunched in his seat before Lord Justice Taylor, looking a little uncomfortable as he gave his evidence on Hillsborough.

Much of the story, at least as it pertained to the FA, was already well known. How Liverpool were unhappy over the choice of the venue, much nearer Nottingham than Merseyside. How their chief executive telephoned the FA to complain at the club being allocated the smaller Leppings Lane terrace – and for the second year running. How some fans therefore blamed the FA for what they saw as a significant, avoidable part of the disaster.

What was new was the minutiae of such big matches, the money made and the costs, of the ground hire, policing, first aid and so on, which were incurred. Kelly provided the information: the FA banked more than £250,000, although most of that was passed to the two competing clubs; hosts Sheffield Wednesday received more than £34,000, the police in excess of £31,000 and St John Ambulance, for its team of volunteer medics, £31.20.[2] Less than the price of six tickets for the Leppings Lane terrace.

The skewed symmetry of the figures shocked me as I noted them, ready to report for the university student newspaper. Long after the note was transcribed, long after the piece was published, they stayed with me, the disparity a financial snapshot of the appallingly run business, one obsessed with security and unconcerned with safety, which resulted in death on the terraces. Proper journalists, those who attended the hearings every day, had collected a series of human stories which recalled the day in greater detail, often in more gruesome detail. But the statistics seemed, to me, to tell the story in a much simpler way. The simplest way. Partly, too, because of the flat, bureaucratic tone of their delivery – from the most important man in domestic football.

On the day of the disaster, Kelly was at the ground, although largely by chance. He could have been at either of the semi-finals, Everton–Norwich at Villa Park or Hillsborough, but FA chairman Millichip opted for Birmingham, so Kelly, the other half of the governing double act, headed for Sheffield. His job was supposed to be a semi-ceremonial one, representing the FA as its main trophy, English football's main trophy, the world's most famous trophy, reached its concluding stages. He attended the pre-match lunch and afterwards took up a seat in the front row of the directors' box. But by then his role was beginning to change.

When Superintendent Greenwood dashed to the referee and the players began to troop off the pitch, Kelly made his way to the players' tunnel to try to discover what was happening – and was greeted by furious words from some of the players. Liverpool's Steve McMahon, who had friends on the terraces, shouted at him, 'Now you know why we should have had the other end of the ground.'[3] He moved on, walking towards the police control box, and fans yelled similar opinions, with similar, perhaps even greater, anger. In the box

Chief Superintendent Duckenfield pointed to the gate which
had been opened to ease the crush outside and told him,
'That's the gate that's been forced; there's been an inrush.'
Soon afterwards Kelly began a series of media interviews in
which he repeated what he'd been told, but also reported the
other story which he'd heard from fans, of the gate being
opened by police.

Almost ten years later I saw Kelly again in a surprisingly
spartan office behind the imposing façade of FA headquarters
in Lancaster Gate. High above the distinctive portals which
have featured as the backdrop to thousands of breaking football stories, he acknowledged the pivotal role that one spring
day played in revolutionizing football: 'The changes might
have happened, but there is no doubt that they came much
more quickly because of Hillsborough.' But his memories of
the day itself were sketchy, featuring little of the detail of
events, more of the consequences of them.

'I remember parts of it very vividly,' he said. 'The realization
that it was so bad came very gradually during the course of
the whole day, probably more quickly in the evening. The
aftermath was very, er, intense. In addition to the incident
itself, the tragedy itself, we had to determine whether the FA
Cup would be played to conclusion that season, so there were
important implications other than actually dealing with the
tragedy itself.' The first came when he returned from the police
control box and convened an ad-hoc meeting with club and
other officials, including the referee, to discuss the situation
and whether or not the game would be abandoned. Once
it was, others followed, most when he finally returned to
Lancaster Gate past midnight.

The basic question was whether the cup should be abandoned for the season. By Sunday afternoon it was decided
not. Instead the final would become a memorial match. The
pre-match celebrations could be cut and the winning team
asked to forgo the traditional lap of honour. Kelly recalled,

'There was a very strong feeling within the FA that the competition should be completed that season. The overwhelming
body of opinion within football was that it should carry on to
its proper conclusion during the season. I think I probably
went up to discuss the matter with the board of directors at
Liverpool and Kenny Dalglish and they had to be allowed
time to come to terms with what we wanted.'

In fact Liverpool officials could barely conceal their fury at
being asked to consider the rescheduling of the semifinal
before the victims were even buried, especially as many of the
relatives didn't want it played at all. Chief executive Peter
Robinson described the FA's request as 'insensitive' and said
no decision would be made until after the funerals. In his
autobiography Kenny Dalglish later went further:

To me, football wasn't important. But it was to the Football Association, who were talking about the Cup on television before 4 p.m.
while the bodies were still being taken out from behind the fence.
That was despicable. All the FA's talk about deadlines was stupid
... Liverpool were going to set the deadline. Not when the players
were ready, because they might not have been ready, but when the
people of Merseyside were ready, when there had been a reasonable
length of time for mourning.[4]

Similar searing criticism of the FA was aired at the Taylor
hearings. The FSA and others attacked the choice of ground
and allocation of ends. Kelly admitted that he had failed to
inform the committee which made the final decision on the
venue of the protest call from Liverpool's chief executive. He
also conceded that 'there was an element of unfairness' to
Liverpool in playing at Hillsborough again. Taylor was more
biting, calling it an 'ill-considered' decision in his initial report,
but dismissing the claims that it was a cause of the disaster
itself.

The final report on the game was even less comfortable

reading for the FA. Taylor noted that both it and the Football League, where Kelly had spent twenty years, almost ten as its general secretary, had been more concerned with pitch invasions than ground safety. He highlighted the fact that the FA had failed to consider fully the safety aspects of the semifinal, neither inspecting the ground nor meeting with representatives of the host club or officials from the local council. Its unimpressive record on dealing with violence on the pitch was also recorded. Poor leadership was mentioned more than once and a more positive approach demanded; insufficient regard for the health, and views, of supporters was highlighted and improvements in safety culture and consultation called for; and the weakness and unwillingness of the authorities to act decisively were criticized and an end to such complacency ordered.

I asked Kelly if he thought the criticism was fair. 'Probably not. Any collection of clubs in an organization like football is going to be conservative by nature, it's going to be resistant to change, because the vast majority of its members' pace of change will be dictated by the slowest. For example, he [Taylor] was saying all-seater immediately and the leadership of the game was saying let's phase it in gradually; we can't do it overnight. There's an immediate dichotomy between someone who looks at the game from the outside and someone who's a director of a club who may have guaranteed an overdraft at the bank.'

There were plenty of fans, however, who agreed with Taylor's assessment of the administrators, many people who thought that Hillsborough would bring a complete overhaul of the game's outdated and out-of-touch government, perhaps even the demise of some of those who had run it. Was there any talk of resignations, I wondered? Kelly replied, 'No, that didn't arise. Certainly not in football anyway.' Perhaps there might have been if the disaster had occurred in Europe, I suggested. 'Um. I don't think it happened after Heysel. It doesn't arise. If you haven't done anything wrong you don't resign.'

Everything, though, had to change after Hillsborough, or so it seemed. All of the ailments, administrative and otherwise, both their symptoms and causes, had to be treated. Officials in blazers sitting in the stands knew it as well as the masses huddled on the terraces, perhaps even better. The only questions were, what would the medicine be and how big the dose?

Now the apparent health of the game – at least at its pinnacle – is as clear as its ills once were. The dark, introspective days of the 1980s have been replaced by the sparkling spectacle of the Premier League, the wealthiest league in the world. Some of the greatest players in the world grace its pitches, their quality and star status helping to popularize football with whole new sections of the community, crossing class and gender divides in a way that has never happened before. And the recruitment of new fans has helped ensure that crowds have increased every year of the Premier League's short life, so that last season's average of 29,189 per game was the highest in the top division for twenty-one years. Business is booming.

Kelly clearly took some personal pride as he talked, in the peculiar monotone falsetto familiar to anyone who has heard or seen an FA Cup draw, of the revolution in his decade and a bit in charge of English football and of its current state of health. 'By and large the game has changed for the better,' he said. 'It's become so much bigger. The television audience is huge. People are going to want to go to football more this season. More kids are going to want to go. More families are going to want to go. The general feeling is that the game is very successful and on the back of that there will be commercial involvement. What we have to do is to make sure that the money we generate on that basis – from television contracts and commercial sponsorship or endorsements – is reinvested in the game. By and large we're in very good shape. If you look back a few years, who'd have thought we'd be having a new national stadium – it just didn't seem to be on the horizon; who'd have thought we'd have been bidding for the World Cup – we were the pariahs of Europe; or that top clubs would be developing youth academies. So much has changed – and for the better really.'

The game's ruddy well-being could be seen as the crowning glory of Kelly's career in the sport to which he has devoted his life. He was a fan as a short-trousered schoolboy in Blackpool when the Tangerines won the FA Cup in the so-called Matthews final of 1953. He can still reel off the names of the numerous subsequent successors to Matthews he saw playing for Blackpool reserves. He even went on to play for the club himself, albeit at third-team level, before realizing that he would be unable to forge a career on the pitch. He joined a bank and worked there for a couple of years before getting a job in the game, joining the Football League, based in nearby Lytham St Annes, in the late 1960s, under its domineering leader Alan Hardaker, and finally succeeding him as secretary in 1979.

Just over a year before Hillsborough he left the League for its historic London-based rival, the FA. The former had been established to deal solely with the professional leagues and the clubs in them, its only link with the FA the resolution of basic disciplinary matters. The latter, governing the game as a whole – upholding the laws, managing the England team and, via county FAs, overseeing the grass roots – was responsible for internationals and park players alike. They coexisted, as they had since the professional game's evolution in Victorian times, although, over time, with an ever greater recognition that the double-headed structure was an anachronism.

The divisions which had first led to two separate authorities – amateurs versus professionals, gentlemen versus players, South versus North – were long gone. The modern disagreements which flared between them, most often epitomized in club versus country disputes, were harming the game, as was the lack of clear, distinct leadership. Pre-Hillsborough the government was calling on them to 'speak with one voice'. Just over a year after the disaster the League responded by producing a plan, even entitled 'One Game, One Team, One Voice', which suggested a merger and a new slimmed-down bureaucracy governed by a twelve-strong joint board made up equally of representatives from Lancaster Gate and Lytham.

On the surface Kelly's move to the FA suggested a similar new, closer working relationship between them anyway. A man with a foot in both camps would have been an ideal candidate to see through a unification. But it was not to be. He and his new employers viewed the League's proposals as a ploy to bolster its power at the FA's expense. To succeed, the plan had to be approved by the very body the joint board would replace: the ninety-strong FA council. And, to use the phrase always invoked when reform of the FA is debated, turkeys don't vote for Christmas. So while the councillors mulled over proposals they were only ever going to reject, Kelly set to work on drawing up an alternative plan for restructuring, a rival vision for the future of football, based around those at Lancaster Gate retaining the dominant role.

The resulting 'Blueprint for Football' was in fact drawn up by experts in various individual fields and the content overseen by a committee. But the most significant influence on its content came after the meal, a month after the League's plan was announced, hosted by Greg Dyke, of ITV.[5] The discussion of a new television deal for the top clubs prompted a delegation from them to visit the FA and ascertain its views on a possible breakaway from the League. The clubs needed FA sanction, otherwise the split would appear to be merely an exercise in greed; the FA in turn needed the big clubs to line up on its side in its power struggle with the League. The result was the conception of the FA Premier League.

And so it was that the structure of the FA, the main target

for those who regarded Lancaster Gate as fusty and out of touch, remained unchanged. As long ago as 1968 Oxford don Norman Chester recommended reform: 'A council of 84 members [as it then was], though excellent for broad discussion and for representing the interests of the game in every part of the country, cannot be an effective policy-making body.' Now a council a tenth bigger again and dominated by men in their seventies drawn overwhelmingly from the amateur game, with as many of them representing Oxbridge, the public schools and the armed forces as the Premier League and the Football League, are in charge of a multi-million-pound business. At the same time as the likes of Alec McGivan and the man who first recruited him, director of public affairs David Davies, have begun to spin a revolution, the old, labyrinthine power structure, with its endless committee sessions and council meetings, has remained.

Kelly defended it, of course: 'The FA works magnificently. It is a very great organization. Despite its image, it looks forward, it responds, it takes the game forward, it tries to work for unity within the game and all our time is spent trying to work for improvements in the game. We've got a good number under our belt and more to come. We work very well with the structure we've got. That's not to say that it can't be streamlined or improved, but some of the council members are very resistant to change. We'll keep trying to devise a structure where the council retain their influence in the parliament of football as representatives of the game, while devolving management to a smaller, more dynamic body. But I argue that it isn't unwieldy – it's my job to ensure that it isn't.'

Indeed he skilfully steered the 'Blueprint' – 'my document', as he called it – the most radical manifesto for reform ever, through the various committees and council and into reality, so ushering in one set of revolutionaries, the chairmen of the big clubs, while seeing off another, those from Lytham. One of the document's key themes was the need to 'end . . . the power struggle' in football by allowing the FA to take the undisputed lead role, while one of its main aims was to improve the England team's chances of success. The League's power has withered, while Glenn Hoddle's side qualified for the World Cup with a mature, confident performance in Rome, so Kelly might appear to be justified in the satisfaction implied when he said, 'The theme of the "Blueprint" has certainly been implemented.'

But the details, like his qualified language, tell a fuller, and slightly different, story. The most obvious example of where fact has not matched philosophy is with the Premier League itself. The justification for offering FA endorsement of it was that it would consist of eighteen clubs, so cutting the number of games for the top players, the England players. A breakaway league was the only way to achieve such a reduction in size and fixtures, the 'Blueprint' claimed, because most clubs would always veto change for fear of the impact on their finances. And an FA-endorsed Premier league would prevent the breakaway being driven purely by the commercial considerations of the eighteen clubs over the rest of the ninety-two.

The Premier League of eighteen was due to start three years ago. But by then it had long become clear that the will of the FA to impose the theory of the 'Blueprint' was gone – partly because their ability to do so had also gone. The league was formed on a one-member one-vote basis, with any notion of FA leadership fading into the background once the League was vanquished, as if that was its job done, and so the very situation the breakaway was supposed to avoid – clubs refusing to accept a smaller league – occurred anyway. Power shifted markedly to the chairmen, but the Premier League ones rather than all ninety-two. And instead of ending the power struggle, a second front was opened up, with the Premier League soon to overshadow both the FA and League.

Kelly said that the eighteen-club league might still come to pass, but his words indicated exactly who would make the decision: 'We're currently looking at that again. The vast majority of clubs want to stay at twenty – I think eighteen would want to stay at twenty and two would want to go to eighteen, Arsenal and Manchester United for obvious reasons. I'm not absolutely convinced we need to go down to eighteen to improve the England team, but that's without any more changes in European competitions. If we get further changes there, I might have to think again. But I'm sure the clubs who aren't the big ones and the fans won't want to see less games.'

His mention of fans also touched upon one of the other core recommendations of the 'Blueprint', one of the most important in that it was intended to repair a gaping hole in the running of the game: the absence of any link between the FA and fans. Ever since it was formed, the FA had been run on behalf of, and by, those who were seen as the main constituents of the football world: the players, officials and administrators. It oversaw the rules and disciplinary measures for breaches of them, both on and off the pitch, but it was utterly unconcerned about the well-being, or anything else, of those who watched the game. The 'Blueprint' suggested a new supporter-friendly approach, even echoing another of Norman Chester's long-overdue reforms: greater involvement for fans.

An entire chapter was devoted to the subject, outlining possible ways of encouraging a general improvement in behaviour by forging links with non-hooligan supporters. It quoted favourably a report from Parliament's Home Affairs Select Committee which said, 'The current "them and us" mentality means that fans resent the way they are treated by clubs . . . As long as the fans are not represented in any formal way at a decision-making level, the pressure for improved facilities and conditions at grounds is missing an important element.' It praised the FSA and the 'embassy' it ran (to provide information and help for fans) at the World Cup in Italy. Generally, it called for better and more direct links with supporters – and even suggested the establishment of a new supporters' organization to be funded to the tune of £100,000 per annum by the FA. A member of it would liaise directly with the FA and all the authorities.

But it was never heard of again. While the Premier League was established and quickly snowballed, while other, smaller elements of the 'Blueprint' were acted upon and while the greatest chance for much-needed reform waited, nothing happened. Kelly admitted: 'It never got off the ground. It was never really developed.' For any particular reason? 'Um . . . I can't remember. Nobody was . . . We developed closer links with supporters' organizations and started having fans' forums with the Premier League clubs[6] and then the Football League clubs started doing that too and it just never . . . Nobody really ever considered it.'

The consequences were clear for all to see at a photo call on a glowing pre-season day, on an almost luminous green pitch at the Valley, south London home of Charlton Athletic. Football's unlikely saviour was making his public debut – by trying to kick a ball straight. Ex-Tory Cabinet member David Mellor, along with his mentor, Sports Minister Tony Banks, was trying to satisfy the photographers' desire for a picture to illustrate his surprise appointment as head of the newly formed Football Task Force. But where Banks was as elegant and well balanced as anyone wearing a suit and smart shoes could be, Mellor's arms flapped as he semi-skipped towards the ball and toe-poked it. Kicking like a girl, someone said, in the sort of comment the Task Force might frown upon.

Mellor's surprise appointment, though, and the creation of the Task Force confirmed a new government commitment to examine football, its schizophrenic health and its lingering ailments – largely from the perspective of the supporters. Other members of the group included, as well as Kelly and officials from both the Premier and Football Leagues, a couple of

members of the FSA and its co-founder Rogan Taylor, ensuring the sorts of concern rarely on the agenda in Lancaster
Gate or Lytham would be aired. A series of evidence-gathering
sessions and public meetings would be staged around the
country, it was also announced, giving the ordinary fan the
chance to raise issues of concern.

The open sessions varied in content and tone from city to
city. In Liverpool families of the Hillsborough victims used the
meeting to continue their campaign for justice. In Manchester
Andy Walsh and his group made sure that almost every question came back to terracing and the case for its reintroduction
– an issue which was omitted from the Task Force's remit. Then
in Southampton fans furious at the stock-market flotation of
the club and the financial rewards enjoyed by the directors
posed some awkward questions, in particular about the £1-
million profit of one director, a certain Keith Wiseman, the
chairman of the FA. When Kelly claimed ignorance of the
issue, he was laughed at; when a fan offered him a recording
of a programme about it and Kelly said he didn't have a video
player, he was laughed at even more.

Most of the sessions, though, Kelly claimed to have enjoyed:
'You get an interesting mix coming from all sorts of different
areas. You hear some interesting views and it's a good debating
forum. The open meetings for the most part I've enjoyed,
they've been good fun. There've been two or three I didn't
enjoy: the Liverpool one for two reasons – one it was a poor
attendance because it was local election night and secondly
because it concentrated on Hillsborough for a significant part
of the evening. Nobody would say they enjoy discussing Hillsborough. You just have to listen to the people who've been
affected and try to answer their questions as best you can.
Mellor's written to Jack Straw since, asking further points.
But you wouldn't say that was enjoyable. I didn't enjoy the
Manchester one because that was hijacked by the terracing
lobby, the pro-standing lobby, so it wasn't a great meeting,

and likewise I didn't enjoy the Southampton one because it was hijacked by the anti-Southampton board lobby and it became a bit of a slanging match.'

His aversion to some of the more important issues raised was no surprise. A popularity poll between Graham Kelly and David Mellor might be an extremely close-run, and low-scoring, event, but there is a fundamental difference between the two and the bodies they represent. Kelly and the FA appear unwilling or unable to recognize problems or address them, unaware of anything beyond the narrowest definition of the game's health; Mellor and the Task Force are concerned only with the wider picture, the tensions caused by commercialism or consumer dissatisfaction.

Almost every interview with Kelly carries a section which notes that his friends and colleagues insist his lacklustre personality disguises a man with a keen sense of self-deprecating humour who is absolutely devoted to the game – watching lower-division and non-league football as often as the top Premier League action. But the longer he went on, the less that seemed to matter. He made the weak quips – about his 'unfortunate start in life' as a Blackpool fan – but his answers to the live issues in the game, those thrown up for Task Force debate, were weaker still.

On the soaring cost of going to a game, he said, 'To a certain extent is there anything you can do about it? I can't see what the FA can do about it. Chelsea presumably will say that if you want to have good facilities and watch the top stars in the world, you've got to pay for it. They would probably also say, "We have to maintain our ground, unlike foreign clubs, who lease them." I don't know what the FA can do about ticket prices quite honestly.'

On the fiasco at Doncaster: 'I think the situation there has far more to do with the way the club's been run down. I think it's very difficult to see what the FA could do. Doncaster is a limited company and there are people there to run the club.

The FA couldn't run it. People who feel passionately about clubs get involved in them and most of the time they do a good job.' Of his appearance at Belle Vue, he added, 'Oh, I watch matches everywhere.'

And on the possibility of the government establishing a regulator for football: 'I just can't see how it will work. Will it say to Ken Bates at Chelsea, "Well, you can't put prices up x per cent, only by y per cent"? How will it do that? By law? It seems a strange concept to me. But maybe it will happen.'

Perhaps his problem was that he was too honest. There were no attempts to disguise his position, no effort at holding answers which acknowledged whichever concern and promised a thorough investigation. But perhaps that was because he knew nothing of the sort would happen. The FA's record over the years has been lamentable. As long ago as 1923 and the inquiry into the overcrowding and mass pitch invasion at the so-called White Horse FA Cup Final, it was clear that Lancaster Gate was aloof; no one from Lancaster Gate even appeared before the hearings into how its major competition came close to ending in utter disaster. And a similar approach is still all too apparent.

Three years ago a Manchester United European Cup tie in Portugal was marred by a crush around the turnstiles, caused by ticket chaos, before kick-off and police firing rubber bullets at departing fans after the final whistle. A full, damning report of fans' treatment was on the FA's desk within a couple of days. But its author, Adam Brown of the FSA, told me when I was in Manchester, 'They obviously didn't read it. Kelly just wrote back to say, "Your comments have been noted." People could easily have died and all they could say was, "Your comments have been noted." I don't think anything has changed significantly since Hillsborough in that sense. In significant areas they are obviously unable or, more likely, unwilling to take action. I'm sure you or I or any number of other people could do a better job. They seem to run on a mix of incompetence combined with complete disregard for the fans.' The difference now is that Adam is also a member of the Task Force.

Kelly's antipathy towards Mellor was obvious from the unusually impolite way he referred to him merely by his second name. But, as he began to sound more and more weary of questions about problems, I asked what his overall view was of the Task Force. He said, 'I think they've had two tap-ins to start with – racism and access for disabled. Once they get into ticket pricing, players' wages, commercialism generally, it's going to be far more difficult. The test will come on issues it has to face.' Which, coming from Graham Kelly, a nice man no doubt, but head of football's most unloved relic and the chief defender of it, might be taken as being as rich as the Premier League he helped to create.

players

For many fervent followers, the men on the pitch are heroes to be revered and emulated.

Lord Justice Taylor's final report, paragraph 131

In the bar of a pub close, but not quite close enough, to Leeds city centre, another afternoon of nothing much was drifting by. The barman busied himself wiping away the detritus of the lunch-time drinkers who had returned to work in the surrounding industrial estate and polishing, then storing, glasses. The landlord sat at a small, round table hosting the only customers, just two of them, chatting over a cup of tea as they each supped a pint. The conversation centred on the subject of the day – the latest self-inflicted stain on the career of Paul Gascoigne – but it was a rather distracted debate, punctuated by the afternoon's horseracing being shown on the TV set just above them.

The landlord, the largest of the three, middle-aged and carrying some spread, had just returned from taking a crying-off call from one of his Sunday morning side – a call which no doubt helped inform his stern views on Gazza and other problem players. The most senior of the three, skin weathered and worn, but radiating the wisdom of an elder, was largely silent, the merest hint of a nod of his white-crowned head indicating his agreement on the need for discipline. The least memorable of the three also had his views, but not, frankly, the 1,000-plus appearances for sides as famous as Juventus, Roma and Don Revie's Leeds, the 500-old goals and the sixty caps of the other two. They, Peter Lorimer and John Charles, seemed rather better qualified to comment.

The pair are bound by history. Lorimer is Leeds' most potent goalscorer – a record which will never be beaten; Charles is second in the scoring list. Lorimer is also sixth in the club's all-time league appearances table, trailing five of his team-mates from the title-winning teams of the late 1960s and early 1970s; Charles, the greatest all-round player the club ever had, is twentieth. And, in one of the playing coincidences which herald the succession of a new generation over the old, when Lorimer made his debut as a fifteen-year-old winger, Charles was the veteran centre-forward at whom his crosses were aimed.

They are also united in the present. When that Sunday morning side, made up of ex-Leeds players and managed by Lorimer, trots out for its part-charity, part-exhibition, but wholly competitive, matches, Charles can usually be spotted on the sidelines, shyly signing autographs. Visitors to Lorimer's pub, a fifteen-minute, exhaust-choked walk around the city-centre traffic loop, are regularly rewarded by the sight of Charles enjoying a quiet pint. Scandinavian supporters are among the more frequent callers, snatching autographs, photographs and a few seconds of history with one or both of the ex-players, but lingering stars, from other countries – Scotland in Lorimer's case, Wales in Charles's – and another time.

In the future, too, they will continue side by side, in the pub, at the park matches, in any line-up of the greatest-ever Leeds team, in the record books, but most of all in hearts and minds. A schoolboy talent might, just might, one day break

Lorimer's record as the club's youngest-ever player; far more likely, a veteran, perhaps a goalkeeper, might surpass the second part of his unique double as its oldest player too. But even then Lorimer and Charles, and every other hero and every other bit-part player, will be remembered, because their exploits made the club what it was, what it is and, in some cases, what it will be. They are the thread which binds its history.

It's exactly the same at every club. There are the old legends, the record-holders, the players-turned-managers and the home-grown heroes. There are also the knackered old-stagers, the record-buy disasters and the one-game wonders. But all of them part of what makes the club the club. And so all one of us.

In the 1950s, when Charles left Leeds for a new, pioneering life in Italy, he was already an archetypal sporting hero: his ability and athleticism exceptional, yet his character and class as ordinary as those of anyone watching.

He had begun his professional career, aged seventeen, at Elland Road as a centre-half and was invincible, his barrel-chested six-foot-two frame an impassable object. He was switched to centre-forward in his early twenties and his lightning speed and skill saw him scoring forty-two league goals in a season, a new club record. He was the Alan Shearer *and* Tony Adams of his day – except that he was Welsh and his wages when he scored at the rate of a goal a game were £14 a week.

In 1957 he left Leeds, reluctantly. Perhaps unsurprisingly for a man whose mother told him that he would need a passport to travel from Swansea to Yorkshire, he was wary of moving again – and moving abroad. But when Juventus bid a world record £65,000 for him and Leeds decided they needed the money, he became the first British star to play in Europe – and is probably still the most successful.

In Italy he quickly became a legend, adored for unfailing sportsmanship which saw him always calm, despite swinging elbows and lashing kicks. Perhaps loved also for the records, sung in Italian yet with Welsh tones. But worshipped above all for his unique talent and the triumphs it brought. He scored ninety-three goals in 155 games, despite the stifling new innovation of the sweeper – and then often dropped back into defence to preserve the 1–0 lead – as Juve won three championships in five years.

In Wales too he was acclaimed. He became its youngest-ever international when he made his debut aged eighteen. He was the heart of the side which went to the 1958 World Cup – the only major tournament finals his country has ever played in – and reached the quarterfinals, where he played against another juvenile player who stood out even among the best, a seventeen-year-old called Pelé, who scored the only goal of the game.

At the time it was Charles, not Pelé, who was known as the World's Greatest Player. On the terraces he had other nicknames. One, King John, showed the esteem in which he was held; another, the Gentle Giant, one of the reasons for it. The only time he threatened an opponent was when an Austrian defender kicked his brother Mel, the Welsh centre-half, so hard that he was out of the game for more than three months. In Italy, where he was subjected to similarly fearsome tackling, his serenity and skill were acknowledged in translation when he first became *il gigante buono*, and then also *il campione preferito* – Footballer of the Year.

When he had joined Leeds his possible rewards were fixed by the strictures of the maximum wage: £10 a week in the season, £7 a week in the summer; the signing-on fee for any transferred player was £10. When he joined Juve his wages doubled to £20, but he also received win bonuses of up to £500 and a signing-on fee of £10,000. A rent-free flat and a car were also thrown in for good measure. It was wealth beyond the imagination of his shackled ex-team-mates back home – a package which could have set him up for life, if he'd had advisers and an agent.

Instead his brilliant and speedy ascent was followed by a tarnished, lingering decline, so common among the heroes of his era that it has become a living cliché. Five years after leaving, he re-signed for Leeds as ambitious new manager Revie realized a coup which he hoped would invigorate his side and its lethargic support. But within weeks, having watched him training, Revie concluded, 'I don't think the big man can do it any more. He's gone.' Charles went back to Italy to play for Roma for the rest of the season. He returned to Wales, for three years at Cardiff, then became player-manager at Hereford and then, aged forty-two, at Merthyr Tydfil for £40 a week.

When he finally accepted that his playing days were finished, and that managing was not for him, he followed generations of his predecessors behind a bar to become a landlord. Later he ran a toy shop, then a children's clothes shop. But in all three the self-effacing manner and happy-go-lucky personality which helped make him a hero on the pitch were the opposite of the drive and determination needed to succeed in business.

It wasn't that he was workshy: in his younger days he would wear a boot only on his weaker left foot in shooting practice to ensure that he improved it; and in the summer he would be at the deserted ground every day, trying to increase his aerial power by firing a ball against the stand and heading the rebound between two sticks. Or that he was unwilling to make sacrifices: by the time he was twenty he had lost cartilages in both knees, the lasting collateral damage of fouls aimed at quelling his talent. By the time his career ended he had undergone six operations on legs punished for the ability they bore.

It was just that Charles's genius was for football. He did well from it for a time. So did others, though: only half of the fee from Juve was used to fund replacements; and when he made his much-anticipated return to Elland Road the admission price suddenly went up by half a crown. But once that genius was diminished by age, and once clubs and fans had found new idols, he was stranded. He was of the generation of whom ex-England international Wilf Mannion said, 'They should shoot old pros when the time comes to hang up their boots.' Their lives were already over in many ways, because their careers were.

Of course, he is still remembered. In 1988 he was awarded a belated, and shared, testimonial. Juve have maintained a link, even inviting him on an all-expenses-paid trip to witness his successors in the European Cup Final in 1996. Two or three times a year he goes back to Turin and is still occasionally recognized as Gian Carlo. In between he watches every home game at Elland Road. And in the merchandising catalogue at the club shop, alongside a Lorimer sweatshirt, there is a Charles fleece jacket, price £55.

But, even so, when John Charles, the ex-World's Greatest Player, a man of few words but so many memories, signed me an autograph and said, 'There you go. All right?', part of me just wanted to ask him if he was.

In the 1960s, when he was aiming crosses at him in Charles's short second coming at Leeds, a fresh-faced Peter Lorimer was growing up in a new family, in a new era, one which was ushered in partly as a result of his centre-forward's transfers to and from Italy.

Revie had been in such a hurry to get to Dundee to sign a lad who scored 176 goals in a season for his school team that he was caught speeding. His haste was prompted by the fact that Manchester United's chief scout had also called at the Lorimer house as the minutes until Peter's fifteenth birthday slipped by. A couple of days earlier Revie had also seen Chelsea manager Tommy Docherty jump on a train carrying the Lorimers back to Dundee to try to woo the emerging star.

Another thirty clubs were also interested in the precocious talent.

But Revie succeeded because he was almost one of the family. He had befriended Lorimer's parents two or three years earlier. He travelled to see them regularly. He promised they would be allowed frequent trips to Yorkshire to see their son. He outlined the bright future he foresaw for the club, how he was aiming to emulate the success of the greatest club in Europe, Real Madrid. In short, he spoke to them in the same language of concern and aspiration as any parent.

Revie started his reign as player-manager, but he was always a players' manager. His own career as a renowned centre-forward had almost been ended by injury twice – first by a broken leg, then by an appalling nose wound which was so bloody that it threatened his life too – and was littered with instances of players being treated shabbily. So when he took charge he was determined that facilities for his side – from training balls to train travel – would be the best. He was determined that the players would be looked after as they deserved.

And by the time Lorimer signed, in 1962, that recognition of players' rights had also been extended to their pay packets. Charles's transfer had helped illustrate the absurdities of the maximum wage and its long-overdue abolition came in 1961. For the first time players could be paid what they were worth, limited only by what clubs could afford. A direct link between the presence of the men on the pitch and the numbers of those in the ground became common. Lorimer and his team-mates, the first of the breakthrough generation of properly paid professionals, were eventually paid a bonus of a pound each if the crowd was greater than 35,000 and another pound each if it went past 42,000.

Wage negotiations, of course, brought disputes, but they were rare. Lorimer had only one, with Revie, in twenty years at the club. He said, 'We'd had a pretty good season, I think we'd won the title, and I'd had a pretty good season too, so I said to myself, I'm going to get £200 a week. I was on £130. Don used to live around the corner from me, so he phoned up and said I should go to see him. I told him what I wanted. He offered £190 and said I would be one of the best-paid players at the club – but he said the same thing to everyone. In those days the tax rate meant that £10 was £4 cash in hand. I thought it just didn't seem worth the argument, so I said, "I don't want to fall out with you over four quid" and it was settled.'

The other half of the discredited system governing players – a transfer system which could hold a player to one club for life, even against his will – was also abolished in the early 1960s. But it was a freedom players still rarely exploited. At Leeds Revie kept special files on each player, on who had bid for him and when the bid was turned down. The manager refused to let any of his players leave; none wanted to go anyway. Lorimer said, 'We'd all grown up together, me, Eddie, Billy [Bremner], Johnny [Giles], big Jack [Charlton], Norman [Hunter], all of us, and we all saw Don as almost a father. We were almost like a family. We worked together and worked for each other from the early days. None of us wanted to leave. We were successful, we liked each other's company and anyway we got paid as well as we would have been anywhere else.'

But football family life had differences from the real thing. Lorimer said, 'You miss out on the things other kids do. You miss all the lads going out for a Friday night out, or any night out really, and when you're a lad of twenty, twenty-one that's all you want to do, but you can't. Then, when you're older, you miss out on your family growing up and seeing your own kids and so they miss out on things other kids are getting. It soon becomes a job – and a harder and harder one to play at the top level if you're not 100 per cent fit and you're playing game after game after game. I remember one season we played seventy-six matches.' But would he have had it any other way? 'Absolutely not, no way.'

The extent to which it was a job became clear when I asked about his memories – perhaps of the hat trick in the famous, imperious 7–0 win over Southampton which was shown to an enthralled audience on *Match of the Day*; or of the controversially disallowed opening goal against Bayern Munich in the European Cup Final; or of the goal-bound shot miraculously saved by Jim Montgomery in the FA Cup Final against Sunderland. He can remember only the latter – and then because of television.

'I've seen the Sunderland save a million times on telly, so I remember that, but to be honest I'm hopeless. If someone goes through it with me, I can sometimes remember them then, but at the end of the day it's the same as when people ask you about winning or losing cup finals: you don't really remember, mostly because we were playing so many games, you just finished one and moved on to the next. There was always another big one coming along. After we won the cup against Arsenal we had twenty-four hours before our last league game, at Wolves, which was going to decide the title. Twenty-four hours, can you imagine?' And as if to prove his point about his memory, it was actually two days.

The family doesn't need set-piece reunions because, ten years after Revie's death, they are still in touch on a regular basis. The crying-off phone call in the bar was from Eddie Gray saying he would struggle to make kick-off in the veterans' match on Sunday. Lorimer's ex-midfield partner Bobby Collins turns out too and so, occasionally, did Bremner before his death – although his health was a concern even then. Injuries sustained in their professional days prevent Hunter, Alan Clarke and Mick Jones – whose career was abruptly ended by knee damage – from joining in, but they still meet up for a drink or a round of golf.

'Sniffer' Clarke sells extractor fans, Jones sports clothes and

Collins was a driver for Leeds University. Some of the family have stayed in football, from Charlton and his exploits with the Irish in the World Cup to Paul Reaney, who runs courses for schoolchildren. Some, notably Giles, who wisely ensured that all of them invested some of their earnings when they were playing, but also Hunter, work in the media. None are rich. Lorimer said, 'We were the most successful team in the country for twelve years, but none of us could have not worked again when we stopped playing. Paul Madeley is the only one that I'd say is well-off – and that's through a family business, not football. In our days it was still impossible to earn big money.'

In the 1970s, when team-mates such as Lorimer were collecting medals at the rate of at least one a year, Eddie Gray was learning to live with disappointment and starting to dread the future.

He was the most gifted player at the club at the time, possibly ever. His ball control was effortlessly sublime, his passing and distribution on a par with the best midfield visionaries, his sprint speed – especially for his six-foot frame – electric enough to take him past any defender even without recourse to the shimmy, the twitch of the hips, which would have beaten them anyway. There was no more terrifying sight for any side than Gray advancing on them, ball at feet, stroking it forward with the outside of his left boot, but head up, alert, like a latter day, and turbo-charged, Stanley Matthews.

Clarke reckoned Gray was as good as George Best. Bremner called him a genius who was poised to become one of the world's greatest players. Shortly before he died, he said:

'[He] was a fantastic player. There were no attributes in the game he didn't have. Eddie could go past you on your left or right side. He would go past people for fun. He could take it with his left, he could take it with his right, he came at you side on. He could bend balls, and could hit them with the outside or inside of his foot. Also when he went past people, he immediately had his head up to pick colleagues out. I've never seen a boy do so many tricks with a ball as Eddie could . . . A great, great player.'[1]

Except for the niggling injury which dogged his entire career and almost ended it. In 1974, as the team won its final trophy of the Revie era – its final trophy for eighteen years – Gray was a frustrated spectator. He had played only eight games before undergoing a fifth operation on the thigh injury he had first collected ten years earlier. When Brian Clough arrived the next season as Revie's replacement, his blunt assessment was, 'If you had been a racehorse, you would have been shot long ago.' But when Clough's brief reign ended, new manager Jimmy Armfield proved to be the saviour of Gray's career. He said, 'I was in my mid-twenties and I thought I was going to have to pack the game in. But Jimmy said do a bit of coaching and a bit of training and through that I learned how to play with it.'

Sitting on the edge of the penalty area of a lush pitch at Leeds' new training complex, nestling in the North Yorkshire countryside some twenty miles from the city itself, Gray stretched his leg out and pulled his shorts back to show the lasting damage. He left thigh was muscular and toned, his right concave, with a livid scar running down its length.

The potential lost to the injury was the biggest disappointment in his career, he said in Glaswegian tones softened only by a lifetime in Yorkshire: 'I was probably a bit foolish when it first happened. Medical supervision wasnae what it is at the present time and I probably came back too quickly. I developed calcification in the muscle which caused me problems all the way through my career. Today, it wouldnae have happened; how things would have been done would have been different, but that's progression. I believe I would have been a lot better player without the injury. I don't really think I got the opportunity to fulfil to the maximum the ability I had. That's a disappointment. Having said that, I still had a good career, I still enjoyed it, but I just wish I'd been fit all the time. Ask any footballer and they'll say that's the most important thing: stay clear of injuries.'

Behind us was the proof. Gray had suggested we sat outside to avoid the banter and brrrrr-ing of phones in the dressing rooms and offices. Instead the only sound was the steel buzz of a sit-on lawnmower fading in and out of the afternoon as it created broad swathes of freshly cut grass. Driving the machine was John Reynolds, groundsman, longest servant of the club and an enormously gifted player who never had the chance to shine. Gray explained: 'They say he was going to be a really wonderful player, but he got a real bad injury when he was seventeen and could never play again. So instead of the club sending him back to Wales with nothing to do, they took him on the groundstaff. Of course, if they'd had the medical facilities we have now, he would have been all right too.'

Much else has changed, of course, in the thirty-three years between Gray arriving at Elland Road on the groundstaff and moulding the players of tomorrow as youth team coach using state-of-the-art facilities. He was from the last generation to learn the game in the way the likes of Matthews or Tom Finney did, with makeshift balls in the back alleys behind rows of the terraced homes close to whichever heavy industry employed their parents: 'We used to roll our socks up, shove paper into them and tie them together to make a ball. Anybody who had a real ball always got a game – in goal if he was a really bad player. You'd be kicking a ball around the back streets and whatever space you could find. It was jerseys for goals, throw your jumpers down and off you went. When you played on grass it was so much easier, but you had the skills.'

When he arrived at Leeds, another recruit of Revie's Scottish scouting network and paternal personality, he became very familiar with the grass – weeding the Elland Road pitch with the other young players in just one of the jobs which often had to be done before they played any football: 'It was all part of the job – cleaning the ground down, sweeping the terraces, getting the kit in, weeding the pitch. The first thing you did when you got in was your jobs and you'd train in between doing them. It all depended on what the groundsman wanted. The Monday after a home game was always a busy day because, as you can imagine, the stadium was filthy with all the rubbish and it was the young players who cleaned it all up. There'd be two or three of you allocated to different parts of the ground and you'd have your brush and your bag and away you'd go. It'd take a long time too. Sometimes it'd take a couple of days to do it – and then there was a midweek game.'

When poor weather threatened, the boys were also pressed into service as the insurance policy against postponement: 'If there was a forecast of frost before a big game, we were all out putting straw on the park for the night and then taking it off again the next day. We'd bring sandwiches in to eat, sleep the night in the players' lounge and then be up at the crack of dawn because it took a long time to get straw on and off a football park.' And it all became part of their education as Revie and his backroom staff provided refreshments and put on a film – usually of Real Madrid's greatest games.

Some of Gray's goals were as good as any scored by the so-called Kings of Europe. In one game, a televised one against Burnley in 1970, he scored two classics, the first a driven chip from thirty-five yards, the second more remarkable still. And his memory of them highlights a fundamental difference between fans and players. For fans, the first goal wasn't that memorable because it looked a little like a hit and hope; the second, on the other hand, was impossibly skilful. For Gray, though, the first was impossibly skilful, a calculated and per-fectly executed effort against a top goalkeeper who was a fraction off his line; the second just a routine, if rare, display of skill which came more or less naturally. He said, 'The second's no' something that sticks out in my mind, I must be honest with you. I can understand why people might look at it and remember, but to me it wasnae anything out of the ordinary. I enjoyed the first goal I scored that day rather than the second, the one where I chipped the goalkeeper from a fair distance. That gave me more satisfaction than the second, which was just something I could do.'

Which, as quickly as possible, just in the time it takes to read about it, was this: beat a defender to the ball as it bobbled around the left-hand edge of the penalty area, nick it past him and chase hard. Trap it on the byline, midway between the edge of the area and the touchline, and then drag it back with the studded sole of the boot. In that instant television viewers were bemused – until a midfielder executing a now embarrassing sliding tackle skidded into view and helplessly out again. Turn to face the full-back closing down, knock the ball to the right of him and sprint to collect it again on the corner of the area. With the full-back and one of the centre-halves as well shutting down the space, feign to shoot with the right foot, but instead cut back inside the first defender, stop in front of the second, draw the tackle and execute another exquisitely timed dragback to take the ball away and then past his lunge. Now, with the midfielder running back on to the pitch and sliding in with another tackle, swerve to the right to escape it and, in the same movement, as the last two defenders close in, jab a shot between them and past the goalkeeper.

When time finally came to stop playing, Gray wanted to stay in football and fifteen years later he still is. As one of his protégés, Harry Kewell, walked by en route for the training session Gray was about to take, I asked if he ever wished he had been born thirty years later: 'I wish I was earning the money they do now, of course you do. Young players coming into the game now and even established players with maybe six or seven years of their careers to go should be secure for life.' Which he certainly would have been after a nineteen-year career. 'Aye, it's a nice thought – being paid for nineteen years at that sort of salary – but it's only a thought. I'm just delighted to still be involved in the game. I enjoy this side of the game, coaching. I enjoy working with players. It's a satisfying job and I'm still in football. I was always going to have to work. I'm just glad it's in football.'

And while he lamented the passing of the team spirit, and players setting scoring and appearance records, he approved of the new freedoms and financial rewards: 'We came through together. Don gave the boys a feeling that we were all together and that we'd stick together through the years. You just couldnae do it now. Everyone moves on. It's a pity. It would be great for clubs. But, from the point of view of players, you can't go back to the days when they were tied to their clubs for the rest of their careers. It was ridiculous. Now the players have a lot of power – and it is more difficult for managers. I just hope players realize that at the end of the day it's the game that's given them a living and not outside interests and it's the game they should concentrate on, 'cos everything else falls into place from there. You work on the game and keep producing the goods, it'll look after you.'

His first coaching experience was at Elland Road, when he was injured, and his first managerial job too. Gray, the last senior player of the great Revie teams left at the club, was appointed after his ex-team-mate Clarke was sacked following relegation in 1982. He cleared out many of the older players who had failed to avoid the drop and introduced younger ones, such as a full-back called Denis Irwin, centre-half Andy Linighan and play-maker John Sheridan – both later scorers of cup-winning goals at Wembley, for Arsenal and Sheffield Wednesday respectively. Alongside them was Lorimer, aged thirty-seven, several months older than the boss who brought him back from the failed experiment of the American league.

At the start of the season there was optimistic talk of promotion, a quick return to the club's supposed rightful place in the First Division. But the inexperience of the side, perhaps, pulled it up just short. The slump in attendances caused by relegation – under 20,000 as opposed to almost 50,000 in the early 1970s – meant there were no funds to buy new players; indeed, previously signed expensive ones were sold cheaply to balance the books. The club was £2 million in debt and lost £1.5 million in its first season in the Second Division. Gray wanted to spend just £20,000 to buy Linighan's brother, but he was told there was no money. When Lorimer was reluctantly granted a new pair of boots he was told to make sure he handed his old pair down for the youth-team players to use.

The chairman even issued a dire warning of the threat of receivership, but the cause of it, the real issue he was warning about, was the fines imposed for hooliganism. In Gray's first season there was disgrace at Grimsby, Chelsea and Derby, as well as during a home game against Newcastle. A relatively quiet second was followed by trouble at Oxford, Barnsley and Huddersfield in the third – and then the riot in Birmingham. Gray admitted he sometimes despaired: 'When you've been at a club a long time and you've got feelings for a club, you don't like to read that the fans are terrible because you know that it's only a certain minority of them that were like that. But that minority can lead to a lot of trouble, which was a disappointment, because every game you were going to, especially games away from home, you were always thinking to yourself, I hope there's no trouble today. Especially when you're manager, because you knew that if there was once again the club would be in the spotlight for the wrong reasons. No one would be talking about football, again.'

When the next season started, Gray was so sick of hooliganism that he banned his family from going to games. But there was no question that he would walk away from the club where he'd spent twenty of his thirty-seven years. The young players were maturing into a good side, one which had been strengthened by the signing of Doncaster's England under-23 international Ian Snodin and the emergence of another promising full-back, another future international, Terry Phelan. There was again talk of promotion. Then Eddie Gray was sacked.

In the 1980s, when some of Gray's young guns were in tears at his departure, David Batty was worried that his career might have stalled before it had even started.

There was turmoil at the club. The players, led by an appalled Lorimer, warned the directors that they were considering a protest strike. One of the board who had voted in support of Gray resigned in disgust at the dismissal. The following Saturday the fans too vented their fury, demanding that the board itself, rather than Gray, should have been sacked.

The tremors extended to the roots of the club too. Three months earlier, when Gray had signed what turned out to be his last batch of apprentices, Batty was among them. Now he thought he would have to work hard to impress a new manager, one who might not be as convinced as Gray that he had the potential to become the club's right-back. And he was right.

Bremner arrived as the new manager and immediately remembered the blond-haired defender as a midfield battler in his own mould whom he'd once watched in a schools match. He switched Batty back to the middle of the park, groomed him in his own image, gave him his debut aged eighteen and kept him in the side from then on, chiding him and encouraging him more than any other. Bremner could often be seen willing his protégé into the thick of the midfield skirmishes, and occasionally, perhaps less helpfully, even flashing him a thumbs-up when he was booked.

In the almost deserted and surprisingly spartan players' lounge at Newcastle's training ground a few months after his mentor's funeral, there was more than a tinge of sadness in his voice when Batty said, 'I think he saw a lot of himself in me. It was a bit embarrassing at times how much. I mean, he did genuinely love me. He took me under his wing and treated me like his son when I was there – and some of the lads used to have a laugh about it. But it was a great relationship we had. I always said, "If I achieve half of what he did I'll have done well." People obviously likened me to him, but it was a great honour just to be mentioned in the same breath.'

In fact he has matched Bremner's haul of two league championship medals and may yet pass it. He is well past half-way to matching Bremner's fifty-four international caps. And, of course, his financial rewards – from transfers worth almost £8 million and the associated earnings – absolutely overshadow Bremner's wealth from the game; Batty earns, roughly, as much in a fortnight as Bremner did in a year at the peak of his playing days. He shares an image with Bremner too: hot-headed, a midfield terrier always snapping at ankles and with a scowl to match. But it's an image that's been foisted upon him and he's never countered. Off the pitch he is one of the more erudite players, reading encyclopedic history books on the coach to away games, and a total family man, always keen to get back home to be with his wife and twin sons.

Football isn't his life, it's his living. When he was injured for a year he didn't see a game. When I met him he was injured again and spending match days at home; he has only recently started watching televised games – and then just highlights. He wants nothing to do with the game's current glamour either. In an age when his team-mates have included models, drinkers, film stars, a restaurateur (who is married to a television star), a newspaper columnist, a self-confessed gambler and Faustino Asprilla, he seems like a throwback to the simple days of straightforward heroes such as Charles. Nor does he want any share of the limelight: 'I think a lot of players speak to reporters 'cos they think they might get a bit of praise in the paper, but that's never bothered me one bit. If I don't want to talk to anybody, I just don't talk with them.'

In another way, too, he was a throwback to the old days: he played for his home-town club. His first organized games were on Sunday mornings in parks around Leeds after his mum spotted an advertisement in the local paper from a team looking for players. To begin with he was a centre-forward, only moving back when a midfielder was injured – and the goals had dried up. He said, 'I enjoyed it more anyway because I liked running round, which is what my game's all about.'

He was also a supporter, too, one of those players – like Alan Shearer – of whom it's often said, 'If he wasn't on the pitch, he'd be on the terraces.' Except that it's rarely true – and less and less so these days. Players play, at whatever level they can. They might support a club, but on Saturdays they turn out for another and that's where their passion for the game lies. If Batty hadn't been spotted by Leeds, he would have been turning out on a park elsewhere in the city: 'I just wanted to play at whatever level I achieved it. I just loved playing.' His dad did take him to Elland Road, but also all over Yorkshire to see other teams, and the one he remembers best was the Doncaster one managed by Bremner and featuring the Snodin brothers.

The bond with the Elland Road crowd, recognizing one of its own, was a real one though – a bond no better illustrated than in the almost four-year saga of waiting for a goal. He scored his first for the club in his sixth game, but then nothing. In the first season the lack of finishing was noticed, but barely remarked upon. In the second, as players who appeared a quarter as often managed a goal, it became his idiosyncrasy. In the third it became a joke, with shouts of 'Shoot!' every time he took the ball over the half-way line and exaggerated 'Oohs' for anything that even managed to trickle out for a goal kick. The goal finally came in the fourth season and 145 games since the last. On the Kop there was absolute bedlam, the release after three years and nine months of waiting.

A smile spread across Batty's face as he remembered the

days: 'I scored a good goal after about six or seven games and didn't attach too much importance to it. I thought, there's more to come because, although I'd never been prolific, I've always got a few. But then it just never came and the reaction was unbelievable. If I had a shot it got more applause than anyone else scoring. The feeling of the fans for me at that time was unbelievable. When I actually scored they were as pleased, if not more pleased, than me. I can still remember that feeling. Tremendous, it was. Tremendous.'

If there was one player who seemed set for a one-club career, to echo that of his mentor Bremner – even after he was sacked and replaced by Howard Wilkinson – it was Batty. His place in the club's history, his part as the latest strand in its long thread, was reinforced when he appeared in Charles's testimonial, a benefit match shared with another of Revie's first signings, Collins. But it was a Leeds side with a difference which took on Collins's ex-club Everton, one which included Michel Platini and Ian Rush, representing Juve and showing the esteem in which Charles was held, and Kenny Dalglish too. And the irony was that it was the night which led to Batty's eventual departure, in a transfer as shocking and unsought as Charles's had been.

Dalglish took note of the impressive tyro winning the ball for him. He asked for first refusal if Leeds ever sold and the day came five and a half years later. Batty had no desire to leave. Wilkinson had no wish to sell. But the club, again, simply had to. In the summer the board had approved the purchase of one of Batty's ex-Leeds schools team-mates, Brian Deane, expecting to fund the fee with an overdraft to be quickly repaid by the sale of another home-grown star, Gary Speed. His transfer, however, fell through and the loan needed repaying by October. Batty, the loyal servant, the fans' favourite, became an asset, sold for exactly the £2.7 million which Deane cost, gone within a day.

The deal was as much of a shock for the player as it was for fans: 'Usually if there's transfer talk it goes on for weeks, it's in the papers and you hear about it, then it goes through. It was a Monday morning when Wilkinson said they'd had an offer from Blackburn and that the directors had told him to ask me if I wanted to go. Well, once they say that, they're willing to let you go and it's time to go. I called Kenny from Elland Road and went over to see him that afternoon and signed then. It was that quick it was unbelievable. 'Cos my mum and dad were back in Leeds, I was aware of the outcry – phone votes, front and back pages on the papers and everything – but it was the right time to go. I'd become a bit stale. I had some great times there and even now there's a lot of people who say, "You know we need you back at Leeds." It's been four years since I left, which is a long time in football with the turnover in players now, and it's nice to know that they still think of me as a Leeds lad and they'd like me back. You never know, one day . . .'

One day he will also have to stop playing. Like Lorimer, he has no desire to stay in football: 'You have to fill your life in some way when you finish playing. As it is I've no interest in staying in the game, and I've no real interests outside the game, so I don't know what I'll do.' The difference is that he won't have to find a job, run a pub or whatever, to meet the bills: 'I'm all right. If I stopped playing tomorrow, if I were injured or whatever, I'd be all right. I'm fortunate. I realize that I'm lucky that I can choose what to go into – if I want to go into anything. I might just opt for playing golf or whatever. But it's great to have that option.'

When he signed his first professional contract Batty earned £250 a week. How much now? He laughed again and said, 'I'm all right. It's gone up a little bit with inflation. But you don't think of money or what you're going to be doing or earning ten years from when you start. You don't do it for the money, although it's changed a little bit now because money is the be-all and end-all to a lot of players. Whether that's right or wrong, it's immaterial, 'cos if that's what motivates them, that's what motivates them. But I never thought ten years ago I'd be financially secure. I just played for love of the game. I still do.'

And he appreciates more than most what it's given him. His dad is a binman, always has been and still is now. One closed season, just before he won his first England cap in 1991, he joined the round. Several fans living on it got a shock when they saw their club's brightest young talent humping bin bags for hour after clammy hour. Batty remembered: 'Some people were surprised to see us. But it was good bit of training – you got a good sweat up. I did it for a couple of days, like, but I wouldn't fancy doing it for a living and it makes you appreciate what you've got. My dad still does it. It's hard work. He does well for his age. I tell him to pack it in, like, but he enjoys it, has a good crack with the lads. That's what he'd miss.'

It's what players often say they miss when they retire too – and it was easy to see why. The room had filled up with familiar faces, but wearing unfamiliar expressions, at ease, reading papers and pointing out the gossip, shouting out jokes. There was John Barnes, idly watching Sky Sports as he had been – and lobbing laddish comments at the screen and at 'Batts' – when we walked in. There was Philippe Albert, lumbering around slightly stiffly in the three-striped and discreetly numbered training kit everyone but me was wearing. And somewhere behind me was Alan Shearer, the real Alan Shearer.

At first I didn't even notice him as Batty chatted away in front of me, the background noise levels rising as the room filled up. Then a disconcerting grin spread across Batty's face before he laughed out loud and shouted back over my shoulder. I turned around to see who it was aimed at and Shearer looked back, wearing an expression of utterly bemused innocence. Face as blank as a poker player's, he lowered his eyes to his paper and read as if that was exactly what he had been doing before. Batty laughed again and resumed our interview.

ɾor years no profile of Shearer has been complete without mention of his supposedly dour character. I'd asked his agent months before about interviewing him with his dad – the sheet-metal worker whom Shearer often mentions – to try to meet him in his family habitat, but got no further than 'a polite "no"'. But I'd probably have learned no more than in just that split second of seeing the real him – an ordinary bloke, gifted with extraordinary footballing ability and therefore also extraordinary profile and wealth – with his team-mates, enjoying an atmosphere little different, I suspect, from his dad's metal works or on Batty's dad's bin run.

When I'd finished my interview with Batty, I had to wait around. He went off to the gym to work on his fitness, ready for his comeback, while the rest of the squad went to the training pitches. A couple of hours later I was still waiting when he re-emerged. In between I'd watched the school holiday auto-graph-hunters gather at the front entrance of the centre, most wearing the ubiquitous black and white stripes. A man in a suit had walked in past them and they hadn't even looked up: Freddy Shepherd, the director who'd ridiculed the loyalty of such fans, but had recently slithered back into the boardroom.

When Batty and I wandered to the entrance and out through it to try to take a look at the county cricket match on Durham's luscious Riverside ground opposite, the pack stood still for a second, unable to believe that one of their heroes was just standing there, and then swamped him. I left him to it – and when I wandered back outside a good fifteen minutes later he was still there, signing away. Freddy Shepherd was nowhere to be seen.

In the 1990s, not long after he won a championship medal with binman's son Batty, Gary Speed was given a new nickname by a bloke in front of me on the Kop: Golden Bollocks.

It was hard to know what he objected to most – Speed's curly ringlets of long hair, his supposed, and I suspect related, absence of Northern grit or, most outrageously of all, the sideline in modelling. But object he most certainly did.

His discontent seemed polite, though, compared to the language used a couple of seasons later on Merseyside when Speed's desire to leave the club he had joined from Leeds, the club he supported as a boy, Everton, became known. Some supporters sent hate mail. Discontent rumbled across the back pages of the newspapers, especially when it was claimed that Speed had turned down a new contract which would have doubled his wages.

Here, apparently, was the latest example of the selfish, modern footballer, a playing successor to Charles, with the same Leeds and Wales pedigree, the same ability to play terrifically all over the park, but the size of his salary – and the Premier League players' *average* is now £175,000 a year – away from the sort of glowing humility and fidelity displayed by the Gentle Giant. Speed submitted a written transfer request, refused to travel on the team bus to an away game and was stripped of the captaincy. A week later he got the move he wanted, to Newcastle, who had bid for him three times, for £5.5 million.

For months I had been trying to arrange an interview with him, and with Batty at the same time, through the club's press office. When it was agreed and I finally travelled to the training ground, I was told to just grab him as he entered. So I did and he said, 'Oh no. I can't now.' The selfish stuff of back-page legend, or so it seemed. But not that surprising when seen in the context of the parade of famous, but largely sour, faces that was also trooping in.

It was a Friday and reporters were milling around by the front door, poised to fire interview requests at whichever player they wanted for the pre-match previews. The players in turn wore their noncommittal public faces. Keith Gillespie, mobile phone to ear, steering with his knee, drove in first, not meeting any of the eyes which followed his progress in or from his car.

John Barnes parked his executive saloon with blacked-out windows, strolled towards the door nonchalantly chewing gum and walked through a reporter's request with a brusque, 'No, not today.' Manager Kenny Dalglish was one of the last in, managing a put-upon smile and a 'Morning, boys' as he locked his top-of-the-range Jaguar.

But inside, while Dalglish took the formal press conference, the players relaxed before training. Speed soon came up as I talked to Batty and apologized, explaining that he'd been running a bit late, suggested that we chat later on and, when I had to cancel that to get a train, gave me his mobile phone number, unprompted, to arrange another time. When I met him for the second time he briefly put me off again because he had an urgent call to make – and then called his wife to say an extra training session had been ordered and he wouldn't be home to baby-sit until later.

In fact he had little to say beyond what I'd already heard. Like Lorimer, he was a juvenile record-breaker – the youngest-ever player for his county and a serial scorer, once netting in twelve consecutive Leeds youth-team games – but struggled to remember specific incidents (apart from when he first captained his country). Like Gray, he was a gifted left-sided midfielder who fondly remembered team spirit, in his case of the title-winners of 1992, and its loss. Like his friend Batty, he happily recalled the help Bremner gave on the training pitch and the thrill of the championship season.

His career highlights were the same as the others, the medals he'd won, but more importantly the fact that he'd avoided injury. The lowlights similar: failures such as losing in the Coca-Cola Cup Final and missing out on the World Cup finals, but luckily no serious injuries. And he was well aware of his good fortune: 'It's the best job in the world. You're outside, playing football, then going home in the afternoons a lot of the time. There's a lot of pressure at times, but you get well paid and you're doing what you love doing.'

Perhaps most revealing was that while, like Batty, he needn't work again, he wanted to – and, like Eddie Gray, in football, because he simply loves the game: 'I just couldn't sit at home doing nothing, I'd have to do something when I finish playing and I hope it's in football. I'd like to play until I was thirty-five or something and then move into coaching or managing. I just love being on the pitch. I love being outside, playing football. That's what I'd want to keep doing.'

Then the water bomb sailed past and exploded with a plop at our feet. We were sitting on a bench overlooking the training pitches, where a few of the fringe members of the squad were knocking long passes to each other and practising a few juggling tricks. But the bench was also below the window and balcony of the players' lounge, from where the loaded plastic bag came, and fatally with its back to the building. 'That'll be Shearer, won't it?' Speed laughed. But it was Batty who soon afterwards appeared on the balcony, grinning.

We continued talking for a little while longer – him swerving out of the way of another water bomb, which he saw coming after wisely rearranging himself so he could watch the balcony at all times – about how nights out, which he used to manage occasionally, are no longer possible because of the added pressure of the game and its demands on fitness; about his favourite position – central midfield – and his hope that he might be able to convince Newcastle to play him there more often; about why he gave up the modelling – for Top Shop – because it was a distraction from playing.

I left him to get back to the afternoon training, to the well-paid job which means that if he does move into management and one day gets sacked, he won't have to worry about how he'll support his family. No doubt, he's lucky to be wealthy beyond any dreams he could have had; no doubt he and Batty and the others are privileged (but, remember, exceedingly talented too). What I always come back to, though, alongside Eddie Gray's *second* goal against Burnley, Batty's four-season goal drought and watching Speed play at Wembley in that Coca-Cola Cup Final, our first cup final in twenty-three years, is that we're privileged to watch them. And that some players have still got only memories.

Peter Haddock helps to run a bakery shop. As the 1990s come to a close, with the next generation such as Rob Bowman and Andy Couzens in Carlisle and elsewhere, 'Fish', as he once was, cashes up at the end of every day and tries not to think about the past. But struggles to think about the future too.

He was still finishing up at the shop when I arrived at his modest house on a modern estate on the outskirts of the ex-pit village of Cramlington, near Newcastle. His oldest son, also Peter and almost a teenager, was kicking a ball against the garage wall and dribbling around the drive – a common enough sight except for one thing: here, in the heart of what Newcastle chairman Sir John Hall called the Geordie nation, where black and white stripes are the uniform, Peter was wearing a Liverpool top.

Inside he sat quietly and listened to the story which explained the red shirt. His dad told it as best he could, but with longer pauses, in more faltering sentences, as he went on. Gary Speed had recalled it with a shake of the head and described it as 'a horror story'. David Batty too had re-membered Fish in an instant and said, 'He was a great lad was Peter and a great player too, vastly underrated. Probably us on the pitch were the only ones who really appreciated the job he was doing. He was so adaptable, he could play in all the different positions, he had the pace and he could play. It was terrible how his career ended.'

In the easy chair in his living room, remembering the days he played with Batty and Speed, he looked different, though. The 1980s long-at-the-back, short-on-the-sides haircut was gone and the moustache too, while the newly exposed, clean-shaven face was slightly chubbier, an indicator of the few extra pounds he was carrying compared to his playing days. But it's difficult to stay in trim when you can barely run. 'I've got arthritis in the knee. It doesn't bend or extend properly and I just get pain in it all the time,' he said, almost matter-of-fact, in his gentle Geordie tones.

The pain is about all he has for fulfilling his dream, every schoolboy's dream. Ever since he could kick a ball he wanted to be a footballer. He played in the same boys' side as Peter Beardsley and was signed by Newcastle when Beardsley was initially ignored. He broke into the first team in 1981, but only after one of his friends trekked into the city centre on a Friday night to find him and tell him he had to get to London. He explained: 'One of the lads who travelled down to QPR had gone down with blood poisoning or something on the Friday night, so I had to get the train down on Saturday morning and get a cab from King's Cross. But I was out on the Friday night and me mam didn't have a phone, so they had to get a hold of one of me mates and he had to come find us.'

At St James's Park he had another local lad, a fizzing cocktail of hyperactive humour and ability, as his bootboy: one Paul Gascoigne. Peter said, 'He couldn't even clean the boots properly – he'd be off doing something else, something he wasn't supposed to, all the time.' He also witnessed the transformation when Kevin Keegan arrived as a player in the early 1980s to stage his first messiah act at a club which was otherwise on a relentless downward slide. But Peter was a bit-part player in the gathering momentum, sidelined by a series of injuries, including a serious knee ligament one which took the best part of a season to overcome, and then only a squad player when fit. In all he played sixty or seventy times in five seasons before, 'sick of not getting a game', he agreed to join Bremner at Leeds.

In his first season he was again restricted by injuries, but still managed to play in the FA Cup semifinal at Hillsborough. He scored his only goal for the club in the game the following season in which Batty made his debut. He went on to win supporters' club player of the year. When Bremner was sacked the next season, he won over new manager Wilkinson too and was at the heart of the defence which won promotion the year after, in 1990. In the aftermath of the celebrations Wilkinson said that he was his personal player of the year. Then in the summer he signed a new centre-half and Peter began the new season, what was to be his last season, as a squad player.

He was in the team, as left-back, for the biggest game of the season though, the League Cup semifinal second leg against Manchester United. Along with his team-mates, he was a mere ninety minutes from a possible Wembley appearance. But also playing his last minutes of first-team football, about to see his dream shattered in front of a full house at Elland Road. It was an innocuous incident: 'I went up to head a ball with Paul Ince. The pitch at the time was terrible, unbelievable – there were massive holes all over it – and when I came down my foot landed in one and my leg twisted as I fell. I felt the knee go. I was waving at the bench straight away. I just knew it was serious from when I'd done my knee, the other one, before.'

He was carried off on a stretcher, changed out of his kit in agony in the dressing room and went off to hospital, where it became clear just how serious the injury was. Two ligaments in his knee were snapped, as was the cartilage under his kneecap. The doctors told him it would be months before he could even walk again, let alone consider playing. He began the lonely and tough route to recovery, first light workouts once the plaster came off, then weights and harder circuits. Meanwhile, the team was only adding to his unhappiness – by flourishing, hammering Villa 4–1 and Wednesday 6–1. He said, 'That was one of the worst things. You're in the club all the time, trying to get fit, and you see the success, the team spirit, you see what you're missing out on, and you can't help thinking, I should be there as well. You have to put a brave face on, but it was awful, just painful in itself.'

So when Batty and Speed were holding the league trophy aloft in front of an endless ocean of glee gathered in the centre of Leeds, Peter was there, but not there. He was at the civic reception, but his part in the celebrations was muted. For a start he lacked the medal the others had won. But he was also beginning to realize that he wouldn't be playing with them again. 'I knew when I was coming back, training, that it wasn't right. I was getting terrible pain in it, I couldn't bend it properly. It took about eighteen months and a couple of reserve games before I realized. Then eventually I just stopped going in. It was too painful and I knew it wasn't worth it. I wasn't going to play again.' An operation confirmed the diagnosis and, as his team-mates defended the title, he was forced to retire.

There was more pain to come, however. Leeds paid up his contract, a relic of the pre-Sky days and only enough to put towards a small business or save for a drizzly day, but there was quickly talk of a testimonial too, with Newcastle the obvious opponents. At the end of the season he spoke to his former team-mate Keegan, who was then manager of a side newly promoted into the new Premier League. 'He said he'd send a team, no problem. It was all agreed. Then I got a call off Freddy Shepherd, who cancelled it. He said they had too many pre-season games to play and they just couldn't help.' A game was played, against Bradford, but it drew a fraction of the crowd a rejuvenated Newcastle would have against the recent league champions.

In the living room the red of Liverpool suddenly made sense. Peter finished the story, tears in his eyes now, but there is no happy ending. He carried on living in a Yorkshire commuter village for a while, looking for a job in football, but nothing came up, so he sold up and moved home with enough to buy the bakery shop. But he's not happy: 'It's not what I want to do, but I don't know what else I want to do. All I ever wanted from the age of fourteen was to be a professional footballer, that's all I thought about and that's all I did and now that's gone. It's been devastating. You just don't know what to do with yourself. An absolute nightmare.'

A couple of times he's seen Batty and Speed playing at St James's Park, but he is, unsurprisingly, no regular. Instead he has his memories, collected in a small bar area just off the living room. There's a signed shirt from his testimonial and photographs of the night. There's another shirt, the one worn in the promotion season when he was player of the year, and the trophy itself nearby, along with other mementoes. And there's a third shirt, an England one, also donated for the testimonial (thanks to Batty approaching its original owner), but kept as a memento – and from the man often cited as representing all that's wrong with players: one Paul Gascoigne, the bootboy who remembered where others forgot.

france

When our supporters go to Europe, they are preceded by this [tarnished] reputation. It is expected they will behave badly, so whether they do so initially or not they are likely to meet a hostile reception from their counterparts. Thus incidents are provoked and the syndrome continues.

Lord Justice Taylor's final report, paragraph 57

In the end it was actually easy, remarkably easy. I sat down for an early breakfast at one of the cafés overlooking the Place de la Comédie, the grand plaza which is the tranquil heart of Montpellier. I sleepily thumbed through my guidebooks, plotting a route to the stadium and working out how long I had to find a ticket. I moved on to my copy of the information leaflet that I'd picked up in London and before I could even get to its fourth point – 'If you do not already have a ticket, you will not be able to get into a match' – the first tout, in the uniform of baseball cap and puffa jacket, strolled up. It had taken me fourteen hours to get to the World Cup, and roughly fourteen minutes to get a ticket, without even trying.

The idea was to get to as many games as possible. I had drawn up a list of up to nine which could be fitted in a schedule initially based around the South of France and which, more importantly, might be among those with tickets at less than absurd prices. That meant no matches involving Brazil or Jamaica, no Holland–Belgium and no Iran–USA, which would all have been on an ideal itinerary. Instead my first target was Paraguay–Bulgaria: the least glamorous South American side against the most impoverished European competitor. I guessed that it would be the worst-attended game of the tournament, the one for which the black market would be nearest to a budget buyer's market.

And it was. For a little over the face value of £15 – the average weekly wage in Bulgaria – the tout handed over one ticket to the multicoloured, multiracial and multinational carnival which is the greatest sporting occasion on earth. In fact I had even more than that. As an afterthought I'd asked about availability for another game on my list, one later that day in Marseilles, an hour away. Yeah, the tout shrugged, fumbling about in his bum-bag, peeling another ticket off his wad, and, for a combined price of £55 compared to a face value of £40, I was also going to see the host country play in its first World Cup finals fixture for twelve years, against tournament debutants and probable future hosts South Africa, in the best stadium after the Stade de France, among fans supposedly the most passionate in the country. Easy.

The only question was whether I would get into either ground, or any ground. For months television advertisements aimed at deterring the ticketless from travelling had been showing an Englishman who was conspicuously not the Jean Pierre Baptiste named on his ticket being turned away at a turnstile. The Foreign Office-produced leaflet, which I'd quickly put back in my bag with the tickets and was the second prong of a £1-million campaign, clearly reinforced the message: 'All tickets sold to French residents will have the name of the buyer printed on them. If you buy a ticket with someone else's name on, that ticket becomes invalid.' The French authorities also claimed that there would be three sets of checkpoints – and indeed that afternoon at the Stade de la Mosson there were.

None of the police or stewards, however, asked me to prove I was a Monsieur Grevstad – perhaps because I wasn't wearing an England top like the man in the advertisements. A few feet away from the first of the checks other touts were holding bundles of tickets, selling at below face value as kick-off approached. Four months earlier, as Home Secretary Jack Straw had launched the 'Don't Travel' campaign, the French officer in charge of World Cup policing had said, 'If we see a group of organized touts we will move in and arrest everybody, those who are buying and those who are selling.'[1] But the clusters of police closest to the thriving black market were as utterly uninterested in it as their colleagues were in me. Remarkably easy.

In Marseilles in the evening no one asked me to prove I was with the local council, as my ticket suggested, and there was an even larger coven of touts, spreading from the exits of the underground station. The most organized were local youths flanked by mates and outriders on mountain bikes, the most sheepish offered one or two tickets in broad South African accents. Again prices tumbled in the countdown to kick-off; again the police, line after line of them, looked impassively past the buyers and sellers – and even the incredible sight of an early stray from the Tartan Army. It wasn't his kilt and big boots, however, which made him remarkable, although the locals were as amused at his attire as all of France would be for as long as Scotland were around, but the spare ticket he was struggling to get rid of – even though he was giving it away.

The Bulldog was the first reminder of why the journey, the overpriced tickets and football, in fact, were worth all the effort.

José Luis Chilavert was just a name and an indistinct face

in a magazine picture of the Paraguayan team until Montpellier. He was supposedly one of the world's best goalkeepers,
but was as famous for a fiery streak as colourful as his kit. His
temper explained his blurred image on the photograph, his
features frozen in a wide-eyed scream of support for his slightly
cowed-looking colleagues; and also the tussle with a ballboy
which resulted in a three-month jail sentence in Argentina,
where he played his club football; and the subsequent comments on the Argentinian justice system, which had to be
soothed with the diplomatic help of the Paraguayan ambassa-
dor in Buenos Aires; and the attack on Faustino Asprilla which
almost cost his side its World Cup place.

Without him, suspended for four games, the defence went
to pieces, conceding as many goals in three defeats as it had
in the previous ten qualifying games. They had lost more than
their goalkeeper and captain, but their backbone and general
inspiration too. The attack was blunted as well, as Chilavert
was the side's free-kick specialist and penalty-taker. He had
scored more than forty goals, including four for his country,
one of them a crucial strike against Argentina in qualifying.
And he had just one individual ambition in the World Cup:
to become the first keeper to score in the finals.

In the dying minutes against Bulgaria his chance came. In
the pre-match warm-up he spent more time practising his aim
than his catching, so, as soon as the referee blew for a free-kick
on the right-hand edge of the Bulgarian box a little under
ninety minutes later, there was no doubt who would take it.
Chilavert jogged upfield, while his right-back dropped back
to guard the net, and stood over the ball, incongruous in his
black and orange kit among team-mates in blue and white.
Left-footed, he hit the ball with power and precise curl, and
watched it clear the defensive wall and arrow towards the far
corner and history – until his Bulgarian opposite number,
Zdravkov, flung himself high to his right and deflected it away.

On television it would have been the highlight of a dull 0–0 draw. A Bulgarian shot against the post and then a sending-off were the only other moments of real note. In the flesh, though, it was a reminder of what makes football great: the sublime skill, of course; but the sounds too – the thud of the ball, the gasp of the crowd and the applause which washed around the ground; and, most of all, the delighted supporters who delivered it, and who gave Chilavert a standing ovation all the way back to his goal while he muttered to himself darkly and ruefully shook his head.

Again, it was a matter of being there, of almost being able to say, 'That goalie who scored? Yeah, I saw that.' To hear the anguished scream of Bulgaria's Chilavert-tempered forward Stoichkov too, and the thump when he kicked the advertising board right in front of us after he carved an opening, only for a team-mate to waste it. To see Balakov have his head swathed in a bandage which made him look like a hapless extra in *Casualty* (and play like it too) and the terrifying size of Ivanov's thighs. To hear and see the supporters: the Bulgarians, at the other end of the ground, who'd spent the morning gathered on a fountain in the city centre singing songs no one else recognized or understood, but everyone enjoyed and applauded anyway; and in our end the Paraguayans, a South American stew of red, white and blue, Latin beauties and bad trumpeting. And, of course, the inevitable strays from the Tartan Army, two of them this time, wearing comic ginger wigs.

Being part of it, like the hard-drinking New Zealanders on the train from London (City workers; tickets off someone they knew) and the softly spoken Irishman next to me, and nineteen empty seats, in the ground who was at his fifth successive World Cup (tickets off touts). To chat to the Yorkshireman in the Leeds shirt leaving France–South Africa about the performance of our club's captain, Lucas Radebe, in the game and the lad in the Welsh top at Montpellier station about the nationality of a player who shares his home town with Gary

Speed, who broke Ian Rush's schoolboy scoring record and who appeared for Welsh school sides, but plays for England: Michael Owen. And to boycott the irritating Mexican wave, which circled the Stade de la Mosson ground a tiresome five times.

Even to be part of it when you weren't at a match. I returned to Montpellier after a night in Marseilles hoping to see a unique event: a replay of the 1986 Brazil against France quarterfinal on the giant screen set up at one end of the Place de la Comédie, with two orchestras – one for each team, obviously – accompanying the action. Luckily, the date had been changed, so instead I was treated to an even greater show: Spain against Nigeria, and the people of Montpellier.

To begin with there were perhaps a couple of hundred of us, augmented by Saturday afternoon shoppers who stopped for a moment or two to see what this World Cup was about. Then the drama hooked them. Hierro scored, a free-kick, for Spain after twenty-one minutes; Adepoju equalized for Nigeria three minutes later. Raul, who had almost scored after twelve seconds and hit the bar after four minutes, finally found the net at the start of the second half, smacking a volley home after watching and waiting for a long ball to drop over his right shoulder on to his already swinging left foot. Then the Nigerians equalized again, Lawal dancing through the defence and crossing for Zubizarreta to deflect into his own net.

By then the crowd had swelled to fill the entire area in front of the screen. Those still heading to the modern shopping centre whose entrance faced the screen had to push through the rear of a crowd 'oohing' and 'aahing' every few moments. Among it were more black faces than I'd seen in all of France so far, all cheering the Nigerians. So too most of the rest of the crowd, in a city so close to Spain itself. Then the ball came to Sunday Oliseh, who hit a drive so unstoppable, so unbelievably powerful, that he ran off celebrating wearing a look which said, 'Did you see *that*?'

Almost the entire length of France away, a crowd now at least 1,000-strong in the centre of Montpellier jumped up and down (the black guys) or high-fived each other (the students in backpacks and trainers or Spice Girl wedges) or just clapped and grinned (the rest of us) at the goal, at Oliseh's joy and the greatness of the game, not Spain–Nigeria, but The Game. Nearby, a giant version of Footix, the mascot of France '98, had been screeching '*Buuuuuut*' every hour of every day in the countdown to the kick-off of the tournament. Even the earache from that would seem worthwhile if the World Cup was all going to be as spectacular as this.

In fact, it was a bit of an illusion. There were more treasured moments to come, more afternoons and evenings of football and festival – indeed, one of the best of them in my next destination. But the shortcomings of the tournament, the problems, old and new, were beginning to become apparent. Problems which even the greatest games couldn't disguise. The first was the ticketing system Michel Platini had defended at the Stade de France.

I was travelling to Toulouse to try to find a Japanese called Asahi Ueda. When I finally caught up with him, I quickly realized that his English wasn't great, despite the year he spent living in Milton Keynes. Or Miro-Cans, as he called it. But between his valiant mispronunciations and the vast pauses as he struggled for vocabulary, he managed one almost comically sophisticated phrase with easy fluency: the black market.

It was no surprise. Asahi was just one of the best-organized, most devoted and worst-treated fans in France – the estimated 30,000 who made the furthest journey from any competing country. One of the many who spent up to £5,000 for a trip to the World Cup, only to find just one thing missing: a ticket. On the eve of the first game, the one for which I was heading, against Argentina, at least eight travel agents aborted trips, leaving 12,500 fans who thought they were going to France at home.

On the train I read that they were not alone: as many as 25,000 fans in Germany were reported to have been fleeced, with many trips to their country's first game with the USA cancelled; thousands of Dutch fans, more than 500 of whom had won tickets in the national lottery, had fallen victim to the spate of unofficial ticket agencies which took money but didn't provide tickets, as had 20,000 Belgians heading for the match against the Dutch; and 700 Brazilians and 400 Scots who were also said to have been ripped off by another unauthorized operator.

Many were indirect victims of the collapse of a single London-based firm, Great Portland Entertainments, which was supposed to be supplying tickets to many of the agencies. Tickets which came from Football Associations and from elsewhere on the blackest of black markets. One alleged scam even involved the head of the French subsidiary of FIFA's marketing arm, who was arrested in connection with the sale of 30,000 fake tickets. The response of the French organizing committee? Simple: it's not our fault – and we'll sue anyone who suggests otherwise. And Sepp Blatter of FIFA, which would be an estimated £50 million richer after the tournament? Straightforward too: I'm sorry for the fans, but what can we do about it? But another promise to review the ticket policy.

In Toulouse the human cost of the incompetence, and hand-washing, was obvious when I received my first desperate plea for a ticket within seconds of stepping off the train. All the way through the city centre miserable-looking huddles of Japanese held scrawny pieces of cardboard all with variations of 'I want ticket.' By the time I got to the Place du Capitole, the central square, the going rate on the black market was FF10,000. About £1,000. Every local who loitered for a couple of seconds to admire the World Cup spectacle, a party which was beginning to go a bit flat, was surrounded by eager, then disappointed, faces.

For the fans the fiasco was an utter calamity following the complete joy of reaching the World Cup finals for the first time. Or as Asahi put it, 'I was really disappointed as if I were in hell.' Being there to see the team was part an act of devotion, part an act of vindication: confirmation that Japanese football had arrived on the world stage. Coach Takeshi Okada said, 'When we kick off against Argentina the world will see us in a new light, as one more member of the family of football nations.'[2] And at the last possible tournament before it hosts that family by co-staging the next World Cup.

The shaggy-haired, cheery-faced Asahi played an important role in securing the 2002 finals by organizing a petition of 200,000 fans in support of the bid. That was part of the reason I wanted to see him. To find out more about football in Japan, as well, from the leader of the Ultras Nippon and the man responsible for a touchingly cross-lingual World Cup record, '*Allez Japon*'. But mainly because he's a Leeds fan and I was intrigued to find out how and why. The answer was simple: because they were the best team at the time he was studying in England earlier this decade. Like almost all Japanese fans, his loyalties have been that recently formed.

For Japan is the national home of New Football. One of the teams in the J-League – the country's first professional league, established only in 1993 – is even called the Red Diamonds in honour of the Red Devils. The difference is that the league went from Newton Heath to the Theatre of Dreams in a matter of months. Foreign talent was recruited to help launch it. Fans quickly found their favourites and started chanting and singing in support of players such as Gary Lineker and Zico. Now, the devotion is still such that many supporters head to the ground hours early to make sure of their place, and a high percentage of them are women. Pre-World Cup, attendances were up by 30 per cent and Japanese players were even being signed by European clubs.

Toulouse was alive with the evidence of what the estimated

£400-million investment in football, from sponsors and club owners such as Nissan and Panasonic, has achieved in a country where the national sport is baseball. There were fans with their hair bleached white and a red sun dyed in the middle, others in kimonos, but almost all in replica kit – most in full replica kit: shirt, shorts, socks and trainers – as if the world's most numerous five-a-side team was in town (and showing why the J-League made more money in merchandising in its first season than baseball had in its entire history). Some had the name Kazu, one player who had been transferred to Europe, on the back of their blue shirts (although his move to Italian club Genoa was later said to have been encouraged by one of its shareholders, Toyota). And while the fans desperately hunted for tickets, two-thirds of the Japanese FA's official allocation was reported to have gone to sponsors and VIPs – which is hardly a good sign for anyone wanting to travel to the 2002 World Cup.

Asahi too was at the ground hours before the kick-off, as usual, leaving me to speak to him later. I wasn't going to get a ticket, so I just concentrated on enjoying the atmosphere of watching the match on the big screen set up in a ribbon of parkland running alongside the river which ambles through the city centre. I strolled along the riverside walkway which overlooked the park and the screen itself, watching hundreds and hundreds of ticketless Japanese and Argentinians who had settled for second best drape their flags and themselves over the wall at the edge of the path. An hour before kick-off every spot was taken, every plastic chair claimed and being used by those in the back row of the five-deep crowd. At ground level, though, there were hundreds of empty seats lined up in front of and corralled by metal barriers. I walked through the entrance gap and was stopped by an urgent '*Non, non*' and the large bouncer who barked them. They had been reserved by Japanese corporate hospitality.

*

I bumped into Sir Bobby Charlton at the station after the game. I even helped carry his bags on to the train. He was standing there on the platform with the delegation from the 2006 bid, who had also been at Argentina–Japan, but in the stadium, to talk to the next hosts and continue the charm offensive. Alongside Sir Bobby, Alec McGivan said he was pleased at how it was going.

He had reason to be – and not just because another of his ambassadors, Geoff Hurst, had coincidentally just been knighted. Far more importantly, the election for Joao Havelange's successor as FIFA president had been held just before the tournament started and the FA had taken an enormous political gamble – and apparently won handsomely. A matter of days before the ballot was held it made a high-profile switch from supporting UEFA president Lennart Johannson, as almost all European countries were, to backing Havelange's number two, Sepp Blatter. The reason was simple: Johannson was thought to back Germany's 2006 bid, often citing the disputed deal which the FA was alleged to have reneged upon; Blatter thought it only right England should bid.

When news of the switch broke, Johannson, the man who personally cleared the way for English clubs to return to European competition after the post-Heysel ban, and who had Sir Bobby endorsing his campaign, was furious. He said, 'The English have shown yet again that they do not keep their word – they did the same over the bid for the 2006 World Cup.'[3] Some Premier League chairmen were said to have been unhappy at the U-turn, fearing the Swede might take out his anger on them whenever much-mooted discussions on the lucrative reform of European competitions took place.

Neither was Blatter exactly pro-England 2006. His preference was for South Africa. But, with crime at epidemic levels and questions being asked over the logistical ability of Nelson Mandela's country to hold the finals, McGivan was quietly hoping that being second best for the moment might become something more soon. 'If the World Cup is coming to Europe in 2006, it is coming to England,' he said. 'A year ago we were told we would not even be allowed to put ourselves forward. Now we are the leading European candidate and, we believe, the best in the world.'[4]

On the platform at Toulouse station he gave me the same confident message. He didn't mention the other 2006-related news from Paris: the split between the English and Welsh and the Scottish and Northern Irish FAs over Britain's automatic vice-presidency[5] of FIFA. The English was still keen for Keith Wiseman to replace David Will and the Welsh were supporting them – in return, it was reported, for £700,000 a year over six years. But in contrast to the unfolding action of the tournament, it appeared to be nothing more than a diversion, albeit a generous one.

Soon the train came and he went off to find the first-class seats for Sir Bobby and himself. For the journey to Marseilles.

A matter of weeks before Italia '90, there was a superb example of how not to ensure a trouble-free match. The starting point was when the fixture list scheduled a game loaded with the potential for violence. The catalyst was allowing the obviously inadvisable kick-off time, and day, to stand, even though it gave the significant unruly element among the large, and largely ticketless, travelling support a weekend of drinking – and in a seaside resort too – in which to lubricate their tempers. Finally, a merely likely riot became bloody fact as final escape clauses such as an alcohol ban or other measures to prevent the ticketless from gathering around seafront bars were over-looked.

In Bournemouth, the result was that a sunny Bank Holiday weekend became the stage for a weekend of destruction and a pitched battle. A drunken mob went on the rampage, smashing bars, cars and shops, fighting with locals first – mugging them for tickets – and police later. Hundreds of ticketless fans confronted officers outside the ground, hurling bottles, bricks and stones. Eventually more than 120 people were arrested, twenty injured – including seven police officers, one a woman who was punched in the face – and the bill for the damage estimated at up to £1 million. And the visitors were, of course, Leeds.

Football League officials confirmed that they had received two pleas from the police to reschedule the game, one as soon as it had first been listed eleven months earlier, the other, from the Chief Constable, a matter of weeks before kick-off. In between Taylor had written, 'It may well be sensible to limit the availability of alcohol, especially before a high-risk match' and 'There is . . . much to be said for an early kick-off especially in a high-risk match. It gives less opportunity for prolonged drinking sessions . . . less time for early arrivals to kick their heels and lift their elbows in bars.'[6] But the League men sheepishly admitted that its management committee had not even been informed of the police requests.

Reaction was the same as ever. Leeds said they had done all they could and were fined, again. UEFA president, one Lennart Johannson, mused out loud that the ban on English clubs in Europe might remain despite his efforts, but indicated that he would do what he could. Home Secretary David Waddington said he hoped that the football authorities would be more aware about scheduling in the future and also pointed to powers fresh on the statute book which would help suffocate hooliganism: restriction orders.

In Marseilles, there were the same factors, with an even worse result. England were drawn to play by the seaside – but in a sunny city with a violent underbelly of disaffected immigrants, many of whom supported opponents Tunisia; it was a game loaded with the potential for violence. The kick-off was confirmed for a Monday lunch time, even though it gave the significant unruly element among the large, and largely ticketless, travelling support a weekend of drinking, and in a seaside resort, to lubricate their tempers. And the alcohol bans, which had been imposed wherever England played in Italia '90, were deemed unnecessary. Restriction orders, we already know about.

The result was never in doubt. On the Saturday there were the first, relatively minor skirmishes, the usual eve-of-game preliminaries of running around the streets, hurling bottles and, no doubt, singing 'No Surrender'. But it was on Sunday, the real eve of the action – in this case both on and off the field – when the real riot, the proper violence and the 'C'mon, England' charges began. When a couple of hundred fans, a tiny fraction of the English in and about Marseilles, ensured that everyone who shared their nationality would be viewed as a hooligan – and all at risk from random attacks.

A group of Tunisians, waving their flags and banging drums, were the victims in the incident from which everything else stemmed. They paraded through England fans drinking in the Old Port under the late afternoon sun. The outward journey was peaceful, but when they turned around to march back the first bottle was thrown and shattered the peace. The Tunisians, including children, were attacked from both sides and chased up a street. The two sides exchanged bottles and stones. The riot police arrived and fired the first of hundreds of rounds of the tear gas which was to become an almost constant mist drifting over the centre of the city for much of the next two days.

About 200 England fans – not cat Cs, but beered-up Bs – regrouped and sang their songs and shouted their shouts and threw their bottles and did what they thought was right, and their right – and thereby put the lives of anyone English in danger as the fighting simmered until after the match. For the first two hours they fought a series of skirmishes with police and locals. A group managed to steal a Tunisian flag from a teenager and set it alight in front of the watching cameras. For three more hours, as the city streets darkened, the English threw bottles and the riot police fired tear gas. Shop fronts were smashed. A few petrol bombs exploded. Cars were overturned and set alight.

Just before 10 p.m. 300 English and Tunisians ran into each other, fists flying and feet kicking, especially anyone on the floor. Some of the English threw punches so drunken that they missed their target entirely and sent the brawler to the floor, comically overbalanced. But plenty of others hit home. Seafront hotels also had windows smashed. The police arrived again and fought with the English until eventually the night appeared to calm. And then an innocent Englishman, guilty only of walking back to his hotel and sharing a nationality with the likes of Paul Dodd, was caught by a young *beur* – a Frenchman of North African origin – and had his throat slashed.

I was miles away, in a hotel in Montpellier, watching the television coverage of what was undoubtedly the most bilious and brutal English hooliganism for years. As with Bournemouth, I should have been congratulating myself for staying away. But instead I was fascinated by reaction which seemed so familiar. The FA's security adviser, Sir Brian Hayes, managed the most predictable: 'This is nothing to do with football.' Sports Minister Tony Banks, hoping the 2006 bid wouldn't be damaged, described the hooligans as 'drunken, brain-dead louts'. But a friend of James Shayler, a Leeds fan so proud of his country that he has its flag tattooed on his beer belly, said, 'I don't care what Tony Banks says, if you had 400 Tunisians after you, you would not walk away.'[7] And in the background chief of police Michel Sappin was left wondering about the wisdom of the fixture's timing.

Arriving in Marseilles on the morning of the game was to wander into the scene of a crime and immediately become a prime suspect. At the station armed police bristled with weapons and barely disguised disdain. In shops the eyes of staff betrayed contempt and confusion – where they could bring themselves to make eye contact and shame failed to

prevent you returning it. McDonald's even had bouncers on
the door. On the streets gangs of youthful but hard-faced
beurs clustered with intent, snarling dogs and the occasional
ill-concealed stave. Walking alone was terrifying, although
probably safer than being in a gang.

At the station I heard the first renditions of 'No Surrender'.
Soon afterwards I passed the first hastily boarded-up shop
front. At the Old Port evidence of the night before was even
more apparent. The English calling cards of broken glass and
occasional puddles of various bodily fluids stained the streets.
More gangs of *beurs* were shuffling around, closely watched by
squads of riot police, ready for the return of the fighters from
the night before. But they were already heading either for the
stadium or for the beach and its giant screen, some singing,
'We're white and we're proud of it.' Trying to work out the best
way to the stadium without following them, I made the mistake
of hanging around the port too long and was tear-gassed – as
the police tried to disperse the *beurs* – for the first time.

The second was three hours later. Three hours in which the
stadium PA had blared out 'All You Need is Love' before
the game started and Alan Shearer's opening goal prompted
renewed rioting in front of the giant screen on the beach. The
toll was two more supporters stabbed and another ten injured.
A reporter was also beaten unconscious. And so also three
hours in which the running battles had moved from the beach
back to the Old Port, where I saw a group of middle-aged,
Middle England fans board a coach which was about to be
sent on its way with its windows smashed – except that the
man who was pulling a concealed two-foot metal rod from
his jacket sleeve spotted the riot police arriving.

Slowly, the skirmishes spread back towards the station, the
sounds of crashing bottles, pounding policemen's boots and
wailing sirens marking the progress of pockets of departing
English. The noise got louder as I reached the approach to
the station – back past the clusters of *beurs* and snarling dogs

and an English woman wiping away tears with her Preston shirt and screaming at her boyfriend and his mates to stay where they were and not head back into town. In their wake, as they walked away from the station, came the acrid taste of tear gas, drifting down the street once more.

At the top of the grand staircase which links the station with the streets below perhaps a hundred England fans glared down; below them, beer in hand outside a bar, another cluster was seething silently; in between two *beurs* were dancing, a few yards from where a gang of mates were sitting, store of bottles undisguised, watching and laughing. The duo sang, 'Ing-lan', and then followed it with two swift thrusts of the pelvis of the sort last seen in the job-centre scene in *The Full Monty*. Then it was funny. Now it had an almost surreal comic value – except that in a minute or two it would lead to a final exchange of bottles and the riot police moving in for what might have been the final time, but probably wasn't.

Inside the station I slumped on the floor, tear gas still burning my eyes. A beautiful olive-skinned local woman, with her four friends at her shoulder, walked past and half-smiled, unsure if I was what she was looking for. She moved on and found her man about ten yards away. His salmon-pink skin from three days in the sun gave him away, but less so than his replica England top covered in blood and a face swollen, bruised and bearing a raw gash. He too was leaning against the wall watching the departure board, conscious of his appearance but wearing a look of sullen pride and battered arrogance. She walked up to him, leaned towards him and said in her best pidgin English, 'Fug you', over and over and over again before walking away, cackling.

For the first time in France I found myself thinking back to the words of a senior police officer after Bournemouth: 'Six of my men are in hospital and what are we talking about? A game. Is it all worth it?'

*

Then, just as it always does, it grabbed you again, engaging all of your emotions, reminding you why you loved it in the first place.

On the night before England played Romania a week later, the Place du Capitole, back in Toulouse, was covered in fans running in every direction – in a mass kickabout. The action pulsed back and forth across the square, many of the players wearing the same raw colouring as the rose-coloured stone of the town hall which towered above them. The calls for the ball cut across some singing from the bars lining the square and in the end added to it as the game degenerated in a mass rendition of the unofficial English World Cup song, 'Vindaloo', and climaxed with dozens of fans doing what any *Tiswas* watcher will remember as the Dying Fly.

On match day itself the square hosted another kickabout, this one a dress rehearsal for the real game that afternoon. And Romania won in the morning too. Every inch of the town hall façade which was within reach was covered with gaffered-up crosses of St George in every size and from towns and cities the length and breadth of the country. I counted fifty before giving up and watching another one fixed up by a man who shinned about thirty feet up a drainpipe. Max Wall was there, or at least someone dressed as him, leading a re-creation of the 'Vindaloo' video. Homer Simpson too and a bloke with the outline of a football shaved into his hair. And the locals were getting photographs of their children with the English fans and their flags. Yes, with the English fans, the supposed monsters of Marseilles.

At one point a trio of local youths began to taunt some of the English and even threw a punch. But the incident fizzled out as quickly as it had flared when plain-clothes police moved in and arrested the three. Perhaps for the first time ever several hundred England fans applauded an arrest. The good relations were fostered further when the volunteers from the FSA's mobile embassy went around the square collecting the discarded bottles and cans and were thanked by the police. Alison Pilling, once one of the Leeds anti-racism campaigners, now one of the leaders of the FSA, explained what they were doing in France: 'Fans still need help and advice – and no one else appears willing or able to provide it. We're also the conduit between fans and the rest of the world, hearing about what was going on and getting that across in the media. Perhaps pointing out the lessons that need to be learned for the future too.'

In the ground at least half of the tickets had found their way into English hands – just as in Marseilles. The Sheffield Wednesday band, reinvented as the England band, thumped out 'The Great Escape' and 'Rule Britannia', perhaps not the most PC compilation but drowning out any efforts to start 'No Surrender'. When Michael Owen came off the bench to score a late equalizer, the noise from the English must have sent a tidal wave down the river which encircled the ground. In front of where I was sitting a giant of a man named Ashley White began to parade up and down, jigging along this side of the touchline advertising boards Nobby Stiles-style, with a four-foot World Cup in one hand and a similarly oversize red rose of England in the other. I asked him, later, why he was carrying his accessories – which were seen at every England game: 'I just wanted to show that we're England, but we can have a good time, we can have fun and enjoy ourselves like everyone else.' Then, just when it appeared that everything was fine, Romania scored the winner.

Even so, the city centre was mostly peaceful after the game. There were one or two scuffles – Old England against New England in one case – but nothing of note to British eyes. Some pushing, some shouting, nothing more. But I'd also seen the day through French eyes. On my first trip to Toulouse I'd quickly discovered that the Japanese thousands had booked every single hotel room in the city. But my accommodation crisis had been solved when I sat down at a bar for a drink before heading for a bench at the station. Before I'd even finished my first beer a group of twenty-something locals had invited me to have another drink with them, join their meal and stay at one of their flats. When my hangover and I left the next morning, I suggested that we should meet up again before the England game.

My host and her sister turned up, looking terrified. They'd read about Marseilles, they'd seen the pictures. They were even more afraid after reading about the riot policeman who had been attacked by Germans in Lens the night before and who seemed likely to die. But at least the Germans had apologized: the head of their FA broke down in tears and offered to withdraw the team from the competition. Half of Germany agreed, while street collections and a media appeal were held to raise money for the policeman's family. More than £100,000 was collected. The German FA also collected £200,000 from its clubs and police. Late it printed up 18,000 T-shirts with 'German fans against violence' on them and handed them out free. In contrast, the English didn't appear to be very contrite.

The sisters ordered a drink and chatted to their overworked friend the barman about the enormous quantities of beer he was serving. They eyed each and every English fan suspiciously and whispered to me, 'And 'im? Izzy 'ooligan?' Fortunately, their English wasn't quite good enough to understand the exact nature of the filthy suggestion from the group at the next table. Ordinarily, the sisters would have spent the night before at the annual Fête de la Musique, a national carnival with events held all over the country – except, in 1998, in Toulouse, because England were there. When we drank up, they headed home and locked themselves in their flat. They weren't football fans when I first met them; they certainly weren't now and said they wouldn't be watching the match.

Neither would anyone who had previously enjoyed games on the big screen. When I walked past it on the way to the ground it was draped in white sheeting, turned off for one night only. Most of the rest of the bazaar around the riverside walkway was closed too. Somewhere nearby a reporter was being hospitalized after being set upon by a gang who accused him of giving England supporters a bad name. An extra 800 police were on duty compared to the other games in the city. Later, an England fan would be rushed to a life-support machine after being stabbed. And this, you had to keep reminding yourself, was being deemed a success.

The party continued, for a little while anyway, in St-Etienne, a city of two tales – one Scottish, one English, very different from each other but with the same conclusion: the end of the World Cup.

The Scots cemented their position as the most welcome, perhaps even the best, fans of the entire tournament. Not the most sober – in fact, probably the drunkest – but also the most entertaining.

I warmed to them immediately when I walked down the length of the Place de l'Hôtel de Ville and was greeted by a home-made banner which read, presumably partly quoting some player or pundit: ' "The archetypal Scottish midfielder is 5' 4", has a poor disciplinary record and ginger hair." Billy Bremner, RIP.'

But the locals were won over by the rest of the display surrounding the lone banner on the steps of the town hall. Several hundred singing Scots had taken over the spot and were facing the rest of the square, teeming with kilts and tartan, sort of serenading it. They roared, 'Stand UPPP if you hate England', voices bellowing, arms raised, four times; then all squatted down and stage-whispered, 'Sit *down* if you hate England', four times too. Then up again and shout; then down again and whisper. Over and over again.

Shoppers stopped in their tracks and looked on in bemusement. Passengers stared out of the windows of trams which clanked past. The clusters of police a few yards from the bottom of the steps just folded their arms, shook their heads and occasionally stepped forward to make sure the road around the square was kept clear. Except one young woman among the officers closest to the singing, who sidled up to a stray who had peeled away from the steps, sheepishly lifted his kilt and then squealed hysterically. Meanwhile, the staff at the surrounding bars kept the beer coming as the Scots drank the city dry, apparently downing 125,000 litres of beer. Each, I would have said.

The soundtrack kept changing. 'Flower of Scotland', then 'Scotland the Brave' and 'Irn Bru', to the tune of 'Vindaloo'. Then 'England's Going Home', '2–1 to Romania' and songs about Jimmy Hill. The sights were constantly changing too: the fan who clambered his way up one of the statues at the side of the steps to stick a cigarette in its mouth; the stragglers who occasionally staggered away to shake hands with policemen; and the various T-shirts, many about Hill again, but the sharpest one listing England's Player of the Year: Southgate, '96; Brolin, '92; Waddle and Pearce, '90.

Then the *beurs* arrived, this time supporting Morocco, Scotland's opponents in the decisive third group game which would decide who would reach the second round, who have to go home. And the party just carried on, but with North African drums pounding away under the songs and new, unrecognized melodies mixing with the Scottish ones. The sea of tartan and blue gained a smudge of red and green in the corner, but remained calm – or as riotously calm, colourful and friendly as it was before. A Moroccan flag was taken into some Scottish hands, but only to act as a makeshift trampoline for one of the African fans to bounce skywards in time to the tunes.

Of course, not all of it was pretty. A few of the dozens of tubs of fuchsias which had inadvisedly been left on the steps got a watering of a sort not recommended in any horticultural book. Some of the pots were accidentally knocked over and smashed. A few were decorated with regurgitated lager. A couple of the little old ladies who stopped to watch the visitors were shocked when a section of them turned around, lifted their kilts and displayed areas where the French summer sun rarely reached. But the women just laughed, their hands clamped over their grins, before tottering away still smiling.

I know it's a cliché that the drinking Scots are the well-behaved antithesis of the fighting English, but that doesn't mean it's not true. I'd heard the common theory – aired by Tony Banks during the World Cup and perhaps correct – that the Tartan Army was so well behaved because its members wanted to be seen as the polar opposites of the English and their hooligans. (Even if the more nationalistic songs in their repertoire could hardly be described as peaceful paeans to good neighbourhood.) But all that mattered in St-Etienne was that a country whose fans were once as feared, as loathed and as notorious as the English had the best party at the World Cup.

Guessing that he might be among the more sober, I asked one of the bagpipers, a middle-aged man named Jimmy McGovern, why. 'It's 'cos we come here just to have a good time. We know we're nae gonna win – and we'll probably get beat tonight – but we want to enjoy ourselves and have people remember us enjoying ourselves too. We got the ferry over wi' some English and you could see the difference. They have this attitude that they are the best, they're gonna beat everyone, they even think they're gonna win the cup, and then they don't understand why everyone hates their attitude. Then they've got a few daft lads who want to take it out on others and the atmosphere is totally different. I mean, this is fantastic, is it not? I've never known anything like it. No one in Scotland wears a kilt, but out here and we've all got them on. I don't know where they've all come from, but it immediately just creates a different kind of an atmosphere or an image to the locals – even if you've been having a few drinks. The English just don't seem to have anything like it.'

He was right several times over. Not least in that Scotland were stuffed 3–0 and, as usual, were sent home in ignominy. And when the ticketless members of the Tartan Army drifted away from the giant screen in the centre of St-Etienne where they watched the almost inevitable defeat a few, faltering voices managed a new song: 'Toy-k-yo. Toy-k-yo. We're the famous Tartan Army and we're goin' to Toy-k-yo.'

The almost entirely disagreeable interlude before the finale back in St-Etienne was in Lens, the least likely World Cup venue imaginable and, even for a few hours, the least likeable. The reason that its civic dignitaries had lobbied for the tournament to come to town was obvious mile upon weed-covered mile before the train pulled into the small ex-mining town haunted by its industrial past. Stacked alongside the track, on flattened ground where they had once been laid, were hundreds and thousands of disused railway sleepers, remnants of the track which had carried the coal trains but which had become as redundant as the miners. In the background slagheaps littered the horizon.

The journey had already been dismal enough. At the station in Paris I found myself swamped by an aspect of the tournament that I had so far managed to avoid: the corporate and commercial. On the concourse in Paris PR women, all crisp blouses and beaming efficiency, led small groups to their trains by holding in the air signs carrying various company names. The station announcer joined in: 'A special train chartered for Snickers will be leaving platform 12 at 4.49. Thank you.' But then he failed to announce the departure, or indeed the arrival or platform, of the train a few dozen of us ordinary fans were supposed to be catching. When we finally boarded another – having been told our tickets were no longer valid – I found a space on the floor of the buffet car, closed to satisfy a belated, and draconian, alcohol ban and sat down. Above me a man in chinos, moccasins and a Newcastle shirt started talking far too loudly, in an accent I never heard in three years living in the North-East, about business opportunities in Eastern Europe.

I was thinking of the West, however. Swindon, to be precise. A couple of months before the riot at Bournemouth I travelled there to see Leeds play. It was an overcast, grey day. We were met by massed police at the station and accompanied to the ground. There was no chance to stop to get brunch – not that there appeared to be anywhere open to serve us anyway as it was Sunday. Kick-off had been put back not for television but for unspecified security reasons. At the ground, the away end was uncovered and just before kick-off it began to drizzle. We lost. Then when we were let out we were marched what was clearly the long way back to the station. When we asked a policeman why, he said it was because the other way went past the back of a stand which was so unsafe in winds above twenty m.p.h. that it might collapse on us.

All aspects of the game supposedly gone now, of course. Except that in Lens the whole atmosphere was back again. The only people on the streets were bored fans, thousands of them without tickets, bored police, watching the bored fans, and bored reporters, watching the bored police watch the bored fans. The booze ban meant many of the bars were closed and so there were very few places for the ticketless to watch the game as the town's giant screen had also been switched off for the evening. Each of the few bars which were open featured the sorry sight of fans outside, pressed up against windows, standing on chairs, trying to catch a glimpse of distant TV screens.

It was easy to understand the reasons for the restrictions, just as it was in the past with Leeds' away record. In Lens, elsewhere in France and even in Belgium, the hooligan element was justifying action against it: a group of 300 threw bottles at the police in Lens itself and thirty-five were arrested; in nearby Lille another thirty were arrested; in Ostend, Belgium, another fifty-seven; at Calais more than 330 fans were refused entry to France and returned home; and, of course, Paul Dodd – spotted the week before in Toulouse buying a ticket for the England game there and trying to sell the story for £10,000 – didn't even make it that far, having been arrested at Dover for stealing a bottle of gin.

But there comes a point when you can't help thinking that sometimes the major effect of such all-encompassing policing is to alienate the ordinary, decent supporter so much that they wouldn't possibly want to go any more, leaving just the undesirable rump – the morons of Marseilles and those like them – whose presence the measures were aimed at dealing with in the first place. A point when you also can't help wondering exactly how far we've come since Hillsborough. And that's how Lens felt to me.

The ticketing fiasco only added to the misery, with the small stadium and enormous number of potential customers pushing the touts' prices up from the £100 which had been the norm at other England games to triple that or more. I managed to get within a couple of hundred yards of the ground, into the hotel where it appeared most of the corporate groups were based, and ordered a drink in the lobby while I waited to meet a friend. I watched the Snickers-jacketed and Coca-Cola-tagged pass by, steering a wide path around a group of lads without logos but with armfuls of beer. A nervous-looking young man sat down next to me and started chatting. Once he'd established that I was ticketless, he glanced around, leaned over and wondered if I might want his – which had come courtesy of his job with the company responsible for the perimeter advertising boards – for £250.

But I'd given up on watching games when the black market prices went past £100. I'd managed four in all – the two on my first day and two England games, for which I had non-black-market tickets – and decided that was good enough. Instead I had a ticket for the small cinema which put its giant screen to good use and allowed a few hundred England fans to watch the action – for £10 each.

As the second half started, I stood in the foyer, chewing on a cheese sandwich and slurping a can of pop – neither of which I was allowed to take into the auditorium itself for security reasons – and realized that, what with Bournemouth and Swindon, the World Cup appeared to be panning out as a reprise of that entire 1990 season. A match at Wolves then was even the last time I went to a game I really wanted to see without a ticket. At least, I thought, that season, for all its trials, ended in the glory of promotion and on-pitch triumph to wash away the off-field blemishes. I almost began to look forward to the return to St-Etienne.

Back there, inside a small bar on the Place de l'Hôtel de Ville packed with so many people that it was like being on the Kop again, the sense of *déjà vu* was stronger than ever. A few early arrivals had grabbed the seats and tables on the small platform coming out from the back wall where the video screen was. Most of us, though, were left to stand behind the wooden banister penning the platform in, pushed against it or, ten or more deep, each other. There was even a wooden panel on the far left which obscured the view of the screen for those at the edge of the crowd – just like the foot of a floodlight, a roof support or even a perimeter fence at an old ground.

Earlier, the city-centre atmosphere which the Scots had created was absent, but there seemed to be far fewer English fans in the city, far fewer than there had been at any of the other games. Part of the explanation was the pitiful official ticket allocation of just over 2,000 in a 36,000-seat stadium (which again was made all the more laughable by the black market). No doubt the extra distance into central France also deterred some fans from travelling on the off-chance of being able to buy a horribly expensive touted ticket. Finally, the miserable experience in Lens must have accounted for others.

Some of the same elements reoccurred. The giant screen, which showed the afternoon's Romania–Croatia game, was turned off. Some bars also closed, while those that were open were under orders to shut at 11 p.m. (even if there was extra time and a penalty shoot-out, until the FSA pointed out that might not be the best idea). Packs of cameramen waited to record anything untoward – and swarmed when police pinned a 1966-shirted fan into the dusty shale in the area in front of the screen. First the stills photographers, then two-man TV crews, all recording the minor incident and then dispersing when the arrested fan was taken away and his mate tried to tell anyone who would listen that they'd been ripped off by a tout who was still standing nearby and were only trying to get their money back when the police moved in.

But by kick-off whatever had gone before was forgotten. We weren't quite there, in the ground, but we were in the city, squashed shoulder to shoulder in front of a screen. On the sides of the room people were standing on chairs and tables and even a fridge to get a view over the throng. The glasses and bottles behind the bar rattled as 'God Save the Queen' was almost shouted before kick-off and followed by choruses of 'Vindaloo' and 'Inger-lund'. Soon the nonplussed staff, bewildered by the fans and their singing, and drinking, were inadvertently bouncing around too as the floor vibrated from the celebrations of Alan Shearer's tenth-minute penalty.

It was an equalizer to an Argentinian spot-kick four minutes before. Two penalties in ten minutes, you thought. Just hold it steady, you thought, trying to catch your breath. Then David Beckham chipped the ball forward and Michael Owen started a diagonal run. He sped past one defender, and the second, but by then those seated nearest the screen were standing and then those behind them too. All you could see was their backs, then their faces as they turned to jump into each other and shout at the rest of the room. Behind, everyone joined in, not entirely sure what had happened, but celebrating anyway.

Those at the back of the throng ran around in circles in the space by the front door, arms waving and embracing when they crashed into each other. Those in the middle pogoed around, hugging mates and roaring in the faces of strangers alike. The police outside peered in to check what all the noise was – as if they couldn't guess.

The rest of the first half was lost to the buzz about Owen's goal and the ten-minute comeback from 1–0 down to 2–1 up. As the atmosphere settled and the glasses emptied and the air started to become stale, a few people began to glance at their watches, willing half-time and a break. Then England conceded a free-kick on the edge of the box. The wall lined up. But Argentina executed the best free-kick of the tournament and equalized again. Within a few breaths, the mood changed. Angry nerves replaced joy and excitement, bitter tension superseded light-headed assurance and soon 'No Surrender' got its first airing.

I think I could have coped if it had just been the usual sorts, the stupid and the hooligan hangovers from the past. But there were some newer, younger fans standing near me, in replica kit not the casual designer labels of the yobs, accentless and polite as they ordered drinks. One of them was a twenty-something woman. She'd been beaming at the pulsating excitement and atmosphere of the remarkable opening period, casting her eyes around the room to drink it all in, catching the eyes of others and conveying the infectious joy with her wide and wild stare and beaming smile. Now she and others joined in the new song, not quite sure if she should but doing so anyway.

I'd had enough. I walked out into the darkened square, a little tired but more weary, and sat on a bench, swilling back water to counter the heat of the packed bar. I wanted to be at home, watching for nothing with friends and a few drinks, rather than here with ticket touts, bottle-throwing and 'No Surrender'-singing scum, and doorstaff who, when I ambled back in to a bar which had stopped serving, insisted on checking that I was drinking just water and not some cunningly disguised spirits.

By then Beckham had gone, head bowed as he was sent off. The cameras panned on to the England bench, where Glenn Hoddle was jabbing sign-language instructions to his players. On it sat David Batty, waiting for his chance. Almost an hour and a half later he strode forward, calmly juggling with the ball, walking to the spot to take his penalty, and I suddenly remembered the other drama which ran in parallel with the promotion campaign of 1990, which pre-dated it and outlasted it: the epic wait for him to score.

I guessed the World Cup was about to end. I felt like everyone did when Stuart Pearce took a penalty in the shoot-out against Spain in Euro '96, when everyone knew his previous form but hoped that history couldn't be so cruel as to repeat itself. All around me, faces which were innocent as to Batty's record were rigid with nerves anyway. Apparently the only man who wasn't tense was Batty himself. He said, 'Whenever I've seen penalties on telly I've been nervous for them even though I'd never done it myself. But once I got on that pitch, in that centre circle, there were no nerves at all, which was probably a bad thing. Perhaps if I'd been a bit more nervous or whatever I'd probably have put it away, but I just felt no nerves at all. I dunno why.'

It wasn't a bad penalty. It was on target and powerful enough. But as Batty skipped into his follow-through, Roa was already palming the ball away. Looking back, with the perspective of a month or two of ribbing from team-mates in Newcastle, Batty laughed, just a little bit, when he said, 'It was a great save. You just try to hit the target, that's all you can do, and the keeper's gone the right way and that was it.'

In the ground the English fans, who'd kept up a constant barrage of noise, led by the band, as the team fought a valiant rearguard action, trooped away disconsolately. In our bar perhaps a hundred fans drifted to the door and out into the night too. A few minutes later a tiny gang of English marched through the square and exchanged some last bottles with loitering *beurs*. For a matter of moments there were people running all around. One English lad dashed past me, at the *beurs* and ready to fight them, and then staggered sideways as if he'd run into an invisible wall. He scrambled to his feet and ran back past me again, clutching his face where the bottle thrown from point-blank range had hit him and slashed his cheek open.

At home millions of television viewers swore or threw something at the television or cried or just put the kettle on. In London a leader writer on the *Daily Telegraph* turned his thoughts to Beckham: 'this Gaultier-saronged, Posh Spiced, Cooled Britannia, look-at-me, what-a-lad, loadsamoney, sex-and-shopping, fame-schooled, daytime-TV, over-coiffed twerp'.

Meanwhile, his team-mate, whose penalty miss will be forgotten in comparison with the sending-off, turned his somewhat wiser thoughts to home. Batty said, 'As soon as I came off the pitch I forgot about it. There's more to life than football. Although I was disappointed we were going out, of course, it enabled me to see the family a bit quicker. I just thought I'd get home and see the kids.'

But sometimes it's hard to remember that there is more to life than football these days.

I can still recall exactly where I was when I read what was – or what, more accurately, would have been – the most remarkable football story ever, one that was so shocking that I literally had to sit down and study the copy of the *Yorkshire Evening Post* in which it was printed. Banner headlines screamed the news. Billboards around Leeds city centre did the same, assaulting those, like me, who had been innocently walking by, and prompting an almost audible buzz as word spread. But, regardless of the size of the typeface or the reliability of the source, the report still seemed simply incredible. Would Diego Maradona, just a year after the Hand of God and the Goal of the Century which quickly followed it in the World Cup in Mexico, really join an English team – especially one languishing in the Second Division? Would the greatest player in the world really join *us*, for goodness' sake?

Unlikely didn't even come close to describing the idea; unbelievable only just got there. Unfortunately, so did untrue, at least in the sense that the *Evening Post* was about as far as the putative transfer got. Apparently a senior figure at Elland Road had contacted the Argentinian captain's agent and asked to be kept informed about his contract negotiations with a view to Leeds stepping in with an offer (although it was a request which went strangely unanswered). What a story, though, so exciting that it even escaped from the ghetto of the sports pages on to the front page, and from the sports round-up at the end of the broadcast bulletins to the top of the shows.

Now such tales seem to happen every few days. If it's not new kit controversies on the news pages, it's the latest figures from the annual report on the City pages. If it's not record transfers hitting the front pages, it's football records reviewed on their way to becoming hits on the music ones – or players, the new pop stars, allegedly hitting their partners. Ridiculously, if it's not the *Guardian* news editors deciding that David Beckham wearing a sarong is worth several hundred words *and* a photograph, it's *Newsnight*'s Jeremy Paxman being asked to deploy his fearsome interviewing technique to interrogate Kenny Dalglish about Newcastle's cup tie at Stevenage.

Football's ubiquity, its popularity, maybe its importance, but maybe not, apparently knows no bounds – and so you'll probably be aware of what has happened to some of those mentioned so far, whether players and clubs, or fans and administrators. But not, almost certainly, to all of them, so perhaps you'll excuse a swift final round-up.

Chelsea got rid of Ruud Gullit when his wage demands were deemed to be too greedy, then became the first to charge more than £1,000 for a season ticket. The training strip produced by Umbro was in fact yellow, not white, and was even worn on the first game of the new season – and rushed into the shops at the same time.

Leeds also hiked up prices, by more than a fifth. They briefly topped the league for the first time since winning it pre-Premiership, but fell back to contend a European place – the best manager George Graham said we could expect, before he resigned to manage a team with no greater aspirations. Eddie Gray was appointed assistant to new manager David O'Leary.

Trevor Hicks was drawn into the spotlight again as a former South Yorkshire officer was appointed as the new Chief Constable of Merseyside. Norman Bettison was accused of serving in a unit which helped oversee the presentation of the police case to the Taylor inquiry. In Parliament Liverpool M P Maria Eagle accused him of helping to coordinate the 'black propaganda' campaign; on Merseyside 15,000 people signed a petition protesting against his appointment and two councillors resigned with the words, 'If he won't go, we will.'

Trevor and the other Hillsborough families also had cause to celebrate, however. Six weeks before the tenth anniversary of the disaster, Sheffield Wednesday agreed to build a memorial at the ground – but only following talk of a stay-away campaign by fans when Liverpool visited the ground and only, most likely, after the anniversary itself. Even so Trevor welcomed the news: 'It's not an admission of guilt – it is just an act of human kindness and a recognition of human feelings.'

Manchester United and Umbro launched a new away kit, black with lime-green trim – not unlike the type of outfits leisure-centre staff wear – less than six months after the zip-up home one. The club also signed a new cross-promotion deal with Pepsi, worth an estimated £1.5 million. Players will feature in advertisements and the pre-season tour to China, Hong Kong and Malaysia is likely to be known as the Pepsi Tour. At the presentation of the annual report, which recorded that profits were up again, to £30 million before transfer spending, Peter Kenyon revealed the latest plan: the opening of 150 United shops throughout the world over the following three years.

But by then there were more important issues on the agenda. First, proposals for a European Super League leaked out and United were forced, under pressure from the City and after a £100-million increase in value in the weeks since I'd seen Peter in the inner sanctum of Old Trafford, to confirm their involvement in discussions with the marketing company and merchant bank behind the plan. The league would have done away with relegation, the cause of so much financial uncertainty for the clubs. But it was eventually sidelined by a sweeping reform of European competition which will see more games – some almost certain to be broadcast on pay television – in a remodelled and expanded Champions' League, with the clubs keeping more of the money generated. The winners could collect more than £30 million – as long as they come from one of the bigger countries in terms of audience share; a team from Norway, for example, would collect less than half as much. Meanwhile, the fourteen biggest clubs, including United, formed a new group, G14, to put pressure on UEFA over marketing and other future issues.

Then the takeover bid which Andy Walsh and other United fans had been expecting materialized, both surprisingly and unsurprisingly from Rupert Murdoch's Sky TV. Zoë Ball announced herself in favour and so, at the other end of the tabloid scale, did a Nicola Harris, of Carlisle, who had travelled to Old Trafford on a day trip. 'It doesn't matter to me who owns the club, as long as they care for it,' she told the Murdoch-owned *Sun*.

Season ticket prices would be held for a year, fans were

told, another 12,000 seats would be added and the transfer kitty would be swollen to overflowing. Yet Andy, and others, campaigned hard against it. The last time I spoke to him, he was as wildly optimistic of victory as only a man who believes in what he is doing can be. He said, 'It's about the future, about United being a football club, not part of a media empire, about people like me still being able to get in too.' For Martin Edwards, it was about, perhaps among other things, making £88 million from the deal. For other media groups carefully monitoring developments, it was about making similar bids, with Arsenal and Villa among the potential takeover targets. Meanwhile, by the by, Oldham fans such as Gerry Boon were stunned to read that their club was considering a three-way merger with Bury and Rochdale.

Newcastle were the next to follow United's lead, though, and succumb to corporate ownership (and see a discredited chairman, in this case Douglas Hall, pocket almost £90 million – thirty times what his father paid for the club). The new man in charge at St James's Park, an American engineer named Barclay Knapp, owner of a cable television company, admitted that he had never seen Newcastle play, let alone stand on the Gallowgate terrace. In his first interviews he seemed to be making the right noises about fans mattering – until he started equating them with viewers and talking of gaining 'a significant market for sports television'.

Rob Bowman has been a regular for Carlisle, Andy Couzens less so, but the side has been becalmed in the lowest reaches of Division Three. Bournemouth set off with the pace-setters in Division Two, but fell back to contest a play-off place as the superior squad strength of the bigger clubs, such as Fulham and Stoke, told. Elsewhere in the lower divisions, Oxford fans delivered food parcels for staff who hadn't been paid for six weeks and Torquay players were banned from shooting practice before kick-off because of the potential cost of compensation claims for supporters hit by wayward efforts.

Chester, though, were the season's running story of the have-nots. Manager Kevin Ratcliffe had to rush to the bank before one game and withdraw £5,000 of his own money to prevent the ground's water supply being disconnected because of an unpaid bill. Televisions and satellite equipment were repossessed and the firm which did the club's laundry confiscated the away kit, while the coach company which provided the team bus was owed a five-figure sum. Fans helped out by paying the players' petrol money for journeys to training, while opposing supporters at several away grounds also rallied to the cause by holding ad-hoc whip-rounds. Chester fans also formed an Independent Supporters' Association, similar to Imusa, and lobbied Tony Banks, who told them, 'Parliament might end up having to take decisions on the regulatory requirements of football generally.'[8]

Paul Dodd was arrested again, in Carlisle, the week before the World Cup Final and charged with causing grievous bodily harm after an incident in which a woman taxi driver was attacked and her car stolen. Just before Christmas his self-published book came out, with a dedication at the front of 'No Surrender' and an Internet site to help promote it. It shared the shelves with a new tome by one of those who inspired Dodd, Colin Ward, the hooligan writer who first put the Border City Firm in a book, and a novel by another of his role models, Eddy Brimson. He also produced a video featuring a stabbing and other 'highlights' of the English fans' experiences in France. Its producers were Carlton Communications, one of the would-be owners of Arsenal.

England's first away game after the World Cup ended in disgrace as well as defeat when supporters racially abused black Swedish players and then went on the rampage, with more aggression and violence than deployed in France – but without mass-media presence to report it. The FA were fined £27,000. Soon afterwards Stan Collymore almost broke Steve Harkness's leg in a tackle widely seen as a result of the unresolved race row nine months earlier. On *Match of the Day* John Motson said, 'There's been a bit of a history between these two.' Meanwhile, Celtic imposed life bans on two supporters who sang pro-IRA songs during a minute's silence for the twenty-nine victims of the bombing in Omagh.

Sepp Blatter visited Tony Blair, and Alec McGivan, and said that he had no doubt the English would make 'a very professional bid'. A couple of weeks later it was reported that the government was giving up on the 2006 campaign, a claim which Downing Street officials furiously denied. In fact the Prime Minister had invited the entire FIFA executive to London, they said. But just a few more weeks on, the bid backfired to engulf the FA and herald a chance for the sort of modernization which McGivan had previously spoken about – courtesy of the greatest scandal in the FA's history.

Graham Kelly resigned, as the deal with the Welsh FA rebounded spectacularly. He left reiterating his mantra of having done nothing wrong: 'I resigned because at the end of a lot of discussions we [he and Wiseman] were unable to convince the executive committee of the appropriateness of what we did.' Which, exactly, was to OK the loan to the Welsh FA without the approval of the finance committee. For a man widely regarded as the committee man's committee man, it was a staggering mistake followed by a stunning defeat, so much so that, given his manner when I saw him, I couldn't help wondering if it had been subconsciously self-inflicted.

We had met a couple of days after England's exit from the World Cup, in a makeshift office as his own was out of use because of a fire which had scorched its way through Lancaster Gate. Despite England's elimination at the same stage as Paraguay, Kelly was bullish as he claimed it was still too early to see the results of many of the 'Blueprint' reforms: 'When you say improve the performance of the England team you're talking over a period of years – not just one World Cup or two World Cups. You're talking about a ten- or twenty-year period.

When we wrote the "Blueprint" we were looking at consistently successful international teams like Germany and Brazil. Now we have put many of the building blocks in place – Howard Wilkinson's reform of youth football, free Saturdays before internationals – and they will feed through.' But when we moved on to the hooliganism of Marseilles and possible cures for it, he suddenly sounded like a man defeated. 'I don't know why our game has so many idiots surrounding it,' he sighed, 'but it does. It has too many, far too many.'

Following his resignation, his enemies tried to portray him as something more than an idiot. Ken Bates leaked details of a £10,000 loan made to Kelly from the FA at a low interest rate. Kelly responded by saying, again, 'I have nothing to apologize for.' He added, 'It is a piddling matter.' The rather more significant agenda was clear: get Kelly and the old-style FA. His dismissal was reported to be the culmination of an almost year-long campaign by a group of Premier League chairmen, keen to modernize by injecting commercialism and business acumen into Lancaster Gate – to complete the takeover of the FA by what was once just a breakaway of the top clubs. And the biting irony was that the early favourites to succeed Kelly and Wiseman were their opposite numbers at the Football League, the rump whose aspirations were supposedly seen off by the 'Blueprint'.

There were wider results of the resignations too. First, it emerged that the FA was paying the £50,000 salary and expenses of ex-Aston Villa star Peter Withe in his new job as coach of the Thai national side, a country with a vote on the FIFA executive. Then a challenge to the British right to hold a permanent FIFA vice-presidency was reported, with the in-fighting between the English and Welsh FAs and the Scottish and Northern Irish cited as the reason. In the past European countries might have backed Britain, but the ill-will lingering after the FA's decision to switch from Johannson to Blatter was said to have seen pro-British sentiment vanish.

As the fall-out continued, Blatter himself announced that he wanted to stage the World Cup every two years – so that the FIFA rankings of national sides were more accurate – and Rupert Murdoch quickly announced that he agreed with the plan.

Doncaster fans, meanwhile, have celebrated the arrival of a minor miracle, one which has left them at the foot of the Conference but still playing, which was more than many thought would happen. Days before the season started Richardson and Weaver left – taking with them the kit, the balls and even crockery used for hospitality – and a new owner, one who gave up a season ticket at Old Trafford to return to his first love, Belle Vue, arrived. A new manager, the prodigal Ian Snodin, was appointed, but inherited a squad of only five players. For the first game of the season, at Dover, he cobbled together a team from his contacts, including one player who had to be picked up at Watford Gap services. But the week after, the first home game, as players such as Steve Nicol, Neville Southall and even John Sheridan started to sign, kick-off had to be delayed as the fans thronged back to watch the start of the resurrection. In March Richardson was jailed for four years for the arson attack on the stand at Belle Vue.

Mention of Snodin and Sheridan, Leeds midfield partners in the mid- to late 1980s, brings us back to me, I suppose. I've seen Leeds a couple of times, just like I have done for a few years now. But I've also been to watch Fulham and even toyed with supporting them, backing my local team (Chelsea, quite obviously, don't count – even if I could afford the prices) for the first time. I've talked about going to stand on the terraces to watch Bournemouth and Doncaster too, but I'd have the same problem at all of them: I'd never really feel involved, always aware that I wasn't really a fan, because all those years ago I started supporting Leeds and that's that. You can't change. Anyway, with O'Leary apparently determined to bring on a new bunch of young players whom I watched win the

FA Youth Cup again, two years ago, I'm more interested than I've been in a while. And, of course, David Batty re-signed too (forfeiting, in the process, a reported £800,000 in loyalty bonuses from Newcastle).

Even so, on Saturdays you'll find me heading across London on the Victoria Line to Finsbury Park. I travel shoulder to shoulder with Arsenal fans, just as I used to with Leeds. But then I watch the Gooners disappear off to Highbury and I change trains to carry on out to a ground – a muddy school playing field actually – where I play the beautiful game, rather inelegantly. It costs the same as I used to pay to stand on the Kop, but gives me an even greater sense of involvement, with some of the fun and the camaraderie – that word again – that I used to get as a supporter.

I'll tell you one more thing before I go. The first sentences you read, all those words ago, about how it used to be – cheap and easy, and empty – well, initially I wanted to write another, one built around a fourth adjective: better. But I think I would have been hopelessly wrong. No one who can remember the dilapidation and the fighting, the injuries and the death, could possibly suggest that today isn't an improvement on yesterday. But I suspect many of us who were there will also remember yesterday so much more fondly. A contradiction, yes, and probably a mawkish one. Strange, too, in the face of the all-conquering presence of the game now. But, perverse as it might seem when there's big business and flotations and vast TV deals and the rest, football just doesn't seem to matter as much any more. At least not in quite the same way.

notes

changes

1. *Committee of Inquiry into Crowd Safety and Control at Sport Grounds*, final report, HMSO, 1986, p. 2.
2. From Premier League Fan Surveys, 1993/4 and 1996/7: season-ticket holders aged under thirty dropped from 42.7 per cent to 32 per cent; season-ticket holders earning £25,000 or more rose from 17 per cent to 30 per cent; and unemployed season-ticket holders fell from 5.3 per cent to 4.2 per cent.

one spring day

1. *Guardian*, 2 December 1990.
2. Taylor concluded that the surge following Beardsley's effort was the most likely cause of the barrier breaking, but noted that there was no clear evidence to say exactly when it gave way.
3. *When Saturday Comes*, June 1989.
4. *Independent*, 26 January 1990.
5. From *Football and Football Spectators After Hillsborough*, compiled at the Sir Norman Chester Centre for Football Research, Leicester University, 1990.
6. *Independent*, 22 April 1989.

7. Quoted in *Football Grounds of Great Britain*, Simon Inglis, CollinsWillow, 1996, p. 12.
8. All figures from *The Football Business*, David Conn, Mainstream, 1997.

winners

1. Quoted in *Football Grounds of Britain*, Simon Inglis, CollinsWillow, 1996, p. 16.
2. Quoted in *The Football Business*, David Conn, Mainstream, 1997, p. 140.

losers

1. Bank funding of the game fell from more than £130 million in 1995/6 to £3.6 million in 1996/7. From *Deloitte & Touche Annual Review of Football Finance, 1998*.
2. From *Rothmans Football Yearbook, 1998/9*. Football League attendances in 1997/8 were 13,600,502 compared to 11,978,401 the previous year and 7,461,014, excluding the old First Division, in 1985/6.
3. Turnover per spectator for Manchester United, excluding television revenue, £1,482.34; for Brighton and Hove Albion, including television revenue, £188.57. From *Deloitte & Touche Annual Review of Football Finance, 1998*.
4. Figures up to December 1997.
5. Arrest rates in Divisions Two and Three in 1990/91 were 16.3 and 15.5 per 100,000 fans. For 1996/97 they were 19.6 and 16.3 respectively. From NCIS figures.
6. Carlisle's turnover grew at 50 per cent per annum over the last five years, trailing only Colchester and Middlesbrough. From *Deloitte & Touche Annual Review of Football Finance, 1998*.

bigots

1. Quoted in *Out of His Skin: The John Barnes Phenomenon*, Dave Hill, Faber and Faber, 1989, p. 49.
2. *Daily Mirror*, 10 April 1987, quoted in *Terror on the Terraces*, produced by Leeds Trades Union Council.
3. *The Flag*, May 1987, quoted in *Terror on the Terraces*.
4. *Committee of Inquiry into Crowd Safety and Control at Sport Grounds*, interim report, HMSO, 1985, p. 34.
5. *Yorkshire Post*, 26 September 1987.
6. *Guardian*, 29 March 1988.
7. Premier League Fan Survey, 1996/7.
8. All anecdotes are from research conducted by Tim Crabbe, Les Back and John Solomos at Goldsmith's College, London.
9. From 'Kick Racism Out of Football: A Report on the Implementation of the Commission for Racial Equality's Strategies', Middlesex University, 1997.
10. From *Football Against the Enemy*, Simon Kuper, Orion, 1995, p. 206.
11. The Mark Scott Foundation, Pacific House, 70 Wellington Street, Glasgow G2 6SB. Tel 0141 248 6677.

spectators

1. The four British countries have been guaranteed one of the vice-presidential positions since 1946 in recognition of their role in inventing and exporting football.
2. Figures for the 1988 Liverpool–Forest semifinal, also played at Hillsborough.
3. Quoted in *The Day of the Hillsborough Disaster*, Rogan Taylor, Andrew Ward and Tim Newburn, Liverpool University Press, 1995, p. 63.

4. *My Autobiography*, Kenny Dalglish, Hodder and Stoughton, 1996, p. 170.
5. See page 78.
6. Once-a-year sessions held at individual clubs, with the agenda set in advance by the clubs.

players

1. Quoted in *Cup Kings*, David Saffer and Howard Dapin, Bluecoat Press, 1998, p. 75.

france

1. *Guardian*, 28 February 1998.
2. *Daily Mail*, 4 June 1998.
3. *Observer*, 7 June 1998.
4. *Guardian*, 9 June 1998.
5. See page 172.
6. *The Hillsborough Stadium Disaster*, final report, HMSO, 1990, paragraphs 262 and 263.
7. *Express*, 16 June 1998.
8. Quoted in *When Saturday Comes*, February 1999.